Economic Integration in Asia

The Regional Comprehensive Economic Partnership (RCEP) aims to achieve greater integration between the ASEAN region and its six free trade agreement (FTA) partners (India, China, Japan, Australia, New Zealand and Korea). The RCEP is the only agreement to include three economies which are among the seven biggest economies of the world—China, Japan and India. The book opens with an introduction to the current status of economic integration and factors that would affect it and looks at key issues like non-tariff barriers, evolving investment regulations in China (in the context of FTAs), connectivity initiatives to integrate the region, rules of origin in the context of value chain integration in selected sectors as well as region-specific aspects of South Asia and South East Asia which would shape the regional economic architecture going forward. With an attempt to cover key imperatives, the book concludes by noting primary impediments to easier trade and investment flows in the region, highlighting possible policy recommendations to improve economic integration.

Deeparghya Mukherjee is Assistant Professor of Economics at the Indian Institute of Management Nagpur, India and a Visiting Research Fellow at the Institute of South Asian Studies, National University of Singapore. His research interests include international trade and investment agreements, services trade, economics of outsourcing & IT integration in India. He earned his Doctorate in Management with specialization in Economics from the Indian Institute of Management (IIM) Bangalore after completing his Master's degree from the Delhi School of Economics. He is a certified Financial Risk manager [FRM (GARP)].

Routledge Studies in the Modern World Economy

For more information about this series, please visit www.routledge.com/
Routledge-Studies-in-the-Modern-World-Economy/book-series/SE0432

Economic Integration in Asia

Key Prospects and Challenges
with the Regional Comprehensive
Economic Partnership

Edited by
Deeparghya Mukherjee

LONDON AND NEW YORK

First published 2019
by Routledge
2 Park Square, Milton Park, Abingdon, Oxon OX14 4RN

and by Routledge
52 Vanderbilt Avenue, New York, NY 10017

First issued in paperback 2020

Routledge is an imprint of the Taylor & Francis Group, an informa business

British Library Cataloguing-in-Publication Data
A catalogue record for this book is available from the British Library

Library of Congress Cataloging-in-Publication Data
Names: Mukherjee, Deeparghya, editor.
Title: Economic integration in Asia: key prospects and challenges with the regional comprehensive economic partnership / edited by Deeparghya Mukherjee.
Description: Abingdon, Oxon; New York, NY: Routledge, 2019. | Series: Routledge studies in the modern world economy; 184 | Includes bibliographical references and index.
Identifiers: LCCN 2018048177
Subjects: LCSH: Asia—Economic integration. | Asia—Foreign economic relations.
Classification: LCC HC412 .E21769 2019 | DDC 337.1/5—dc23
LC record available at https://lccn.loc.gov/2018048177

ISBN 13: 978-0-367-66270-7 (pbk)
ISBN 13: 978-1-138-48095-7 (hbk)

Typeset in Times New Roman
by codeMantra

Contents

List of figures

List of tables

Preface and Acknowledgements

East and South East Asia have emerged as economically dynamic regions of Asia. In order to facilitate greater economic integration between the Association of South East Asian Nations (ASEAN) and its six free trade agreement (FTA) partners, the ASEAN centered Regional Comprehensive Economic Partnership (RCEP) is being negotiated. India is the only country from South Asia which is a part of the RCEP by virtue of its FTA with ASEAN. As a neighbouring region to East and South East Asia, South Asia offers immense potential for fruitful mutually beneficial economic relations with ASEAN and East Asia.

The key issues involved in the RCEP, the concerns of various participating countries and their expectations from a post RCEP world formed the theme of a workshop organized by the Institute of South Asian Studies, National University of Singapore entitled "Trade & Economic Integration: South Asia, Southeast Asia and Asia Pacific". This book is predominantly a product of the chapters presented by the participants at the workshop. Most chapters of this book have been contributed by eminent scholars, academics, public policy experts and practitioners who made the workshop a grand success. The contributors come from various backgrounds including economics, law, public policy and industry bodies and also from various countries in ASEAN and its FTA partners. A unique component of the book are the perspectives offered by scholars from South Asia, primarily India and Bangladesh about their impression of the benefits that RCEP would bring to the table.

The book would not have come out in a timely fashion without the active cooperation of a number of individuals. First and foremost, we owe our debt to the eminent contributors who completed their chapters and submitted the same in time. I appreciate and thank all the contributors for recognising the importance of the theme of the book and agreeing to contribute. The book proposal was vetted and reviewed by two anonymous referees and their comments and suggestions have further enriched the content and direction of the book. We would like to express our gratitude to the reviewers.

I would like to thank the chairman of the Institute of South Asian Studies (ISAS), Ambassador Gopinath Pillai, for his unwavering support to the initiatives of the Trade and Economics programme at ISAS, the workshop and the book project. Prof. Subrata K. Mitra and Prof. Chilamkuri RajaMohan have extended their support as successive ISAS directors during the time the book was given shape. Prof. L.S. Murty, Director of the Indian Institute of Management Nagpur deserves special mention and thanks for supporting my association with ISAS and also for supporting the book initiative. Thanks are due to Dr. Amitendu Palit (Senior Fellow and Research Lead of the Trade and Economics Program at ISAS) for sharing his vision about the workshop as well as the book from an early stage. A special word of thanks goes to Mr. Hernaikh Singh, Senior Associate Director of ISAS for his support at the workshop and the publication process. Ms. Liyana Othman provided quality research assistance and helped ensure a successful workshop and timely receipt of theme papers. I thank her for all her efforts. The administrative and support team members at ISAS, namely Muhammad Yusuf Bin Yacob, See Bee Lian, Sally Goh Hui Chin, Pang Shi Lin and Sheila Devi deserve my sincere gratitude for their support.

Finally, no book sees the light of day without constant support to the editor or author from immediate family members. No word of thanks could be enough to express my gratitude to my son Devopam, Antara and my parents for always standing by my efforts.

List of contributors

Rupa Chanda is the RBI Chair Professor in Economics at the Indian Institute of Management Bangalore (IIMB). She teaches courses in Macroeconomics and International Trade across various programs. From April to July 2018, she briefly served as the Head of UNESCAP Subregional Office for South and South West Asia in New Delhi, while on leave from IIMB. She has received several research grants and has undertaken research and consulting assignments for many international organizations such as the ILO, WHO, UNDP, UNCTAD, OECD, World Bank and Indian organizations such as ICRIER and IIFT. She is a member of several committees in India and was appointed as a member of the WHO's Expert Committee on International Health Regulations in 2015–2016.

Sachin Chaturvedi is Director General at the Research and Information System for Developing Countries (RIS), a New Delhi-based autonomous think tank. He was also a Global Justice Fellow at the MacMillan Center for International Affairs at Yale University. He works on issues related to development cooperation policies and South-South cooperation. Dr. Chaturvedi has served as Visiting Professor at the Jawaharlal Nehru University (JNU) and has also worked as consultant to the UN Food and Agriculture Organisation, World Bank, UN-ESCAP, UNESCO, OECD etc. He is on the Editorial Advisory Board of *IDS Bulletin* (UK); and is Editor of *Asian Biotechnology Development Review.*

Sanchita Basu Das is Lead Researcher for Economic Affairs at the ASEAN Studies Centre of the ISEAS-Yusof Ishak Institute, Singapore. She is also Fellow of Regional Economics Studies Programme and a co-editor of *Journal of Southeast Asian Economies.* Sanchita has authored and edited numerous books and book chapters, policy papers and opinion articles. She has published in several academic journals, including *Singapore Economic Review, Asian-Pacific Economic Literature* and *Journal of World Trade.* Her research interests include economic regionalism in ASEAN and the Asia-Pacific Region; international trade; and economic development issues like digital economy and infrastructure/connectivity.

Deborah Kay Elms is Founder and Executive Director of the Asian Trade Centre (ATC) in Singapore. The ATC works with governments and companies to design better trade policies for the region. Dr. Elms is also Vice Chair of the Asia Business Trade Association (ABTA). She sits on the International Technical Advisory Committee of the Global Trade Professionals Alliance and is Chair of the Working Group on Trade Policy and Law. She is also a senior fellow in the Singapore Ministry of Trade and Industry's Trade Academy. Dr Elms publishes the *Talking Trade Blog*.

Sudeshna Ghosh is Research Associate in the Economics and Social Sciences area at the Indian Institute of Management (IIM) Bangalore. She received her MPhil in Development Studies with Specialization in Economics from the University of Calcutta in 2009. She completed her Master's (Gold medalist) and Bachelor's in Economics from Visva Bharati University. Her current research interests are in international trade and migration and economic geography. Her publications include "International Migration of Skilled Women: Overview of Trends and Issues", in *India Migration Report: Gender and Migration* 2015, (ed.) Irudaya Rajan, Routledge, co-authored with Prof. Rupa Chanda.

Pranav Kumar is Head of International Trade Policy at the Confederation of Indian Industries (CII). He holds an MPhil degree in Economics from Indian Institute of Technology, Bombay. He has over 22 years of professional experience in teaching, research, project management and policy advocacy with primary expertise on trade and development and regional economic integration. Since February 2012, he has been working as Head of International Trade Policy with India's apex business chamber Confederation of Indian Industry (CII).

Deeparghya Mukherjee is Assistant Professor of Economics at the Indian Institute of Management Nagpur, India and a Visiting Research Fellow at the Institute of South Asian Studies, National University of Singapore. His research interests include international trade and investment agreements, services trade, economics of outsourcing and IT integration in India. He earned his Doctorate in Management with specialization in Economics from the Indian Institute of Management Bangalore, after completing his Master's degree from the Delhi School of Economics. He is a certified Financial Risk manager [FRM (GARP)].

Minh Hue Nguyen works as Trade Policy Analyst at the Asian Trade Centre (ATC). Her areas of focus include ASEAN Economic Community (AEC), Regional Comprehensive Economic Partnership (RCEP), Trans-Pacific Partnership (TPP), Digital Trade and E-commerce. Minh Hue obtained her Bachelor Degree in Economics from Nanyang Technological University Singapore and was among 33 scholars from ASEAN countries under Singapore Ministry of Foreign Affairs' scholarship in 2012. Prior to the

ATC, Minh Hue used to work at Taylor & Francis Academic Publishing as a Journal Editorial Intern. She is fluent in English and Vietnamese.

Amitendu Palit is Senior Research Fellow and Research Lead (Trade and Economic Policy) at the Institute of South Asian Studies (ISAS) in the National University of Singapore (NUS). He is an economist specializing in international trade policies, regional economic developments, comparative economic studies and political economy of public policies. He worked with the Government of India for several years with his longest span being in the Department of Economic Affairs in the Ministry of Finance, India. He appears regularly as an expert on the BBC, Bloomberg, Channel News Asia, CNBC, Australian Broadcasting Corporation (ABC), Doordarshan (India) and All India Radio.

Selim Raihan is Professor at the Department of Economics, University of Dhaka, Bangladesh and the Executive Director of the South Asian Network on Economic Modeling (SANEM). He is the Honorary Senior Research Fellow at the University of Manchester, UK. He is the alumni of the Harvard University's program on "Cutting Edge of Development Thinking". Dr. Raihan possesses vast expertise in empirical research on international trade, economic growth, poverty, labour market, etc. Dr. Raihan has worked for several national and international organizations including the Asian Development Bank, the World Bank, UNDP, UNESCAP, UNCTAD, IFPRI, the Commonwealth Secretariat, FAO, European Commission, ILO, IDRC, DFID, etc.

Rajan Sudesh Ratna is the Economic Affairs Officer in Trade Policy and Facilitation Section, Trade and Investment Division of UNESCAP, Bangkok since July 2012. The current assignment relates to carrying out research and analysis of international trade issues, especially those relating to WTO, RTAs and Green Trade, as well as providing policy advisory, formulating and organizing tailor-made capacity building programmes for ESCAP members. He is in charge of maintaining the Asia-Pacific Trade and Investment Database (APTIAD). He also provides policy advisory to Afghanistan, Myanmar and Mongolia in the negotiations and trade policy making.

Vo Tri Thanh is Chair for the Vietnamese committee for Pacific Economic Cooperation Council. Dr. Vo is currently the senior expert of the Central Institute for Economic Management (CIEM). Dr. Vo mainly undertakes research and provides consultation on issues related to trade liberalization and international economic integration and macroeconomic policies. His other areas of interests include institutional reforms, financial system and economic development. He has received a Bachelor of Science from the Moscow State University, and a Master's degree and PhD in Economics from the Australian National University.

Jhanvi Tripathi is Associate Researcher in International Trade Policy at the Confederation of Indian Industry. While there, she has worked on multiple policy projects related to E-Commerce, Global Trade Architecture, Regional Integration, and India-Africa Trade and Investment. She was also on the organizing team for the Business Stakeholder Consultations at the 19th round of RCEP negotiations. Her recent publication, *"Deepening Africa - India Trade and Investment Partnership"*, written in collaboration with the African Trade Policy Centre of the UN Economic Commission for Africa was presented at the 13th CII-EXIM Bank Conclave on India-Africa Project Partnership in New Delhi.

Heng Wang is Associate Professor and Co-director of UNSW Law's China International Business and Economic Law (CIBEL) Initiative, and University Visiting Professorial Fellow at Southwest University Political Science and Law. Heng spoke at the WTO Headquarters and leading institutions including Harvard, Oxford, New York University and London School of Economics, and taught in Australia, Canada, China, Japan and the United States as Visiting Professor. He has been executive council member of one global, two Asian and all three Chinese societies of international economic law. He studies the frontline of China's international economic law practice (e.g. the Belt and Road Initiative (BRI), and central bank digital currency), its rationale and implications.

Introduction

Deeparghya Mukherjee

In the aftermath of the financial crisis of 2008, the world has tried to address issues of economic uncertainty with mixed success in various regions of the world. Asia as a region has emerged as a hub of economic activity over the last few decades. With limited scope of economic growth in the west, the world looks at Asia as a land of tremendous potential in shaping the future of the world economy. While East and South East Asia have been economically vibrant regions, South Asia is a region with reasonably untapped potential and could benefit significantly through constructing strong economic links with the more economically vibrant Asian neighbours.

A multitude of trade and investment agreements "noodle bowl" have tried to facilitate free trade and investment flows across East and South East Asia already. Currently, one of the most significant mega-regional trade agreements under negotiation, namely the Regional Comprehensive Economic Partnership (RCEP), envisages to do away with tariff barriers and encourage free trade among the ten-member ASEAN group of countries and its six free trade agreement (FTA) partners, namely China, India, Australia, South Korea, Japan and New Zealand. The eclectic mix of countries at various stages of development and its respective objectives for economic development make this a unique and yet exciting agreement. However, the ramifications of the agreement for the Asian region may be explored on various fronts. This is what this book attempts to do.

As the book revolves around RCEP as a backbone for economic integration of ASEAN and its six FTA partners, the first chapter looks at the evolution of RCEP as the ASEAN-centred answer to the "noodle-bowl" effect of the multiple individual FTAs that exist in the region. The negotiation of RCEP was started in 2012 and by mid-2017, officials had gone through 18 rounds of it. While ASEAN has individual FTAs between itself and larger economies, the RCEP brings together all these larger economies with different stands on issues due to their different challenges. This chapter tries to unravel the progress of RCEP negotiations and highlights key attributes.

In Chapter 2, the importance of growth corridors and the economic geography approach to study regional integration is brought out, while Chapter 3 reviews connectivity initiatives in the region and emphasizes the need to fast-tracking the growth of physical and digital connectivity infrastructure to obtain greatest economic benefits for the region in a post RCEP world.

In the next part of the book, specific attributes are discussed. Chapter 4 looks at the importance of and role of non-tariff barriers (NTB) in inhibiting trade. Reduction in tariffs across the world has been accompanied by a disturbing increase in NTBs constraining market access for exports. The Asia-Pacific region has seen a sharp proliferation of NTBs in the last couple of decades. These NTBs are significant challenges for mega-FTAs like the RCEP aiming to create large zones of preferential access in the Asia-Pacific. This chapter studies the nature of NTBs prevailing among RCEP economies and the challenges for RCEP in overcoming these. Arguing for a program of harmonization of standards in RCEP for rationalizing NTBs, the chapter discusses the difficulties RCEP might face in this regard. It also examines the Indian perspective on NTBs in RCEP as a non-Asia-Pacific Economic Cooperation member.

China has been the most sought-after investment destinations among the RCEP negotiating partners. It stands out as the single most economically powerful nation in the RCEP negotiations. Chapter 5 looks at the legal issues of investment rules in the RCEP from the Sino-ASEAN perspective. It argues, first, that there are three models of China's FTA investment agreements (the China-ASEAN Investment Agreement, the China-Korea FTA and China-Australia FTA), and the China-ASEAN Investment Agreement is unique for understanding the RCEP negotiations due to several factors. These factors include the status of this agreement as the only FTA that China signed with more than one economy, and the ASEAN's arguably leading role in the RCEP negotiations. Second, the approach of the China-ASEAN Investment Agreement has three features: flexibility, less rigorous or developed rules, and an incremental strategy. Finally, the key issues in RCEP investment rules include market access, substantive provisions, social clauses and investor-state dispute settlement. Investment rules of China's FTAs vary with partners but reflect a pragmatic approach, and a large number of RCEP parties bring considerable uncertainties and difficulties. Chapter 5 discusses the issues in detail and the ramifications for the region due to China's presence in RCEP.

While studying the regional trade agreements many studies have focused on Rules of Origin (RoO), mostly in terms of their restrictiveness and as a deterrent to regional trade. Only a few studies have discussed the development role that the preferential RoO play. Chapter 6 analyses various components of the RoO with regard to the RCEP to examine if the RoO will facilitate RCEP members to become part of regional value chains or not. The study relies on the various RoO criteria that RCEP members have agreed under the ASEAN + 1 FTAs and then looks at the likely RoO in RCEP, after which it evaluates which criteria can facilitate the intra-RCEP value chain.

The final part of the book at sub-regional perspectives of the prospects of RCEP. Chapter 7 looks at services trade specifically. India has been increasing its economic interests in the Asian region through the last two decades and its approach in FTA negotiations currently focus more on services and investments given its success as a services exporter globally and this could offset any perceived losses in goods trade liberalization. This chapter examines the prospects for and challenges to this approach through a detailed analysis of India's interests in services through its comprehensive agreements which are currently in force in the region. It begins by outlining the status of services in India and its existing and prospective partner countries in Asia in terms of the sectors' contribution to value added, trade, employment, investment flows, important subsectoral features, trends within services and bilateral relations in services trade with its Asian FTA partners. The discussion highlights the complementarities and overlaps in services between India and these countries and identifies potential areas of interest and concerns on both sides. Building on this overview of opportunities and challenges, the discussion outlines the state of play in India's FTA negotiations with respect to services, including the status of commitments by India and its partner countries under various agreements, progress with regard to realization of market access in services and issues and concerns in services under existing and prospective FTAs. The chapter concludes by outlining possible negotiating and domestic reform strategies for furthering services integration with India's Asian FTA partners and effectively leveraging these agreements.

Chapter 8 provides an ASEAN perspective on economic and strategic rationales for RCEP. It highlights some of the negotiation challenges and gives suggestions on the way forward for ASEAN 5 as a group, that is, Singapore, Thailand, Philippines, Malaysia and Indonesia. The perspective of CLMV countries is brought out in Chapter 9. The distinction helps us look at the varied concerns by levels of development across the countries.

Chapters 10 and 11, although the concluding chapters of the book, are unique features of the collection as they bring out the perspective of South Asia and its prospects. Chapter 10 recognizes that India is the only South Asian country present in RCEP but the agreement has ramifications for other countries in South Asia such as Bangladesh. The RCEP can help regionalize the sophisticated global production networks that make Asia the world's factory. However, since RCEP largely excludes least developed countries and small states, there could be various implications for the RCEP, which might include potential loss of market access from trade preference erosion and growth of new standards to trade governance. The chapter presents likely scenarios of gains and losses to other South Asian countries, like Bangladesh or Sri Lanka, if they were to remain away from RCEP or join the RCEP and holds out an interesting analysis.

Finally, Chapter 11 looks at overall economic integration in Asia as a source of generating economic gains for the world as the western world turns increasingly protectionist with moves like BREXIT and the United States's current trade policy. It reflects elaborately on the possibility of Asian integration through value chains in a post RCEP world.

In sum, the book tries to cover a myriad of issues starting with a brief background of the RCEP; it delves into specific issues that inhibit economic integration in the Asian region as well as focuses on specific attributes where integration would have great potential through value chain integration, services trade liberalization and rationalization of NTBs with concentration on issues of connectivity, investment regulations and inclusive growth for the region. The focus on prospects for South Asia and ramifications for it is one of the many unique features that the book offers.

Part I

RCEP, growth corridors in Asia and connectivity

1 The evolution of the Regional Comprehensive Economic Partnership

Deborah Kay Elms and Minh Hue Nguyen

In the beginning

The Regional Comprehensive Economic Partnership (RCEP) has grown out of five existing free trade agreements (FTA) with ASEAN. Meeting at the Seventh East Asia Summit in November 2012, RCEP was announced as a new trade agreement which would further the process of regional integration across 16 countries in Asia: Australia, Brunei, Cambodia, China, India, Indonesia, Japan, Laos, Malaysia, Myanmar, New Zealand, Philippines, Singapore, South Korea, Thailand and Vietnam.

A dialogue for developing trade had been opened between ASEAN and its neighbours through the development of an ASEAN+3 track in 1996 with ASEAN, Korea, Japan and China. This ASEAN+3 process paved the way for Japan and Korea to argue for a common trade deal in East Asia. By 2005, Japan wanted to expand on the progress being made in trade agreements with ASEAN. ASEAN had begun working on FTAs with China in 2002, Korea in 2004 and Japan in 2005. All of these were signed and put into effect in 2005, 2007 and 2008, respectively, coming out of the ASEAN+3 dialogues. ASEAN also negotiated FTAs with India and Australia/New Zealand in 2004 that were signed and put into effect in 2010.

Shifting to regional agreements

Each of these ASEAN agreements, known as ASEAN+1s, moved Asia closer to having an Asia-wide integrated framework for trade. But the dream, pursued in different venues like the Asia Pacific Economic Cooperation (APEC) and promoted by others in the region, called for deeper and wider integration.[1] A patchwork of trade agreements can be difficult for companies to use, especially for smaller firms. Experts have labelled this problem the "spaghetti or noodle bowl" and companies have had to navigate often complex rules to take advantage of preferential rules under existing free trade arrangements. Since each agreement has different rules, paperwork and requirements, sorting out which provisions make the most sense for a company was becoming increasingly time-consuming. Firms were often opting to avoid using the agreements entirely, leading to low utilisation rates for many preferential trade deals.

At the same time, in the early 2000s, the World Trade Organization (WTO) was holding negotiations at the global level as part of the Doha Development Agenda (DDA). A breakthrough in Doha would have meant fewer reasons for regional trade arrangements. But as the years went by and the DDA continued to miss key opportunities, Asian governments increasingly focused on the prospects for renewed trade deals closer to home.[2]

Japan first proposed creating a wider Asia-Pacific free trade zone in the form of Comprehensive Economic Partnership in East Asia (CEPEA) in 2006. From 2006 to 2009, CEPEA's proposal led to the grouping of ASEAN+6, which at the time was a loose collection of all of ASEAN's free trade partners.[3] This was seen as a strategic move to take the lead at developing a larger and more comprehensive economic zone in East Asia.

Since it seemed most Asian economies desired some kind of common Rules of Origin (RoOs) and many studies had identified these as a key factor hindering production costs,[4] officials began looking for an agreement that would satisfy the desire for a regional multilateral FTA. CEPEA research by The Economic Research Institute for ASEAN and East Asia (ERIA) identified India, Australia and New Zealand as key partners in Asia-Pacific trade.[5] Increasing links with these three would not only grow exports, but at the same time make the East Asian economies more resistant to shocks caused by problems in their own industries.[6] In 2009, economic ministers in the East Asian Summit (EAS) agreed to consider carefully the impact of a regional trade agreement.

At this time, the idea of CEPEA was competing with the East Asia Free Trade Agreement (EAFTA), an ASEAN+3 led agreement specific to East Asia, (i.e. with only China, South Korea and Japan and ASEAN) with more specific provisions for their markets.[7] However, since CEPEA also was a better fit within the objectives of APEC to create a Free Trade Area of the Asia Pacific (FTAAP), it became easier to promote a larger grouping. ASEAN members seized the opportunity to repackage the idea, by consolidating CEPEA into an ASEAN endeavour to maximise ASEAN's centrality as a hub and reinforce the importance of the ASEAN Economic Community (AEC).

Consolidation into an ASEAN-Led RCEP

ASEAN had been pursuing economic regionalism as a tool for growth for decades. In 2007, AEC leaders identified their key goals moving forward— fully five years before the development of RCEP. The most important item on their agenda was "ASEAN centrality."[8] The regular meetings of the AEC and economic ministers (AEM) advanced the proactive development of ASEAN trade arrangements.

ASEAN officials pushed for the inclusion of India, Australia and New Zealand in RCEP, even when the East Asian nations feared this would dilute the quality of the agreement.[9] It is important to note that nothing in the origins of RCEP points to the likelihood of RCEP being dictated or driven by China. Instead, from the earliest days, RCEP has been an extension of ASEAN+1 FTAs. China's push for EAFTA, or an ASEAN+3 FTA, was, after all, not met with success.

As noted earlier, ASEAN had concluded five ASEAN+1 FTAs with Australia/New Zealand, China, India, Japan and South Korea by 2009.[10] ASEAN was geographically placed at the centre of the CEPEA countries, but as the largest entity with existing agreements with all parties, could set the agenda for determining which provisions could be included in any regional agreement. While every potential member of the deal had links to ASEAN, not all had connections to one another. China and India, for example, had no existing trade agreement. ASEAN was, therefore, a strategic negotiating partner between ASEAN, the "Plus 3" countries, and the "Plus 6" countries.

In November 2012, leaders of ASEAN+6 nations agreed to launch RCEP, as a consolidation and advancement of trade integration objectives pursued under FTAAP, CEPEA and as a grand consolidation of ASEAN+1 FTAs.

ASEAN+1 FTAs

ASEAN therefore had a position of natural leadership for RCEP. Though FTAs did exist between other members of the grouping, the ASEAN+1 FTAs provided an easier common platform for launching negotiations. The benefits gained from ASEAN+1 FTAs between ASEAN and the other six nations could therein be extended to create a larger area, simultaneously opening up ASEAN as a hub and standardizing FTA provisions.

While many of the provisions in the ASEAN+1 agreements were similar across all five agreements, particularly for market access in goods, there was also fairly wide variation in each.[11] Services and investment were incomplete in some, like the agreements with Japan, Korea and India.[12] Only the deal with Australia and New Zealand could be fairly characterised as a comprehensive agreement, covering topics beyond just goods, services and investment and including topics like intellectual property rights and competition policy. Trade facilitation had remained general in ASEAN+1 FTAs.[13] Straining the noodle bowl—or sorting out the overlapping and complicated RoOs used in different ASEAN agreements—was to be one of the most important tasks for RCEP.

Other bilateral FTAs between RCEP members like New Zealand and India had struggled to get off the ground for agricultural reasons.[14] Indeed, just like at the WTO, agriculture within and between RCEP parties remained a sensitive issue. It was also expected to be problematic in the regional negotiations. Protectionist barriers remained high in many RCEP markets, with rising non-tariff barriers of various sorts in place.

Given that utilisation of the ASEAN+1 FTAs in 2013 was not high, it meant there was an opportunity for RCEP to improve on the status quo.[15]

The Leader's Statement launching RCEP made important provisions for building off existing trade approaches outlined in the +1 FTAs. These base-building areas included "The General Agreement on Trade and Services (GATS) plus" components for services, investment opening and protection, and a general commitment to go beyond existing ASEAN+1 agreements. Most RCEP parties had, by 2012, engaged in various other FTA negotiations that included similar types of provisions, so there was reason to believe that getting a more comprehensive deal done in Asia should be achievable.

ASEAN-Led RCEP—a tough region for economic cooperation

RCEP was thus born as a regional experiment in coordination among 16 very diverse parties. The project and its negotiators began with a belief that coordination and the negotiation process had the potential to add significant value through synergistic negotiation efforts, the sharing of cost burdens between parties and the setting of high ambitions for quality outcomes.

High-quality outcomes could reconfigure the business environment, making it easier and less costly to do business in Asia. Larger regional agreements like RCEP held the promise of more useful trade rules than a collection of ASEAN+1 FTAs could achieve, since larger agreements were a better match for regionally integrated supply chains that dominate the member states.[16]

From the beginning, RCEP also had the potential to change political relations between members. ASEAN has been "in the driver's seat" for the negotiating process. This has been a challenging position, however, to maintain, given ASEAN's own institutional weaknesses and difficulties in arriving at common positions among ten quite divergent members.

Compounding the negotiating difficulties in reaching an agreement in RCEP has been the ongoing process in a parallel FTA, the Trans-Pacific Partnership (TPP). Seven member countries in Asia are members of both RCEP and the TPP as shown in Figure 1.1 below. Balancing the demands of TPP and RCEP has required a delicate touch.

Several members (India, China and South Korea) are present neither in ASEAN nor in TPP. The strength of negotiating relationships that have been built-up across years are thus not as deep, nor are the country positions as well known with these three member countries.[17] Of course, ASEAN had experience negotiating the +1 agreements with each partner country and some individual RCEP members, like China and Australia, had bilateral agreements in place between them. But overall, most of these experiences were not as long or as sustained as the ASEAN integration processes, nor as in-depth as TPP negotiations.[18]

China, as an example, appears to have seen negotiations in RCEP as an extension and formalization of a long history of relations with the South East Asian states. Even in the absence of RCEP, China has become the largest trade partner for nearly every member of the grouping. Hence, any

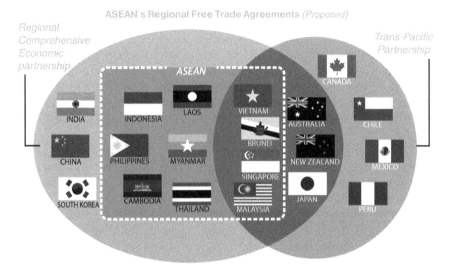

Figure 1.1 Sorting out "The Noodle Bowl."[19]

additional trade benefits that flow from RCEP will likely solidify Chinese economic strengths in Asia—even if the final RCEP commitments are relatively weak.

India has a more complicated relationship with RCEP. On the one hand, India has been following a "Look East" policy and what the then-Prime Minister Manmohan Singh described as the "evolution of an open, balanced, inclusive and transparent regional architecture" with ASEAN.[20] This approach, plus a strong desire to create a competitive, forward-looking domestic economy has pushed India to embrace part of the RCEP agenda, particularly centred on India's traditional strengths in services. On the other hand, India's difficulties in ensuring effective livelihood for farmers and problems with revving up the manufacturing sector have led to strong desires to keep out new imports from RCEP agricultural powerhouses like New Zealand and Australia and manufacturing giants like China or Japan.

The tensions within RCEP have proven challenging for ASEAN to manage. All participating states in RCEP are parties by virtue of their connection to ASEAN. RCEP negotiations take place in "rounds" with ASEAN negotiators central to discussions and negotiators from China, Japan, India, New Zealand, Australia and South Korea known as "ASEAN Foreign Partners" (AFPs). On the first day of negotiation rounds, all ASEAN members caucus separately from AFP members, who are not obligated to caucus concurrently, before all 16 negotiate parties collectively in their respective working groups.[21] RCEP is thus flexibly negotiated via consensus building, using the time-honoured "ASEAN way."[22] The six AFPs may be at the heart of discussions, but they push from the periphery.

Making progress in RCEP

With the common goal of increased regional integration in the minds of its member states, RCEP was first mooted in the 2011 ASEAN Summit in Indonesia. In the next year, the RCEP project was officially launched in the 2012 ASEAN Summit in Cambodia alongside the release of guiding principles in eight areas: goods, services, investment, economic and technical cooperation, intellectual property, competition and dispute settlement.[23] The first round of negotiations began in May 2013 in Brunei and have been ongoing since.[24]

Negotiations have proceeded with ASEAN+1 FTAs and WTO agreements serving as the foundation.[25] Given the variation in quality among the existing ASEAN agreements and the lack of an updated WTO rulebook, it has been difficult to even agree on the appropriate starting point for talks in the early rounds of RCEP negotiations. The Leader's Statement said that the existing ASEAN+1 agreement should serve as building blocks. Even this proved controversial as some members suggested this meant taking the most ambitious agreement of the lot, ASEAN Australia-New Zealand, as the starting point and building up from this baseline. However, other members in RCEP took a look at the commitments contained in ASEAN Australia-New Zealand FTA and decided that this agreement was entirely too bold. ASEAN Australia-New Zealand FTA, as an example, includes tariff cuts for some members approaching all tariff lines and these cuts go all the way to become duty-free in relatively short order. Many RCEP rounds were therefore devoted to the vexing issue of "modalities" for market access for goods—or how much needed to be cut, from which member states, and under what timelines.

Over time, the negotiating agenda in the talks has also expanded. Getting something done with 16 diverse parties on a growing list of issue areas has meant RCEP officials have missed several announced "deadlines" for conclusion; most notably the 50th-anniversary meeting of ASEAN in the Philippines in November 2017. While the talks have been ongoing, negotiating texts have not been released, or even leaked (Table 1.1)

When negotiations began in 2013, RCEP progressed as many high-ambition projects do: with much enthusiasm, but with increasing challenges over time that have slowed progress. The easiest issues are usually tackled first, giving the sense of strong momentum. The harder topics are often pushed back towards the end, leaving officials grappling with the most challenging compromises in what become marathon sessions usually right up against a key deadline for a deliverable. RCEP has not been immune to these pressures.

The very early rounds were largely about determining the scope and pace of the negotiations and setting common expectations for outcomes. It was not until the first half a dozen rounds or so had been completed that officials were able to start focusing on details. Even with the original Leader's

Table 1.1 RCEP negotiation rounds and meetings from 2013 to 2018

Negotiation round	Host country	Time
RCEP round 21	Yogyakarta	February 2018
RCEP ministerial meeting	Manila	November 2017
RCEP round 20	Incheon	October 2017
RCEP round 19	Hyderabad	July 2017
RCEP ministerial meeting	Ha Noi	May 2017
RCEP round 18	Manila	May 2017
RCEP round 17	Kobe	February–March 2017
RCEP round 16	Jakarta	December 2016
RCEP ministerial meeting	Cebu	November 2016
RCEP round 15	Tianjin	October 2016
RCEP round 14	Ho Chi Minh City	August 2016
RCEP round 13	Auckland	June 2016
RCEP round 12	Perth	April 2016
RCEP round 11	Brunei	February 2016
RCEP round 10	Busan	October 2015
RCEP ministerial meeting	Kuala Lumpur	August 2015
RCEP round 9	Nay Pyi Taw	August 2015
Intersessional RCEP ministerial meeting	Kuala Lumpur	July 2015
RCEP round 8	Kyoto	June 2015
RCEP round 7	Bangkok	February 2015
RCEP round 6	New Delhi	December 2014
RCEP round 5	Singapore	June 2014
RCEP round 4	Nanning	April 2014
RCEP round 3	Kuala Lumpur	January 2014
RCEP round 2	Brisbane	September 2013
RCEP round 1	Brunei	May 2013

Source: Ministry of Foreign Affairs and Trade of New Zealand.[26]

Statement directing progress in a wide range of topics, it was not easy to bridge gaps in goods, services and investment, nor to bring in additional topics like intellectual property and sanitary or phytosanitary standards.

Market access for goods

The slowest aspect of the RCEP negotiation from the beginning has been market access for goods. This element of negotiations held back prospects for closure for round after round. The primary debates revolved around the extent to which goods markets had to be opened to one another. While all RCEP parties have existing trade agreements with ASEAN, not all members have opened markets to each other. In particular, the Dialogue partners or AFPs have not had agreements between them, especially between India and China.

Early discussions started with some members pressing for cuts on 65 percent of tariff lines upon entry into force (EIF), and 80 percent or more by full implementation within ten years.[27] Even this starting point remained problematic, as it did not address which tariff lines were to be cut, or whether this target was even feasible for all parties involved. Such relatively low levels of tariff cutting fell far from the aspiration of free trade in Asia.

The problem of cutting a limited number of tariff lines is compounded by the high levels of concentrated trade within RCEP economies. While intra-RCEP trade accounts for a significant portion of total trade, a number of top trade products or items among RCEP are similar among 16 countries. These products are often subject to significant applied most-favoured-nation rates.[28]

Given the concentration of trade between some parties, even relatively high levels of tariff lines might actually exclude most of the tradable items. As an example, of India's relatively limited trade with RCEP countries, nearly three-quarters of the total comes from just the top 20 products.[29] A proposal that opens up even 95 percent of tariff lines sounds very impressive and trade liberalizing, but if these 20 products are excluded from India's RCEP commitments, the overall impact of the agreement will be extremely modest.

Despite the relatively low levels of trade with RCEP economies, India has been deeply concerned about additional goods market opening through RCEP. India tried to press for a three-tier proposal that would have provided for differential trade access for members. India wanted to offer 42.5 percent of tariff lines for China, Australia and New Zealand, 60 percent access for Korea and 80 percent for ASEAN. This would have meant, for example, that more than half of all tariff lines would have received no additional benefits or changes at all for companies from Australia, China and New Zealand as a result of RCEP at any point in the future.

By contrast, other RCEP members were prepared to make the same offer of access for all other RCEP parties at 85 percent or 90 percent coverage. Some members argued that the Leader's Statement made clear that RCEP was meant to go beyond existing ASEAN+1 agreements and this meant considerably stepping up the goods market access commitments to include not just a certain percentage of tariff lines but also measure of the value of trade. This latter commitment would have helped take into account the concentration of trade and ensured that members could not open only commercially meaningless sectors while continuing to protect everything of potential importance for firms.

India's three-tier proposal was finally dropped from consideration in 2017 in favour of more flexibility in staging with longer timelines. But the basic questions of how much and how quickly to open in market access for goods remained problematic as ASEAN approached its 50th anniversary and the presumptive deadline for RCEP conclusion. ASEAN leaders broached the subject directly during their visit to India for National Day in early 2018 to reinforce the point that conclusion in 2018 required significant effort to clear the blockages in market access for goods to get the agreement across the line.

India's intransigence over goods negotiations was not only due to difficulties directly with manufacturing or agriculture. Past experience in working with ASEAN showed that many ASEAN members seemed to prefer to work on goods access first and deal with services trade later. The ASEAN-India

FTA started with goods and the services and investment elements were not locked in until several years later. India did not want to repeat this experience in RCEP. In order to ensure that India's primary objective of better services access was met by RCEP countries, Indian officials slowed progress in goods talks until services talks were sufficiently advanced.

For goods, tariff cuts are not the only issue that matters to firms. In order to qualify for preferential tariff rates, companies have to show that products are made within RCEP economies. The related negotiations around RoOs were also slow-going. RCEP opted for product-specific rules, which meant that each of the more than 5,000 tariff lines needed an individually crafted rule.[30] This is not the way that ASEAN has typically designed RoOs, but it can be more beneficial for companies, especially if the agreement allows multiple methods for achieving origin criteria.

The RoOs for RCEP will ultimately be one of the most important deliverables for the agreement, since firms will be able to craft products for 16 countries within, needing to remanufacture items for different Asian economies, and all goods can be shipped using just one certificate of origin or piece of paperwork. This is a critically important element of sorting out the "noodle bowl" that bedevils companies trying to ship goods across Asia using five different ASEAN agreements and an assortment of bilateral deals now.

The working group in charge of creating these rules decided to craft RoOs for each line without worry over whether or not individual tariffs would ultimately be included or dropped in the final agreement. Even with this commitment, the RoO negotiations proceeded slowly with less than 20 percent of the necessary provisions drafted by early 2017.[31] Work sped up throughout the year but working line-by-line through thousands of individual tariff lines simply takes a certain amount of time to complete.

Services and investment

While much of the focus of the negotiations has been on the market access for goods, services and investment discussions have been moving along more quickly. RCEP is a comprehensive agreement where all elements are negotiated simultaneously and the final package agreed as a cohesive unit. This is different from the ASEAN+1 agreements, where commitments on goods typically went first, followed by services and investment (plus any additional items) at a later date. Since the services and investment provisions in the ASEAN+1 agreements (other than with Australia and New Zealand) were often not completed at all, or finished at a considerably later date, RCEP has been working on all elements in parallel from the beginning.

Investment, in particular, has been easier in RCEP as all parties want to encourage inbound investment flows from one another. Hence the discussions on market access for investment have been done on the basis of what is called a "negative list" where all investment sectors are automatically opened out to RCEP parties, unless the sector is listed as closed.[32]

Investment protection is meant to be accomplished through a provision called the investor-state dispute settlement (ISDS) provision. ISDS was originally part of the Leader's statement that set up the agreement. As the negotiations have proceeded, the specifics of ISDS have been put largely on hold until other elements of the agreement have been locked down. When RCEP talks got underway, ISDS was not particularly controversial—it appeared in thousands of existing bilateral investment treaties or FTAs globally and most RCEP members had also included it in past agreements. As the months and years dragged on, however, this specific provision became more challenging for some members at the domestic level.

Services have been tougher to negotiate, as services are ultimately about domestic level regulation. Existing ASEAN+1 agreements had limited or non-existent services commitments to build upon in RCEP. For many RCEP parties, their commitments at the WTO under the GATS are also limited. Members are therefore drawing upon a range of different experiences in past trade agreements, with some members having done agreements only on the basis of what is called a "positive list," like the GATS, where only services that are listed are opened for access to member firms, and others having done both positive lists and negative lists. The "negative list" opens up all service sectors unless these are specifically excluded. To complicate the issue further, positive lists for services typically divide each service and service subsector (roughly 160 subsectors ranging from accounting to construction to tour guides) into four different "modes" of delivery. Negative lists do not worry about how services are delivered and either open subsectors or do not under specific, listed conditions. RCEP reflects this diverse background as the services chapter commitments including both positive and negative list pledges, depending on the preferences of the member.

The services negotiations are also made knotty by India's insistence that services discussions revolve primarily around one specific element of services—the "Mode 4" movement of people. India believes it has a comparative advantage in the provision of services and the skills of the Indian service providers in Asia. Hence it wants to ensure that these individuals are free to move about the region to provide such services as business services, Information and Communications Technology services and the like with fewer restrictions than such individuals face currently. Even if this wish were to be granted, individuals would still be subject to immigration controls, visa requirements and, potentially, licensing and regulatory requirements for specific sectors. It is not clear, therefore, whether including Mode 4 commitments within RCEP would result in a meaningful movement for service providers.

Movement of people collides head-on with a difficulty that most RCEP member states have with accepting foreign labour. This tension is unlikely to be resolved to the satisfaction of India. Instead, India might be better served to focus on the delivery of services online or the broader opening of service sectors where it has a comparative advantage overall. Even if no specific commitments are made within RCEP regarding the movement of service providers, it does not mean that individuals are unable to relocate for work. It simply means that the temporary provision of service providers is not locked in through RCEP.

E-commerce

Among the most important debates in the regional economy is that which revolves around e-commerce and digital trade. As an increasingly integral part of the global economy, e-commerce facilitates cross-border trade with unprecedented speed and reach. This new development is critical to the development of international trade and can no longer be overlooked.

Asia has been at the forefront of e-commerce and digital trade and RCEP has been moving towards the inclusion of new rules in the agreement. It will include provisions not just in the chapter labelled e-commerce but also in other chapters that are relevant, like trade facilitation for smaller sized, smaller value packages that are more typically moved through e-commerce.

Getting an agreement done on e-commerce in RCEP, though, has been more difficult than anticipated. In part this stems from some of the member government's concerns about the movement of information and data and increasing desire to keep data (either all data or some sensitive or sectoral data) hosted locally. It has also proven challenging for RCEP to manage the broader demands of e-commerce and digital trade which touches on nearly every chapter in the agreement, given the relatively isolated working group structure in the negotiations.

Other chapters

RCEP had about 15 substantive chapters under negotiation by mid-2017. In addition to goods, services, investment and e-commerce, officials were also working on intellectual property, standards (for both food and other goods), legal issues, small and medium enterprises (SMEs), development and cooperation, trade remedies and government procurement. These additional chapters were often moving ahead with greater speed than the traditional topics. In fact, two chapters, on SMEs and development, were closed relatively quickly. The remainder were more challenging to close out independently, as progress in one area was dependent on commitments made in other arenas.

Stakeholder involvement

The concurrently developing TPP negotiating process was lauded for an innovative program of stakeholder involvement. Non-governmental entities, business representatives and academics were integrated as part of the negotiation process, providing important information to government officials on what their needs were and how best the agreement might be able to achieve it.

Such a high level of stakeholder involvement would be very helpful in supporting RCEP's efforts to find common ground between 16 entities. But stakeholders have been noticeably absent across the RCEP process. Only a handful of rounds have included an opportunity for businesses and civil society organizations to comment on the agreement. Those involved have largely been specifically invited by the local host. Press access has also been minimal. Few delegations have released information about ongoing talks.

RCEP and the relationship to the TPP

The RCEP was negotiated around the same time as the TPP agreement and the seven members (Australia, Brunei, Japan, Malaysia, New Zealand, Singapore and Vietnam) involved in both agreements were the same, therefore, there has always been a level of comparison between RCEP and the TPP.

The TPP negotiations were concluded and the legal text was signed by trade ministers on 4 February 2016, by 12 members (Australia, Brunei, Canada, Chile, Malaysia, Mexico, New Zealand, Japan, Peru, Singapore, the United States, and Vietnam). The 30 chapters of the TPP included topics that are not often included in trade agreements in Asia, such as state-owned enterprises, deep commitments in intellectual property rights (IPRs), a variety of rules on standards including new provisions on sanitary and phytosanitary measures, e-commerce, labour and the environment. The TPP also contained new rules in digital trade and trade facilitation.

The goods commitments in the TPP were particularly high-quality, with members committed to opening up nearly all product categories, including extremely sensitive agricultural items to one another. Nearly all tariffs were cut to zero and most were cut on the first day of the agreement (or entry into force). The rest were cut on relatively short timelines. For services and investment, members agreed to use negative list scheduling, meaning that all sectors and subsectors were opened to member firms except for those explicitly listed as closed. In practice the level of exceptions was quite small.

However, once the deal was signed, ratification proved challenging. The election of US President Donald Trump dramatically changed the prospects for the TPP. One of his first acts in office was to withdraw the United States from participating in January 2017.

While it initially looked like this would be the death knell for the agreement as a whole, the remaining 11 parties regrouped and spent the remainder of the year meeting regularly to address new entry into force procedures and adjustments to the deal to present to leaders in November 2017. Hence, November 2017 became an interesting tussle once more between RCEP and the TPP as both agreements were scheduled to make big announcements at their respective Leader's Summits (RCEP at the ASEAN Ministerial in the Philippines and TPP at the APEC Leader's Meeting in Vietnam).

As it happened, neither agreement lived up to the billing—the TPP11 was unable to conclude as scheduled and RCEP was barely mentioned in Manila. Instead, the TPP was renamed the Comprehensive and Progressive Trans-Pacific Partnership (CPTPP) and signature was set for March 8, 2018. RCEP rolled over to 2018 as Singapore took up the ASEAN Chairmanship.

TPP and RCEP comparison

RCEP will not be a second TPP. The high standards and level of commitments in the TPP are not acceptable to many RCEP members. Even though the negotiation for RCEP has not been concluded, it is predictable that several advanced areas under the TPP will not be covered, and that RCEP provisions under the same areas will not have as high standards as TPP rules. Getting an agreement done with 16 extremely diverse members is hard. RCEP countries were "drafted" into these negotiations—they did not volunteer to join like TPP members. Their overall level of commitment to regional integration with one another therefore varies.

While the TPP has 30 chapters, RCEP has roughly 15 substantive chapters.[33] Several areas under the TPP will not be covered by RCEP including labour, environment, and (probably) state-owned enterprises.[34] However, RCEP will include areas that are not included in the TPP, such as SMEs and cooperation and development.

As part of the developmental objective, RCEP includes special provisions for developing countries and least developed country members. The TPP, by contrast, applies exactly the same rulebook to all members regardless of their developmental status (with slightly longer one for implementation of a very small number of provisions).

The main areas of focus in RCEP negotiations have been trade in goods, trade in services, investment, e-commerce, trade facilitation and customs, SMEs, IPR and legal issues. Even though RCEP takes into account many key areas of concern for companies and governments in the era of digital and advanced technologies such as e-commerce, IPR or disputes, the rules written for these areas under RCEP are unlikely to be as ambitious as the ones written under TPP.

Due to the substantial existing gaps among RCEP members in terms of economic development, and approaches towards trade liberalization, the potential coverage and depth of RCEP rules will be closer to ASEAN than to TPP.

The first criterion in which TPP is more ambitious than RCEP is the level of commitment on market access for goods. The TPP cuts tariffs for almost all product lines including sensitive goods such as rice, beef and dairy products. On entry into force, the TPP would eliminate around 75 percent of non-zero tariffs.[35] In the long run, 99 percent of non-zero tariffs would be removed.[36] Meanwhile, RCEP might be able to conclude on tariff liberalization for up to 90 percent of products due to the disagreement among RCEP members on the level of trade liberalization the countries are ready to take on, with likely long timelines for reduction for some members.[37] Most agricultural products will likely remain in the 10 percent of items untouched by RCEP liberalization.

The second criterion is services liberalization. Using the negative-list scheduling method,[38] the TPP opened services to an extent that has rarely been seen in trade agreements. These include sensitive areas such as healthcare, hospitality and tourism, education, logistics and professional services.[39] RCEP, on the other hand, uses mostly positive-list scheduling for services chapter.[40] While it is possible to schedule exactly the same commitments using both approaches, in general, positive lists tend to be less market opening than negative lists. Over time, new service sectors are also not automatically opened in positive lists but must be renegotiated by the parties as well.

Investment could be a bright spot for RCEP as all members want inbound investment. Protection of this investment, however, remains unclear as parties are not yet certain about the extent to which they will follow the guiding principles.

The remainder of the agreement in RCEP, including what the TPP officials used to call the "21st century" elements, is more promising. Many of these issues are new to ASEAN and some RCEP parties. Hence any commitments at all that are forthcoming in the RCEP context will be a welcome addition to the regional integration efforts.

China's role[41]

RCEP has often been described as "the China-led" alternative to the "US-led" TPP. As this chapter makes clear, this formulation is not accurate. RCEP has always been guided by the ASEAN. The agreement will be built on the foundations of the ASEAN agreements. The criteria for entry is an existing deal with ASEAN.

Nevertheless, the perception remains that RCEP is China's baby. This vision was reinforced by events in 2017 as the US began to retreat as a leader of globalization and headed towards a more protectionist orientation. China came under the spotlight and showed their strong support for globalization. At the World Economic Forum in Davos in January 2017, Chinese President Xi Jinping emphasized the important role of globalization and economic integration while acknowledging the existence of issues around this area.[42]

Apart from the One-Belt-One-Road initiative, the Chinese President has mentioned RCEP as the main focus of the continuous efforts of Asian countries to expedite globalization and economic integration in the region. This shows China's commitment to support globalization and to strengthen the image of a new progressive China.

Being seen as a China-led trade deal, RCEP also started receiving more attention. Countries are looking for alternative options outside the TPP or are keen to see the future of globalization. Several countries that have considered joining RCEP in the near future include Chile, Peru and Canada.[43] There has been a slow, but steadily increasing amount of news and discussions on RCEP.

India's challenge

While China has not exactly claimed the leadership mantle in RCEP like most outsiders have assumed, India has been tagged with being the anchor that is dragging down the talks. This perception is perhaps also unfair.

While it is true that India has struggled to come to terms with the remaining RCEP economies on market access for goods, it is also likely the case that several other RCEP members are effectively "hiding" behind India—hoping that India will absorb the brunt of complaints and keep the agreement from cutting tariffs too deeply or too quickly. If India were not doing so, other members might have to admit that they also have sensitivities in goods trade as well. As an example, in the ASEAN-India FTA, Indonesia did not make any changes at all to more than half its total tariff lines—compared to India's commitments on nearly three quarters or the rest of ASEAN who agreed to tariff opening for up to 80 percent.

On services trade beyond just Mode 4 movement of temporary service providers, many ASEAN countries also have difficulties and past ASEAN experience suggests limited commitments are likely to be forthcoming.[44]

However, there is a strong case to be made that India should seize the opportunities offered by RCEP negotiations. In particular, while ASEAN and the other +6 countries have extensive links to global trade, India does not. India's existing FTA connections are weak and the country remains outside the manufacturing and agricultural supply chains that dominate most ASEAN and Asian economies. RCEP offers a chance for Indian firms to engage in a serious fashion. For most RCEP member firms, the biggest "prize" on offer is the potential to work more closely with Indian companies in the future.

If India misses this opportunity to more tightly connect to Asia, the countries in the region will simply proceed to integrate without India. Already seven RCEP members are in TPP11, 12 are in APEC, and nearly all have extensive bilateral agreements with other parties including new links with the European Union. The option on the table for India is not RCEP or the status quo where no one has an agreement across Asia, but a 15-party RCEP and a much worse set of options.

Current rounds and latest news

By the end of 2017, RCEP has finished 20 negotiation rounds. The 2018 calendar includes three full rounds: with an all negotiators gathering; a partial "round" with the key working groups meeting simultaneously; many "intersessional" meetings of specific working committees; multiple ministerial meetings planned, culminating in the Leader's Summit in November in Singapore. The fervent hope of many officials is that the agreement can be concluded at the end of 2018.

Under the political pressure of the ASEAN's 50th anniversary, RCEP negotiations made enough progress to issue an agreement outline for all 18 chapters in November 2017 at the Ministerial Meeting in Manila. Two chapters have been officially concluded on SMEs and on economic and technical cooperation (Table 1.2).[45]

Table 1.2 RCEP potential chapters

No	Potential chapter
1	Trade in goods
2	Rules of Origin (RoO)
3	Customs Procedures and Trade Facilitation (CPTF)
4	Sanitary and Phytosanitary (SPS) Measures
5	Standards, Technical Regulations and Conformity Assessment Procedures (STRACAP)
6	Trade remedies
7	Trade in services
8	Financial services
9	Telecommunications services
10	Movement of natural persons
11	Investment
12	Competition
13	Intellectual Property (IP)
14	Electronic Commerce (E-Commerce)
15	Small and Medium Enterprises (SMEs)
16	Economic and Technical Cooperation (ECOTECH)
17	Government Procurement (GP)
18	Dispute Settlement (DS)

Source: Joint Leaders' Statement on the Negotiations for the Regional Comprehensive Economic Partnership (RCEP).[46]

2018 will be an interesting year for RCEP. Under Singapore's chairmanship of ASEAN and the fast-changing trade landscape, the 16 countries will have even more motivation to accelerate the negotiation progress and finish the deal within the seventh year of negotiations.

Acknowledgements

The authors would like to thank Benyamin Jamieson, Isabel Udal Perucho for their assistance with this chapter.

Notes

1 Kim, Sangkyom, Park, Innwon, and Park, Soonchan. "A Free Trade Area of Asia Pacific (FTAAP): Is It Desirable?", *East Asian Economic Review*, vol. 17, no. 1, pp. 3–25 (2013). Retrieved from: www.eaerweb.org/journal/journalDetail.jsp?mgr_no=JE0001_2013_v17n1_3&ejno=JE0001 [Accessed on June 30, 2017].
2 Lester, Simon. "Is the Doha Round Over? The WTO's Negotiating Agenda for 2016 and Beyond." *Cato Institute* (2016). Retrieved from: www.cato.org/publications/free-trade-bulletin/doha-round-over-wtos-negotiating-agenda-2016-beyond [Accessed on June 30, 2017].
3 Risaburo Nezu. "Comprehensive Economic Partnership in East Asia (Part 1)", Fujitsu Research Institute. (2009). Jose, Tojo. "What is Special Safeguard Mechanism under WTO?" *IndianEconomy.net*. (2015). Retrieved from: www.

fujitsu.com/jp/group/fri/en/column/message/2009/2009-9-9.html [Accessed on June 30, 2017].

4 Das, Sanchita Basu, and Reema B. Jagtiani. "The Regional Comprehensive Economic Partnership: New Paradigm or Old Wine in a New Bottle?" *ISEAS* (2014). Retrieved from: www.iseas.edu.sg/images/pdf/iseas_economics_working_papers_2014_3.pdf [Accessed on June 30, 2017].

5 Hadi Soesastro (Ed.). "Developing A Roadmap towards East Asian Integration," 2008, ERIA, www.eria.org/publications/developing-a-roadmap-toward-east-asian-economic-integration.html [Accessed July 31, 2017].

6 Das, Sanchita Basu, and Reema B. Jagtiani. "The Regional Comprehensive Economic Partnership: New Paradigm or Old Wine in a New Bottle?" *ISEAS* (2014). Retrieved from: www.iseas.edu.sg/images/pdf/iseas_economics_working_papers_2014_3.pdf [Accessed on June 30, 2017].

7 Das, Sanchita Basu, and Reema B. Jagtiani. "The Regional Comprehensive Economic Partnership: New Paradigm or Old Wine in a New Bottle?" *ISEAS* (2014). Retrieved from: www.iseas.edu.sg/images/pdf/iseas_economics_working_papers_2014_3.pdf [Accessed on June 30, 2017].

8 Das, Sanchita Basu, and Reema B. Jagtiani. "The Regional Comprehensive Economic Partnership: New Paradigm or Old Wine in a New Bottle?" *ISEAS* (2014). Retrieved from: www.iseas.edu.sg/images/pdf/iseas_economics_working_papers_2014_3.pdf [Accessed on June 30, 2017].

9 Armstrong, Shiro. "Why the RCEP is the Only Game in Town for ASEAN Following TPP Trumping." *AEC News Today* (2017). Retrieved from: https://aecnewstoday.com/2017/why-the-rcep-is-the-only-game-in-town-for-asean-following-tpp-trumping/ [Accessed on June 30, 2017].

10 Das, Sanchita Basu. "Understanding the Regional Comprehensive Economic Partnership and the Trans-Pacific Partnership: An ASEAN perspective." *ISEAS* (2014). Retrieved from: www.brookings.edu/wp-content/uploads/2014/01/11-asia-pacific-economic-integration-presentation-basu-das.pdf [Accessed on June 30, 2017].

11 Lee, Chang Jae, Misa Okabe (Eds.), "Comprehensive Mapping of FTAs in ASEAN and East Asia," *ERIA Research Project Report* 2010-26.

12 Despite a commitment in the Leader's statement for RCEP that called for all members of RCEP to have completed agreements with ASEAN that included commitments on goods, services and investment prior to launching negotiations.

13 Das, Sanchita Basu. "Understanding the Regional Comprehensive Economic Partnership and the Trans-Pacific Partnership: An ASEAN perspective." *ISEAS* (2014). Retrieved from: www.brookings.edu/wp-content/uploads/2014/01/11-asia-pacific-economic-integration-presentation-basu-das.pdf [Accessed on June 30, 2017].

14 New Zealand Foreign Affairs and Trade. "New Zealand-India FTA." (2017). Retrieved from: www.mfat.govt.nz/en/trade/free-trade-agreements/agreements-under-negotiation/india/ [Accessed on June 30, 2017].

15 Das, Sanchita Basu, and Reema B. Jagtiani. "The Regional Comprehensive Economic Partnership: New Paradigm or Old Wine in a New Bottle?" *ISEAS* (2014). Retrieved from: www.iseas.edu.sg/images/pdf/iseas_economics_working_papers_2014_3.pdf [Accessed on June 30, 2017].

16 Fukanaga, Yoshifumi, and Isono, Ikumo. "Taking ASEAN+1 FTAs towards the RCEP: A Mapping Study." *ERIA Discussion Paper Series* (2013). Retrieved from: www.eria.org/ERIA-DP-2013-02.pdf [Accessed on June 30, 2017].

17 Anuradha, R. V. "Liberalization of Trade in Services under RCEP: Mapping the Key Issues." *Asian Journal of WTO & International Health and Law Policy*, vol. 8, no. 2, pp. 401–420 (2013). Retrieved from: https://papers.ssrn.com/sol3/papers.cfm?abstract_id=2385520 [Accessed on June 30, 2017].

18 Of course, it should perhaps be noted that for most TPP member countries, the specific negotiators on the RCEP side were often different. However, many members had tight coordination between teams domestically.

19 ASEAN. "ASEAN Briefing 2014." *ASEAN Briefing* (2017). Retrieved from: www. aseanbriefing.com/news/wp-content/uploads/2014/10/Chart-2.jpg [Accessed on June 30, 2017].

20 Panda, Jagannath P. "Factoring the RCEP and the TPP: China, India and the Politics of Regional Integration." *Strategic Analysis*, vol. 38, no. 1, pp. 49–67 (2014). Retrieved from: 10.1080/09700161.2014.863462 [Accessed on June 30, 2017].

21 Elms, Deborah. "Solving the Many Sides of RCEP." *Asian Trade Centre Talking Trade Blog* (2017). Retrieved from: www.asiantradecentre.org/talkingtrade// solving-the-many-sides-of-rcep [Accessed on June 30, 2017].

22 Fukanaga, Yoshifumi, and Isono, Ikumo. "Taking ASEAN+1 FTAs towards the RCEP: A Mapping Study." *ERIA Discussion Paper Series* (2013). Retrieved from: www.eria.org/ERIA-DP-2013-02.pdf [Accessed on June 30, 2017].

23 Fukanaga, Yoshifumi, and Isono, Ikumo. "Taking ASEAN+1 FTAs towards the RCEP: A Mapping Study." *ERIA Discussion Paper Series* (2013). Retrieved from: www.eria.org/ERIA-DP-2013-02.pdf [Accessed on June 30, 2017]; and Anuradha, R. V. "Liberalization of Trade in Services under RCEP: Mapping the Key Issues." *Asian Journal of WTO & International Health and Law Policy*, vol. 8, no. 2, pp. 401–420 (2013). Retrieved from: https://papers.ssrn.com/sol3/ papers.cfm?abstract_id=2385520 [Accessed on June 30, 2017].

24 Mishra, Rahul. "RCEP: Challenges and Opportunities for India." *RSIS Commentaries*, No. 140 (2013). Retrieved from: http://hdl.handle.net/10220/20111 [Accessed on June 30, 2017].

25 Anuradha, R. V. "Liberalization of Trade in Services under RCEP: Mapping the Key Issues." *Asian Journal of WTO & International Health and Law Policy*, vol. 8, no. 2, pp. 401–420 (2013). Retrieved from: https://papers.ssrn.com/sol3/ papers.cfm?abstract_id=2385520 [Accessed on June 30, 2017].

26 Ministry of Foreign Affairs and Trade of New Zealand. "Regional Comprehensive Economic Partnership negotiating rounds." Retrieved from: www.mfat. govt.nz/en/trade/free-trade-agreements/agreements-under-negotiation/rcep/ regional-comprehensive-economic-partnership-negotiating-rounds/ [Accessed on July 17, 2017].

27 Elms, Deborah. "Cutting tariffs in RCEP." *Asian Trade Centre Talking Trade Blog* (2015). Retrieved from: www.asiantradecentre.org/talkingtrade/2015/9/3/ cutting-tariffs-in-rcep [Accessed on June 30, 2017].

28 Nguyen, Minh Hue. "Concentrated Trade in the Regional Comprehensive Economic Partnership." *APEC Currents*. Retrieved from: https://us9.campaign- archive.com/?u=6fc18e2d4abd250eb5f7b2445&id=2c8ce6b10e&e=abb157e48b# Welcome [Accessed on January 31, 2018].

29 "Policy Brief: Concentrated Trade in RCEP," Asian Trade Centre, April 2016, Number 16-07, https://static1.squarespace.com/static/5393d501e4b0643446ab- d228/t/5752a730f850829dde1c4acc/1465034547365/Policy+Brief+16-07+ Concentrated+Trade+2016+ATC.pdf.

30 RCEP has been drafting RoOs at the six-digit level, meaning roughly 5000 tariff lines will need matching RoOs. This is different from the TPP, for instance, where tariff commitments were made at the domestic heading, or up to ten-digit level of specificity, and considerably more RoOs. For companies, however, more digits do not automatically equal greater benefits, just more clarity on which products fit into which categories.

31 Comment by the chief negotiator, ATC podcast, February 21, 2017, www.atc. org.

32 Conversations with the authors.

33 Elms, Deborah. "RCEP And TPP Compared." *Asian Trade Centre Talking Trade Blog* (2016). Retrieved from: www.asiantradecentre.org/talkingtrade//myvwg5y r21a93pkjc45bwzx3wtbc3z [Accessed on July 14, 2017].

34 Ota, Yasu (2017, April 27). "Think the RCEP is about Free Trade? Think again." *Nikkei Asian Review* (2017). Retrieved from: http://asia.nikkei.com/ magazine/20170427/On-the-Cover/Think-the-RCEP-is-about-free-trade-Think-again?page=2 [Accessed on July 14, 2017].

35 Freund, Caroline, Moran, Tyler, Oliver, Sarah. "Tariff Liberalization." Chap. 2 in Elliott, Kimberly Ann, Caroline Freund, Anna Gelpern, Cullen S. Hendrix, Gary Clyde Hufbauer, Barbara Kotschwar, Theodore H. Moran et al. *Assessing the Trans-Pacific Partnership, Volume 1: Market Access and Sectoral* Issues. No. PIIEB16-1. Peterson Institute for International Economics (2016). This refers to TPP12.

36 Freund, Caroline, Moran, Tyler, Oliver, Sarah. "Tariff Liberalization." Chap. 2 in Elliott, Kimberly Ann, Caroline Freund, Anna Gelpern, Cullen S. Hendrix, Gary Clyde Hufbauer, Barbara Kotschwar, Theodore H. Moran et al. *Assessing the Trans-Pacific Partnership, Volume 1: Market Access and Sectoral* Issues. No. PIIEB16-1. Peterson Institute for International Economics (2016). This refers to TPP12.

37 Philippine News Agency. "RCEP participating countries urged to speed up discussions on trade liberalization." (2017) Retrieved from: www.pna.gov.ph/articles/985848. [Accessed on July 14, 2017].

38 Only listed sectors will be restricted. The rest will be opened.

39 Ministry of Foreign Affairs and Trade of New Zealand (MFAT). "Market access in non-goods sectors." Retrieved from: www.tpp.mfat.govt.nz/assets/ docs/TPP_factsheet_Market-Access-Service-Investment.pdf [Accessed on July 15, 2017].

40 Elms, Deborah. "RCEP And TPP Compared." *Asian Trade Centre Talking Trade Blog* (2016). Retrieved from: www.asiantradecentre.org/talkingtrade//myvwg5y r21a93pkjc45bwzx3wtbc3z [Accessed on July 14, 2017].

41 Chen, Lurong. "RCEP Is Not the Anti-TPP." *The Diplomat* (2016). Retrieved from: http://thediplomat.com/2016/12/rcep-is-not-the-anti-tpp/ [Accessed on June 30, 2017].

42 Parker, Ceri. "China's Xi Jinping Defends Globalization from the Davos Stage." *World Economic Forum* (2017). Retrieved from: www.weforum.org/ agenda/2017/01/chinas-xi-jinping-defends-globalization-from-the-davos-stage/ [Accessed on July 14, 2017].

43 Zhou, Laura. "Latin American Economies Look to China for Free Trade Options." *South China Morning Post* (2016). Retrieved from: www.scmp.com/news/ china/diplomacy-defence/article/2047728/latin-american-economies-look-china-free-trade-options [Accessed on July 14, 2017]; and Patterson, Brent. "Canada explores joining the Pacific Alliance or RCEP at Upcoming TPP-Alternatives Summit." *The Councils of Canadian* (2017). Retrieved from: https://canadians. org/blog/canada-explores-joining-pacific-alliance-or-rcep-upcoming-tpp-alternatives-summit [Accessed on July 14, 2017].

44 See, for example, the *ASEAN Services Integration Report*, 100637. Retrieved from: http://documents.worldbank.org/curated/en/759841468178459585/pdf/ 100637-Revised-WP-PUBLIC-Box393257B-ASEAN-Report-web.pdf [Accessed on February 14, 2018].

45 ASEAN. "The Third Regional Comprehensive Economic Partnership (RCEP) Intersessional Ministerial Meeting – Joint Media Statement." (2017). Retrieved from: http://asean.org/storage/2017/05/RCEP-3ISSL-MM-JMS-FINAL-22052017. pdf [Accessed on July 15, 2017].
46 ASEAN. "Joint Leaders' Statement on the Negotiations for the Regional Comprehensive Economic Partnership (RCEP)." 2017. Retrieved from: http://asean.org/ storage/2017/11/RCEP-Summit_Leaders-Joint-Statement-FINAL1.pdf [Accessed on January 31, 2018].

2 Trade and economic integration for South Asia

Exploring corridors and dynamism in Asia[1]

Sachin Chaturvedi

There is little doubt that we have entered the times when contradictions and counter-cyclical moves become part of the flux that the world economy is going through. The cross-border connects and cross-domain connects are emerging as new realities. The narrow approach to trend analysis is paving way for multidisciplinary approaches. Unease at the top to absorb the granularity along with the ground reality is multiplying.

Analytical efforts to capture these details were missed out in the past. It is in this respect economic geography approach is increasingly being referred to by policymakers for greater understanding of processes and for better practical insights.

These approaches help in mapping the economic landscape in a dynamic fashion, as opportunities come up to explore economic inter-linkages across various policy concerns like employment, production, environment and trade.[2] As a result, we often hear of economic growth corridors, growth triangles, growth quadrangles, and other such approaches where integrated networks, value chains, and intra-regional connects may come in. The earlier idea of close geographic proximity, though is still relevant, but is not the only determinant for success for such initiatives. Political commitment, policy coordination and adequate physical and infrastructural approaches are equally important in exploring commitment for trade and competitiveness and for that matter for processes like Regional Comprehensive Economic Partnership (RCEP).

Economic growth corridor

Economic growth corridors are often mentioned in contemporary development parlance. Essentially, economic corridors connect economic agents (that is businesses and entrepreneurs) in a dynamic setting with economic growth agents (that is policy makers) and help create patterns of regional economic development. Structural characteristics that growth corridors facilitate bring in cohesion across parameters such as trade diversification, value chains, both inter and intra-regional and vertical networks.

The direct advantage of growth corridors is mostly in the form of enhanced combined trade, and travel costs, logistics chain efficiency, comprehensive transit arrangements and inter-connectivity. Excellent and highly efficient supply chains that have come up in East Asia offer a varied lesson to the rest of the continent. Largely what initially started with transport corridor brings in transport and trade facilitation, leading to logistics corridor and finally economic corridor.

The purpose of setting these corridors may vary as they are built on the basis of different opportunities, and more certainly on relative comparative advantages. To analyse the prospects of intra-regional trade, one can look at 'trade complementarity index'.[3] This index shows the extent to which structure of the importers and exporters match. It lies between 0 and 100 where 0 implies no complementarity, that is, no goods are imported and exported between the two countries and 100 implies an exact match of import and export pattern. Trade complementarity in 2016 between India and Japan was 62, between India and the entire South Asian region[4] was 61, between Malaysia and India was 60, between Afghanistan and Maldives was 59 and between Indonesia and Japan was 63.[5] These numbers point towards the fact that there are trade complementarities between the Asian nations and thus giving them a scope to trade more with each other.

Growth poles

Countries in different stages of economic development and asymmetric distribution of factor endowments need to assess terms of technology and quality of human capital endowments when they opt for regional or subregional cooperation. The idea of growth triangles, in this context, assumes greater relevance as it promotes open regionalism through intra-regional human development. They may prove to be an important tool in reducing the income and growth gaps. Fundamentally, the concept of growth triangles is not completely new. It is based on what came out in 1950 in the writings of Francois Perroux on 'Growth Poles'.

Darwent in his 1969 paper, 'Growth poles and growth centres in regional planning – a review' pointed out that 'growth pole' is not the right translation of what Francois intended when he wrote out the concept. However, the term could create its own traction and as Darwent described, "a very powerful intuitive and emotive appeal" among the larger economic community members. 'Poles' were identified as spaces from which centrifugal forces emanated and to which centripetal forces were attracted. These poles may be firms, industries or even industrial mechanisms.

Speakman and Kouvisto in the World Bank's Africa Competitiveness Report, 2013, identified 'growth poles' as simultaneously coordinated investments in many sectors to support self-sustained industrialization. 'Growth poles' bear resemblance to, but are not the same as special economic zones, which are spatially delimited areas within an economy. Examples include export economic zones, economic processing zones, free zones and foreign trade zones. The growth of corridors is intrinsically linked with right identification and nurturing of growth poles. The strategies of corridors are successful when essential epicentres for growth are identified.

New initiatives

South East Asia is filled with extremely rich experience in this regard. The saga of economic growth in the ASEAN region has several fascinating stories of economic corridors and growth poles eventually leading to regional integration. The economies of ASEAN countries could evolve an optimal balance in hard and soft elements that optimize a corridor's competitiveness.

The idea of Belt and Road Initiative (BRI), Bangladesh, China, India, Myanmar (BCIM) Corridor, Asia Africa Growth Corridor (AAGC) are manifestations of similar approaches. With a varied degree of optimality, each option has its own unique gains for the region. The idea of AAGC is to bring in Indo-Pacific in the framework and thereby expanding the universe.

In this effort inter-sectoral multilevel approaches could provide growth impetus for small and medium enterprises. There are due lessons to be learnt on how trade and economic integration in South and South East Asia and Central Asia needs to move forward, as we are moving ahead with the Asian Century.

South-Asia

There have been constant debates regarding progress in South Asia in terms of economic integration and performance of the South Asian Association for Regional Cooperation (SAARC) as an institution.

Efficacy and effectiveness in regional cooperation pursuits are extremely important for retaining our collective competitiveness in the global economy. The regional outlook of South Asia is showing a remarkable upturn compared to rest of the world. The regional macroeconomic situation is gradually improving with partial recovery of the global economy in recent times. According to the Asian Development Outlook, 2017: Transcending the Middle-Income Challenge, updated numbers, South Asia as a whole is expected to grow at 7 percent in 2018.

With the introduction of GST in India, one is keenly waiting to see its impact on informal trade in South Asia and in particular India. Though this is viewed as a manifestation of natural comparative advantage, the existence of trade complementarities and supply-demand gaps across countries in the region with formalization of better incentives may help promote the much-required regional integration. Adding both formal and informal, the intra-SAARC trade would be much higher. While formal intra-SAARC trade stands at around US$ 20 billion, the informal trade estimates turn out to be US$ 25 billion.[6]

In the South Asia Development and Cooperation Report 2016 published by the Research and Information System for Developing countries (RIS), we mentioned that the intra-SAARC formal trade increased by 270 percent between 2003 and 2012; however, informal trade increased by only 112 percent between 2005 and 2012, while it increased by 285 percent between 1990 and 2005.

As we celebrate the 20th anniversary of BIMSTEC this year, two platforms for sub-regional cooperation, namely BIMSTEC and the Bangladesh, Bhutan, India, Nepal (BBIN) Initiative are moving towards deeper integration.

BIMSTEC

The Bay of Bengal Initiative for Multi-Sectoral Technical and Economic Cooperation (BIMSTEC) is a regional organization, comprising of seven Member States and 14 priority areas of cooperation. Each country has identified some lead areas in which to provide leadership. Keeping the current dynamics in mind, I presume, Bangladesh has the most important area to lead BIMSTEC on, which is trade and investment. India has the responsibility for transportation and communication while Sri Lanka can be relied on for technology.

At RIS this year in partnership with the Export-Import Bank of India (EXIM) we hosted the first Summer School for BIMSTEC countries on 'International Trade, Theory and Practice'. More than FTA discussions, I think non-tariff barriers (NTBs) were to be addressed by the grouping on a top priority basis. To capture the essence of NTBs, Table 2.1 below provides some indicators that capture the ease of doing business in BIMSTEC countries. Even though some countries like Thailand have a more conducive environment for businesses to flourish, others like Bangladesh and Myanmar have a long road to cover. The latest report by World Bank on Doing Business[7] shows that overall ranking of Bangladesh is 177 among the 190 economies that are ranked and Myanmar stands at the 171st position. In

Table 2.1 Overview of non-tariff barriers

Country	Ease of doing business ranking, 2017	Cost of business start-up procedures (% of GNI per capita), 2016	Logistics performance index: overall (1 = low to 5 = high), 2016	Mobile cellular subscriptions (per 100 people), 2015
Bangladesh	177	13.8	2.6	81.9
Bhutan	75	3.8	2.3	87.0
India	100	13.8	3.4	78.1
Myanmar	171	40.4	2.4	75.7
Nepal	105	26.1	2.4	96.7
Sri Lanka	111	12.2	NA	110.6
Thailand	26	6.6	3.2	152.7

Source: Compiled by the author using World Development Indicators, World Bank.

the case of Bangladesh, enforcing contracts, getting electricity and register-ing property are the most poorly performing areas. Cost of business start-up procedures[8] is the highest in Myanmar at 40 percent of gross national in-come (GNI) per-capita followed by Nepal at 26 percent. Similarly, logis-tic performance index for most of the BIMSTEC countries remains low at around 2.5. As a proxy for communication infrastructure, we report mobile cellular subscriptions per 100 people.[9] Here we find that barring Thailand and Sri Lanka, across all BIMSTEC countries mobile subscription is not present with every individual.

In light of the new developments at RCEP, better preparedness of the re-gion would prove to be a greater building block.

BBIN sub-grouping

This is an important grouping of South Asian nations which is shaping up well as a potentially important vehicle for regional integration. The bloc would play an important role in linking ASEAN with South Asia. With highly po-larized political opinions on regional integration in South Asia, engaging the public is very necessary. Everyone should welcome the jobs, technology and easier movement that better cross-border links would bring. Regional coop-eration should not remain confined to the government-to-government level, it must also encompass ordinary citizens to make it a success. Think-tanks and other actors would have to actively communicate this responsibility.

BBIN initiatives are advancing through two joint working groups, one focused on water resources and power and the other on connectivity and transit. The first group is exploring hydropower projects that would be undertaken jointly by at least three countries on an equitable basis and on developing grid connectivity. The second working group, which produced the motor vehicle agreement, is looking at ways to improve cross-border movements of cargo and tourists by road and rail as well as how to strengthen actual border infrastructure. One result is the well-equipped Phulbari road crossing between India and Bangladesh. A future initiative could involve visa reciprocity.

The process of heart of Asia

The South East Asia and South Asia connect is to be expanded to Central Asia and the possibility is through the process of Heart of Asia (HoA). This has emerged as an important initiative for connecting Afghanistan with the rest of the Asian countries. In this context, the role of India becomes crucial as India is geographically situated in a manner that it connects South and Southeast Asia with Central and West Asia.

India particularly is in a position to play a more dynamic role in the connectivity projects, especially given the fact that for India the HoA, that is, Afghanistan, is already one of the most prominent destinations of its developmental projects and cooperative endeavours. Due to this, India's role in strengthening connectivity within the ambit of HoA becomes eminently more pronounced. This assumes even more importance as India has the wherewithal to effectively contribute towards the evolution of various facets of connectivity through mutually beneficial cooperative initiatives. One such example is the 1,814-km-long Turkmenistan-Afghanistan-Pakistan-India Gas Pipeline (TAPI) that aims to exports nearly 33 billion cubic metres (bcm) of natural gas annually from Turkmenistan to Afghanistan, Pakistan and India. This project will not only help in supplementing energy needs of the countries involved but will also promote peace between them.

The philosophy of "Borders serving as Bridges" as the economic, physical and transport connectivity between sub-regions of Asia including Central Asia is to be leveraged for further enhancing regional trade in HoA countries. The prospects of development of air transportation, associated with projects like 'Cargo–Kyrgyzstan', could also be harnessed with the help of adequate investment; especially by the construction of a cargo terminal with an expected volume of cargo operation to the tune of 2.5 million tonnes. The agreement on the establishment of "Lazurite corridor", signed by Afghanistan, Turkmenistan, Azerbaijan, Turkey and Georgia on 19th November, 2016, would enable Afghanistan to get the shortest access to the Black Sea and the Mediterranean Sea. This will not only improve the connectivity, but also provide employment opportunities for Afghanistan that faces a low labour participation rate.

25 years of ASEAN-India partnership

While our minds are with the ongoing RCEP process, our hearts are full with the idea of celebrating the 25 years of ASEAN-India Partnership and 50 years of ASEAN. South East Asia is at the core of India's Act East policy for the realization of our dream of an Asian century. It is not only central to our presence in East Asia but is equally essential for connecting with the North East and Eastern part of our country.

It also needs to be underlined that Prime Minister Narendra Modi has been present at the three ASEAN-India and East Asia Summits that took place in 2014, 2015 and 2016, and visited most of the ASEAN countries. This reflects the new salience of the ASEAN in India's foreign policy.

As we see proactive prospects for ASEAN-India trade relationship one also finds another important ingredient for boosting economic engagement, that is, the involvement of Indian companies in regional value chains and production networks. A project development fund for catalysing Indian economic projects in Cambodia, Lao PDR, Myanmar and Vietnam has been announced. It has a corpus of US$ 77 Million. Potential sectors have been identified and pre-feasibility studies will be undertaken soon. It is believed that interactions between policymakers and industry would give a boost to

India-ASEAN trade so that it reaches its true potential, which is estimated to be around US$200 billion by 2020.

It also needs to be underlined that India has accorded preferential treatment to the least developed countries (Cambodia, Laos and Myanmar) by way of duty-free preference schemes for import of goods, preferential treatment for services and liberalized market access, in general. This also involves the movement of people, technical assistance and capacity building. India currently provides a visa fee waiver for Laos, Cambodia and Myanmar applicants applying for Indian Business and Employment visas.

In the entire process of strengthening ASEAN-India partnership, connectivity is a huge enabler not only for development, for improving the quality of life of our people, for encouraging greater people-to-people exchanges but also for stimulating trade and investment. We use the 'trade intensity index'[10] to check the extent of trade between India and the ASEAN member countries. This index is used to indicate whether the value of trade between two countries is greater or smaller than would be expected on the basis of their importance in world trade. It lies in the range of zero to infinity; a value greater than 100 indicates a relationship more intense than the world average for the partner. Table 2.2 provides the trade intensity index for 2016, between India and ASEAN member countries.

Looking at the trade intensity index, we find that India is exporting less than expected to Brunei Darussalam, Cambodia, Lao PDR and the Philippines. Also, trade intensity index with Thailand is just above 100. This shows that there lies great potential for India to exploit and enhance its trade with ASEAN nations.

The partnership with ASEAN provides mutually beneficial gains and paves the way to benefit from the US $ 2.5 trillion ASEAN economy that eventually goes up the US $ 21 trillion as RCEP economy.

At the Economic Research Institute for ASEAN and East Asia Research Institution Network meeting, where RIS is also a member, we have stated

Table 2.2 Trade intensity index between India and ASEAN countries, 2016

Country	*Trade intensity index, 2016*
Brunei	69.20
Cambodia	46.38
Indonesia	139.38
Lao PDR	25.51
Malaysia	146.26
Myanmar	316.17
Philippines	85.06
Singapore	170.89
Thailand	105.57
Vietnam	175.60

Source: WITS Trade Indicator Database.

that RCEP is not only about opening markets but is also about building a community and enhancing the welfare of all its members. It should also seek to improve the competitiveness of services, which includes not only the visible international services like financial services and air services, important though both of those are, but also business services which are embodied in traded goods and are crucial to the operation of production networks. In the process of dealing with services, RCEP must also provide for international investments as many services require investments in commercial presence, and so do production networks. RCEP should also seek immediately to initiate regional agreement on how intellectual property rules.

Concluding remarks

The New World is becoming more specialized and requirements are divided into many areas; multiple requirements need to be responded to, like the coming up of the New Development Bank. We are going through a phase where specific requirements are to be met with special arrangements. Unique approaches of countries, in this regard, would play an important role. As trade within South-South cooperation expands, more flow of resources through FDI and development cooperation would be needed.

There is also a need to emphasize the role of finance in the region and need for us to collaborate in this area for better macroeconomic gains through greater coordination. This is one area, which has not received sufficient attention as we move for greater integration across the regions. The financial crisis of 2007–2009 has made it clear as to how activities outside the purview of regulation may lead to epidemics which individual systems are unable to manage. It is pertinent to deliberate upon how we manage our negative spillovers in an integrated region or sub-region.

Notes

1 Based on the Keynote Address delivered at the Workshop on Trade and Economic Integration: South Asia, Southeast Asia and Asia Pacific, held at Institute for South Asian Studies, Singapore on 3 August 2017.
2 Many attempts have been made by researchers to quantify the impact of trade on employment. For example, Gilbert (2011) found that Asia's growth rate was dominated by improvements in growth performance of China, India, Korea, Thailand and Vietnam which was a result of growth in productivity in these countries (Refer Brooks & Go, 2011 for more details).
3 Trade complementarity Index (TC) between country i and j is given as: $TC_{ij} = 100(1 - \sum_k (|m_{ki} - x_{kj}|/2)$ where, m_{ki} stands for share of product k in country i's total imports and x_{kj} stands for share of product k in country j's total exports. Note that $TC_{ij} \neq TC_{ji}$
4 South Asia includes Afghanistan, Bangladesh, Bhutan, India, Sri Lanka, Maldives, Nepal and Pakistan.

5 Trade Complementarity Indices have been downloaded from WITS Website.
6 RIS (2015).
7 Refer www.doingbusiness.org/rankings.
8 Cost to register a business is normalized by presenting it as a percentage of gross national income per capita.
9 Data on mobile cellular subscriptions is not available beyond 2015.
10 Trade intensity index is given as: $\mathrm{TI}_{ijt} = \left(x_{ijt} / x_{it} \right) / \left(x_{wjt} / x_{wt} \right)$ where, t stands for time, x_{ij} and x_{wj} stand for country i's and world's exports to country j and x_{it} and x_{wt} stand for total exports of country i and world at time t.

References

Asian Development Bank. (2017). "Asian Development Outlook 2017: Transcending the Middle-Income Challenge", doi:10.22617/FLS178632-3.

Brooks, D.H., & Go, E.C. (2011). "Trade, employment and inclusive growth in Asia", in D. Lippoldt (Ed.), *Policy Priorities for International Trade and Jobs* (Chapter 11), OECD. https://www.oecd.org/site/tadicite/50258009.pdf

Darwent, D. (1969). "Growth poles and growth centres in regional planning: A review". *Environment and Planning* 1: 5–31.

Gilbert, J. (2011). "International Trade, Growth and Structural Changes in Employment in Developing Asia", Paper presented at the Conference on International Collaborative Initiative on Trade and Employment, ADB, Manila, 18–19 April.

Research and Information System for Developing Countries. (2016). "South Asia Development and Cooperation Report".

RIS. (2015). *South Asia Development and Cooperation Report*, Research and Information System for Developing Countries, New Delhi.

Speakman, J., and Koivisto, M. (2013). "Growth Poles: Raising Competitiveness and Deepening Regional Integration". In D. Kaberuka, C. F. Bach, K. Schwab, and J. Y. Kim (Eds.), *The Africa Competitiveness Report*. World Economic Forum, 93–106.

3 Connectivity

The key to South Asia's integration with the Asian region

Deeparghya Mukherjee

Introduction

Trade and investment linkages form the heart of economic relations across regions of the world. Communications and transport infrastructure can be found to be the backbone of any such relationship historically. In today's world, connectivity through sea, railways, roads and aviation combined with communications and digital connectivity stands out as key infrastructure facilitating trade apart from traditional port logistics.

Through history, we find enough evidence of improved connectivity improving trade and economic relations. As shipping routes developed connecting Europe to the rest of the world, they quickly transformed into trade routes. The opening up of the Suez Canal in 1869 multiplied trade between Europe and Asia manifold and reduced the costs of trade. The canal had achieved a reduction in distance travelled by about 43 percent for ships previously approaching Asia from Europe through the Cape of Good Hope.[1] Prior to the shipping connectivity, trade routes by land connecting vast stretches of empires from the Middle East to India or the silk route of China are well known. In modern times, connectivity on fronts such as road, rail, air, water as well as digital connectivity has become extremely important in furthering business to business (B2B) or Business to consumers (B2C) trade.

Sea transport remains the cheapest way to transport goods in mass. According to statistics, around 14 percent of country pairs in the world are connected directly, 11 percent through one trans-shipment, 36 percent through two trans-shipments and 28 percent through three trans-shipments, which accounts for 90 percent of country pairs across the world (Fugazza, 2015). Approximately 80 percent of goods transported around the world is through sea or maritime transport (UNCTAD, 2008). Fugazza (2015) finds that the absence of a direct sea connection results in a drop in exports by about 42 percent.

Among various regions of the world the Asian region comprising primarily East and Southeast Asia have come to be major players in world trade over the last few decades. South Asia's involvement in trade is on the rise mainly because of India, which comprises 80 percent of the South Asian economy. As trade among these regions have been growing and South Asia stands out as a region of greater business opportunity analysing possible trade linkages and promoting and inhibiting factors become interesting. Connectivity is one of the key enabling factors to grow trade among the regions apart from complementary comparative advantage of these regions. The Regional Comprehensive Economic Partnership (RCEP) which is under negotiation involving the ten-member Association of Southeast Asian Nations (ASEAN) and its six free trade agreement (FTA) partners which include countries of East Asia and India in South Asia is aimed to facilitate commercial relations. Needless to say, connectivity would play a crucial role in facilitating business relations reaching their potential. In the context of trade in Asia and South Asia's prospective trade with rest of Asia, connectivity thus has paramount importance and this chapter reviews the connectivity situation, the initiatives that are underway analysing trends and ends with possible implications.

South Asia has traditionally been an economically least integrated region. Connectivity within south Asia as well as between South Asia and other parts of Asia have been reasonably low (Kumar, 2015). Southeast Asia has had some success as an economically integrated region with closer trade links and has been working towards a master connectivity plan for 2025.[2] The plan is built on three pillars, including physical, institutional and people-to-people connectivity. As of 2016, about 18 projects on physical connectivity, 15 on intuitional connectivity and 6 on people-to-people connectivity have been completed. The plan is working systematically to achieve sustainable infrastructure, digital innovation, seamless logistics, regulatory excellence and people mobility. The aim is to bridge the economic disparities within the region and evolve as a truly integrated region capitalising on prevalent advantages and adoption of best practices. East Asia has been the most connected region with the greatest extant economic links. There is increased focus in East Asia of further building long-term sustainable connectivity projects with ASEAN. Some East Asian region itself may be rebuilding old ports, highways and railroads (Hong, 2017). In the following section we study some key metrics of connectivity and look at the progress for each of the subregions (East, Southeast and South) of Asia.

Key indicators of connectivity

We now analyse some key indicators of connectivity across the three subregions of Asia. As maritime connectivity is most conventional and relevant for trade, we look at the Logistics performance index (LPI) which reflects efficiency in ports followed by liner shipping connectivity at a bilateral level between countries of south, east and Southeast Asia. This is followed by a look at the number of containers handled in the ports of each country and how it has grown over the years.

LPI

From Figure 3.1 above, countries in East Asia stand out distinctly in terms of their logistics performance through the last decade followed by ASEAN. Logistics performance is least for South Asian countries, but we observe a significant improvement in logistics performance from 2007 till 2016 where LPI increased from an average of about 2.25 for South Asia to about 2.6. The improvement for ASEAN and East Asian countries has been lower than this. South Asia may thus be working towards improving port logistics and port clearance processes significantly. For a country level understanding we look at Table 3.1 below.

In East Asia, Japan and Hong Kong have comparable statistics on LPI closely followed by China, Korea and Taiwan (Table 3.1). Singapore stands out in Southeast Asia with Thailand and Malaysia being the next best in logistics. In South Asia, the level of LPI scores are lower than those of east and Southeast Asia, but improvement is observed over time. While most countries have improved, India has the best LPI scores in South Asia.

While port logistics are important for trade, bilateral shipping links are important and we analyse the shipping connectivity patterns next.

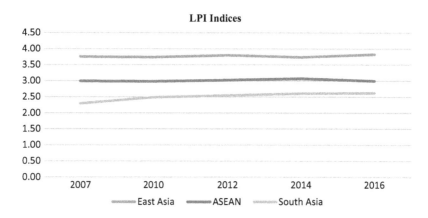

Figure 3.1 Logistics performance index (LPI) for East Southeast and South Asia.
Source: Compiled by the author using World Bank LPI statistics from World Development Indicators (WDI).

Table 3.1 Logistics performance index (LPI) indices by country

Region/country	2007	2010	2012	2014	2016
East Asia					
China	3.3	3.5	3.5	3.5	3.7
Japan	4.0	4.0	3.9	3.9	4.0
Hong Kong, China	4.0	3.9	4.1	3.8	4.1
Korea, Rep.		3.6	3.7	3.7	3.7
Taiwan, China	3.6	3.7	3.7	3.7	3.7

Region/country	2007	2010	2012	2014	2016
Southeast Asia					
Cambodia	2.5	2.4	2.6	2.7	2.8
Indonesia	3.0	2.8	2.9	3.1	3.0
Lao PDR		2.5	2.5	2.4	2.1
Malaysia	3.5	3.4	3.5	3.6	3.4
Myanmar	1.9	2.3	2.4	2.2	2.5
Philippines	2.7	3.1	3.0	3.0	2.9
Singapore	4.2	4.1	4.1	4.0	4.1
Thailand	3.3	3.3	3.2	3.4	3.3
Vietnam	2.9	3.0	3.0	3.2	3.0
South Asia					
Afghanistan	1.2	2.2	2.3	2.1	2.1
Bangladesh	2.5	2.7		2.6	2.7
Bhutan	2.2	2.4	2.5	2.3	2.3
India	3.1	3.1	3.1	3.1	3.4
Maldives		2.4	2.5	2.7	2.5
Nepal	2.1	2.2	2.0	2.6	2.4
Pakistan	2.6	2.5	2.8	2.8	2.9
Sri Lanka	2.4	2.3	2.8	2.7	

Source: Compiled by the author using World Bank LPI statistics from World Development Indicators.

Bilateral liner shipping connections

In Figure 3.2 we plot the intra-regional bilateral connectivity of each regional block in Asia and then the inter-regional country-to-country connectivity across regions. The average bilateral connectivity is calculated as the average of the bilateral connectivity of countries within or across the regions. It appears that bilateral connectivity is highest for countries in the East Asian region, that is, China, Japan, Korea, Hong Kong and Taiwan. The intra-regional bilateral connectivity in Southeast Asia and South Asia are comparable and have also grown on almost similar terms between 2006 and 2016. Inter-regional connectivity is highest between east and Southeast Asia although this is much less than East Asian intra-regional connectivity. East Asia-South Asia connectivity is a close second and is observed to have grown significantly over the 2006–2016 decade. Southeast Asia and South Asia connectivity has been low but almost at the level of their intra-regional connectivity. There seems to be little difference between East Asia's connectivity with Southeast and South Asia. South Asia's connectivity with both East and Southeast Asia has shown impressive growth between 2010 and 2016. Hence maritime connectivity shows some improvement in connectivity for South Asia.

Containerisation of shipments has eased global trade in a big way.[3] Mostly 20-foot containers are used for shipment and then they are transported to the hinterland if required through railways. The number of 20-foot containers handled in each country port gives an indication of how busy the port has been as well as the participation in trade. A growth in these numbers could arise from increased value chain participation, greater participation in world trade in general and also through better logistics services. We study this for the Asian countries in RCEP below:

From Table 3.2, we find that between 2010 and 2016, the countries that have grown their handling of port containers the most are China and Korea in East Asia, and Malaysia, Indonesia and Viet Nam in Southeast Asia. While India has also grown in its handling of port containers, the magnitude of increase is not as much as the other countries mentioned above. Countries like Singapore which were already handling a large number of containers have also shown growth but lower than others. Hong Kong has actually handled a lower container volume in 2016 compared to 2010. Countries with very low container handling include Maldives, Myanmar and Brunei apart from the landlocked countries.

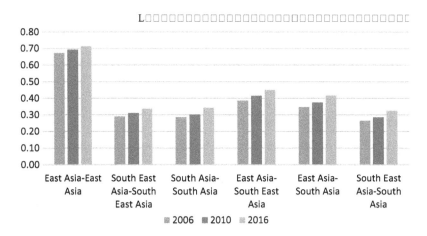

Figure 3.2 Average bilateral shipping connectivity across regions.
Source: Compiled by the author using bilateral liner shipping connectivity index (UNCTAD statistics).

Table 3.2 Number of 20-foot containers handled in ports per year (in thousands)

Year	2010	2011	2012	2013	2014	2015	2016
East Asia							
China	139,358	152,476	163,372	175,805	186,853	194,756	199,566
China, Hong Kong *Special Administrative Region* (SAR)	23,600	24,404	23,100	22,290	22,300	20,114	19,580
China, Taiwan Province of	12,937	14,518	13,878	14,047	15,050	14,492	14,865
Japan	18,115	16,624	17,075	19,108	20,675	20,076	20,257
Korea, Republic of	18,517	20,591	21,535	22,523	24,814	25,477	26,373

Year	2010	2011	2012	2013	2014	2015	2016
Southeast Asia							
Brunei Darussalam	93	105	109	122	128	128	125
Cambodia	224	238	255	286	424	474	482
Indonesia	8,089	9,674	10,428	10,811	11,637	12,032	12,432
Lao People's Dem. Rep.	NA	NA	NA	NA	NA	NA	NA
Malaysia	18,204	20,011	20,588	20,910	22,368	24,013	24,570
Myanmar	335	381	474	567	717	827	1,026
Philippines	5,087	5,315	5,642	5,826	6,176	7,210	7,421
Singapore	29,179	29,938	31,649	32,579	34,688	31,710	31,688
Thailand	6,521	7,036	7,324	7,547	8,119	8,359	8,239
Viet Nam	5,886	6,924	7,372	8,254	8,150	8,842	8,496
South Asia							
Afghanistan	NA	NA	NA	NA	NA	NA	NA
Bangladesh	1,469	1,343	1,469	1,626	1,643	2,045	2,367
Bhutan	NA	NA	NA	NA	NA	NA	NA
India	9,112	9,557	9,577	9,685	11,319	11,883	12,083
Maldives	50	53	55	80	84	84	82
Nepal	NA	NA	NA	NA	NA	NA	NA
Pakistan	2,149	2,132	2,244	2,445	2,535	2,756	2,645
Sri Lanka	4,080	4,263	4,187	4,306	4,908	5,185	5,550

Source: Compiled by the author using Container port throughput statistics from UNCTAD statistics.
(Figures in thousands.)

We note from the above analyses that there is scope to build on connectivity infrastructure across countries and the current levels of connection are disparate. While sea linkages and port logistics capture one part of the connectivity initiatives, sine the region in question is connected by land, road and railway networks play a crucial role. We take a look at the various initiatives and projects underway to improve connectivity across countries in the region.

Connectivity initiatives

We find a number of projects currently underway in connecting South Asia with Southeast Asia. As South Asia is a land of potential with lower cost production opportunities and most products are being produced through regional value chains in Asia, better connectivity is expected to benefit trade and economic relations between Asia. We look at the connectivity initiatives sequentially.

Kaladan multimodal transit transport project

The Kaladan Multimodal project has been one of the most important connectivity initiatives between India and the rest of Asia. It has multiple components: namely, a 539-km shipping route from Kolkata, India, to Sittwe seaport in Myanmar; a 158-km boat route from Sittwe seaport to internal water terminal at Paletwa Jetty through the Kaladan river; a 109-km road route from the Paletwa to Zorinpui which is at the Indo-Myanmar border; and finally a 100-km route from the Indo Myanmar border to Aizawl.

The project was initially due to be completed in 2016 but has met with multiple bottlenecks. The idea of the project has been to improve India's connectivity to the Northeast as well as improve connections with Southeast Asia through the Sittwe port and its connection to the trilateral highway. While the waterway link has existed for a long time and the sea route is an established channel of transportation. The roadways construction has been held up.

It is only around the middle of 2017 that the construction of the connection from Paletwa port to Zorinpui in the Indo-Myanmar border started.[4] It is expected that this will be completed by 2019. However, at this stage it seems doubtful whether the 2019 deadline can be met. There have been multiple bottlenecks in obtaining approvals from either government for getting equipment across to Myanmar for construction, in addition to delay due to weather which has not been conducive to quick progress.

On the Indian side there has been progress in extending the Aizwal-Saiha national highway till the border at Zorinpui (around 90 km) has been on.

India-Myanmar and Thailand trilateral highway

While the trilateral highway was conceptualised in 2012 in a Joint Task Force meeting, the approximately 1700-km trilateral highway between India and Thailand through Myanmar is far from completion. An initial deadline of 2016 for its completion has been periodically extended and it is estimated that this might be completed by the end of 2019 or early 2020.

The highway has been planned from Moreh in Manipur to Mae Soet in Thailand through Mandalay in Myanmar. Along with the conceived Motor Vehicles agreement (MVA) between India, Myanmar and Thailand, this highway would improve connectivity between India and Southeast Asia phenomenally improving trade, tourism and cultural exchanges. The MVA has however been put on hold primarily due to reported concerns of Myanmar about connectivity.[5] There are plans to complement the highway with a railroad connection running parallel to the highway.

Bangladesh China India Myanmar (BCIM) economic corridor

The BCIM project is one particular initiative which can work towards improving linkages between India and both East and Southeast Asia. In order to improve India's competitiveness in trade with the East and Southeast Asian region, the BCIM corridor connecting India, Myanmar, China and Bangladesh is crucial. The transnational corridor was conceptualised in 1998 as part of a track 2 dialogue to promote freer flow of goods and also as a means to attract foreign investment in the region. The economic corridor will be linking the cities of Kolkata (India), Dhaka (Bangladesh), Mandalay (Myanmar) and Kunming (China) thereby building a road approximately 2,800 km in length. The Kolkata to Kunming (K2K) highway plan was unveiled at the tenth BCIM forum meeting in Kolkata in 2012. The route as unveiled flows through Kolkata, Dhaka, Imphal, Mandalay, Lashio, Muse and Kunming. There are two obvious benefits that the region shall gain after the construction of the corridor. First, trade costs between the nations may be reduced significantly. Second, this would add crucial infrastructure to the north eastern region of India which would get better connectivity with the world and act as a road to faster economic development of the region. While some parts of the route already have a road infrastructure, building all-weather roads is underway and the Kolkata-Kunming car rally in February 2013 brought renewed focus on usage of the roadways for transport.[6] However, after this there has been slow progress towards completion of the BCIM economic corridor.

Bangladesh, Bhutan, India Nepal (BBIN) initiatives

The BBIN is a subgroup of the South Asian Association of Regional Cooperation (SAARC) countries aimed at improving regional cooperation. The initiative has a close focus on connectivity and while each of the countries has a myriad of problems with respect to cross-border movement of goods, customs clearance etc. each one realises the need to improve connectivity and ease of goods movement across the borders for quicker trade-led growth. A MVA has been signed in Thimphu (Bhutan) in June 2015 by the four South Asian countries to regulate passenger, cargo and vehicular traffic. Bhutan's parliament is yet to ratify the agreement. The other three members have shown the success of the MVA through trial runs by truck movement between Kolkata-Dhaka-Agartala and Dhaka-Kolkata-Delhi already.[7] However, to make connectivity in BBIN a true success a significant improvement is required in the road infrastructure (roads and bridges). This is particularly true of Bangladesh. About 30 connectivity projects have been identified by the MVA requiring an investment of about US$8 billion. The condition of the roads connecting the countries needs immediate attention and local sub-regional or state level support for this is a prerequisite for progress on this front. In addition to road connectivity, there has been an agreement to discuss the potential for a BBIN rail agreement.[8]

Belt and Road Initiative (BRI)

The belt and road initiative which was earlier known as the one belt one road (OBOR) initiative has been the Chinese government's proposal for a transport infrastructure development strategy between China and its neighbouring regions as well as to key strategic trade destinations. There are a few distinct components to the BRI initiative. First, China would want to connect its inner regions with Europe via land connectivity. Hailing from the historic Silk route, this is the Silk Road Economic Belt. Second, China would want to link the fast-growing south-east Asian region with its southern provinces by sea and this route would be further extended touching the major ports of the Asian region in South Asia, Sri Lanka (Hambantota: which the Chinese have financed already), Africa and Europe through the Suez Canal. There are other relatively smaller segments which are part of the initiative like the China-Pakistan Economic Corridor (CPEC) and the BCIM project. Added to this, there are major railway network building projects within China and elsewhere (Cai, 2017). This would primarily link Asia, Africa and Europe connecting about 80 countries promoting flow of trade and investment, people and ideas. This is the largest connectivity initiative requiring massive investments building ports, roadways, railway lines. The total investment is scheduled to reach US$4 trillion.[9] China has already set up bodies to fund the investment in phases.

The BRI if successful would open up a host of opportunities, especially for the landlocked countries along the Silk Road who would be able to participate in world trade more easily. However, these are mostly the central Asian countries and most of South and Southeast Asia would have incremental benefits (if any) only in reaching landlocked countries. Most of the rest of the countries in the Asian region are connected through the sea and the maritime segment of the BRI would be most relevant for them.

There are a number of developing and emerging economies which also figure in the BRI radar which would have easier access to ports. Many developing and emerging countries find it difficult to fund road infrastructure which is crucial in bringing down trade costs. China currently has an advantage in building physical connectivity infrastructure. It is also ready to fund the building of such infrastructure for developing economies at a concessional rate. This naturally is a lucrative offer for many countries. However, the ability to pay back the debt for different countries is not the same. The experience of Egypt with the building of the Suez Canal could become a reality for a few countries. Sri Lanka has struggled and finally leased out the Hambantota Port and 15,000 acres of land to China for 99 years in order to pay off its debts.[10] The situation could turn out to be quite the same for other countries if they are facing fiscal pressures.

While most countries around the world have welcomed the Chinese initiative, India which accounts for most of South Asia's geography has expressed its reservations about the BRI initiative. While efforts have been on to convince India about joining the project, India's position is firmly placed as it remains in opposition to the CPEC which runs through the disputed territory of Pakistan Occupied Kashmir.

Aviation connectivity

The role of air connectivity in facilitating trade is relatively lower than maritime and road or rail connectivity. This is primarily because the costs of air transportation are far higher and only selected goods which are fragile and or perishable in nature often get traded through air connectivity. However, air connectivity has a tremendous role in forming business relationships, improving the potential of tourism, business travel for investment and entrepreneurial ventures etc. Hence, although trade through air connectivity may not be high in terms of volume of trade, the value of trade could be significant. The need for greater air connectivity has been stressed at various levels including by the Singapore prime minister in his last visit to India.[11]

ASEAN and India have signed the agreements on investment and services and this further necessitates better air connectivity to harness the potential benefits of the agreements. In addition to this, reaping the benefits of a fully implemented RCEP also calls for greater air connectivity to foster business and commerce between the regions. India's national civil aviation policy (2016) emphasizes the need to improve the quality of air cargo services.[12]

While it is recognised that greater air connectivity between India and ASEAN is necessary, currently only five ASEAN members, that is, Malaysia, Singapore, Vietnam, Myanmar and Thailand have direct flights to India. Each of the East Asian countries have better connection. We also note that among the ASEAN members which have direct connectivity, there is a mix of development levels with no flights from the least developed ASEAN members. Indonesia and Philippines are two ASEAN members with which India has substantial business relations but there are no direct flights from these countries to India. India has signed bilateral air services agreement (BASA) with all ASEAN countries as of 2015. Most of the ASEAN country airlines fly to major Indian cities with flights to tier 2 cities seeing slow growth. Flights from and to Malaysia, Singapore and Thailand seem to be very useful and run on full bookings but flights from other ASEAN countries, especially the CLMV, are underutilised (AIC, 2016).

Among the countries involved in RCEP negotiations, China and Vietnam have been found to have high-volume trade by air connectivity. But the figures for the rest are not in the high-growth zone. There is significant scope for growing air connectivity between South Asian countries like India, Bangladesh and Sri Lanka for purposes of improving trade and business relations especially the parts and components trade which would help link the whole Asian region in the most productive manner.

Digital connectivity

Digital connectivity is revolutionising the way business is conducted across the world. The pioneering advances made in communications and digital technology have transformed lives across the globe. The prospect of

conducting most transactions through the digital mode using either the
mobile network or internet connectivity was not so prevalent even at the
turn of the century for most countries. However, over the last two decades,
a significant number of financial transactions have started taking the digital
route. This trend is found to have picked up fast for developing as well as
emerging economies. Some estimates suggest that widespread use of digital
finance could boost annual GDP of all emerging economies by US$3.7 tril-
lion by 2025.[13]

If we look at the growth of the number of mobile subscribers per hundred
people in the Asian countries between 2000 and 2016 (Table 3.3), we observe
that mobile usage has grown the most in Southeast Asian countries. In East
Asian countries where the level of mobile subscription was already significant in 2000, most countries have more than one mobile subscription per
person and in the case of Hong Kong we observe more than two subscriptions per person. In the case of South Asia, countries like Nepal, Maldives
and Sri Lanka have shown maximum growth.

Table 3.3 Mobile subscribers per 100 people

Country	2000	2005	2010	2015	2016
East Asia					
China	7	30	63	92	97
Hong Kong	82	125	196	231	241
Japan	52	75	96	125	131
Korea, Rep.	57	79	102	116	121
Southeast Asia					
Brunei Darussalam	29	64	112	111	124
Cambodia	1	8	57	134	126
Indonesia	2	21	87	131	148
Lao PDR	0	11	64	56	59
Malaysia	22	76	120	144	141
Myanmar	0	0	1	78	96
Philippines	8	40	89	116	109
Singapore	70	98	146	149	150
Thailand	5	47	107	150	174
Vietnam	1	11	126	129	128
South Asia					
Afghanistan	0	5	35	58	62
Bangladesh	0	6	45	81	83
Bhutan	0	5	54	86	88
India	0	8	61	76	85
Maldives	3	64	136	177	190
Nepal	0	1	34	96	111
Pakistan	0	8	58	66	71
Sri Lanka	2	17	86	115	124

Source: Compiled by the author using World Bank World Development
Indicators statistics.

Mobile usage for financial transactions has also gone up remarkably after smartphones are being used for e-payments through portals like Paytm and the growth of e-commerce for selling products in each of the countries across the regions of Asia. Hence mobile usage combined with the use of internet has become more useful in facilitating trade and commerce. We look at the level of internet usage across countries below:

Most of East Asia barring China has grown in the number of internet servers per one million people significantly, with the highest growth recorded for Korea (Table 3.4). In Southeast Asia, Singapore, Malaysia and Brunei stand out by the number of internet servers per million people and in South Asia Maldives emerges as the country that has grown the most in internet penetration. Given the difference in digital infrastructure as can be seen from the above tables, one could expect a difference in the role of digital commerce. However, trends in growth of digital commerce tend to suggest that there is a somewhat uniform growth across countries in using digital channels for conducting business as well as payments.

Table 3.4 Secure internet servers (per one million people)

Country	2005	2010	2015	2016
East Asia				
China	0	2	10	21
Japan	258	647	970	1071
Korea, Rep.	20	1125	2301	2201
Hong Kong	162	456	906	963
Southeast Asia				
Brunei Darussalam	14	67	206	234
Cambodia	0	2	5	7
Indonesia	0	2	8	10
Lao PDR	0	1	3	3
Malaysia	15	42	102	106
Myanmar	0	0	1	2
Philippines	2	7	14	15
Singapore	275	530	932	890
Thailand	5	14	30	33
Vietnam	0	3	14	19
South Asia				
Afghanistan	0	1	1	1
Bangladesh	0	0	1	2
Bhutan		4	17	24
India	1	2	7	8
Maldives	6	47	100	103
Nepal	0	2	4	4
Pakistan	0	1	2	3
Sri Lanka	2	5	14	17

Source: Compiled by the author using World Bank World Development Indicators statistics.

Southeast Asia's e-commerce revenues are set to surpass US$25 billion by 2020. While Malaysia and Thailand have been the largest markets for B2C e-commerce, Vietnam and Indonesia may soon surpass these markets.[14] South Asia has also been in the news for digital networks improving opportunities. In India, the National Agricultural Market (eNAM) was launched in 2016 allowing farmers and traders to view agricultural prices, commodity arrivals and other agricultural market-related information. This helps famers in turn to bid for the best prices across markets.[15] Indian fishermen use their mobiles with apps to get information about the weather conditions in the sea as well as identify areas where the catch may be better on a particular day. This saves their fuel consumption. The app also helps them identify the prevailing rates at different markets and hence they are in a position to choose which port they would approach for selling their catch.[16] The Indian e-commerce market is scheduled to grow to US$200 billion by 2026 from US$38.5 billion in 2017.[17] There has been a commitment to build digital connectivity through the use of Gigabit-capable passive optical network (GPON) technology between India and ASEAN.[18]

Digital connectivity and data flows help improve business possibilities as digitisation of logistic services and border controls ease the process of trading by reducing transaction time. Measures like customs automation, electronic documents and single window clearances are possible using digital technology. It helps increase transparency, reducing costs of risk management while lowering opportunities for corruption. It also helps prospective customers to connect to prospective sellers far more easily as soon as they have access to the digital platform.

This also adds to some challenges of customs officials. With direct interaction between buyers and sellers the number of small consignment as opposed to big ones by wholesale operators increases. This challenges the ability of authorities to monitor enforcement standards, trade in counterfeit products etc. (Jouanjean, 2017).

For B2B trade, digitisation facilitates coordination of production networks. The electronic cargo tracking system enables this in a big way. The role of regional value chains in improving regional trade in Southeast and East Asia is reasonably well known. Countries like India may integrate into certain industries like automobiles and electronics where the usage of digital technology already benefits B2B trade. This could be further improved and South Asia may see greater integration in Asian value chains in the near future. However, digital connectivity alone may not be able to improve trade potential as, end of the day, trade can only happen through physical goods crossing the borders. Hence, digital connectivity supplements the ability to trade only when physical infrastructure like road or waterway connectivity is built in a competitive fashion. (OECD, 2017).

Discussion and conclusion

Issues of connectivity furthering economic relations between countries has been well recognised in the world. Our analysis in this chapter centred around the regions of South, Southeast and East Asia furthering trade and economic relations and its prospects in the backdrop of the RCEP mega Regional Trade Agreement (RTA) that is currently under negotiation.

East and Southeast Asian regions have had significant advances in connectivity through both maritime and other routes and these regions are appreciably ahead of the South Asian region in terms of economic linkages and business through value chains integrated across borders. South Asia as a land of opportunity through lower costs of production and resources can benefit immensely through business linkages with either or both of the neighbouring Asian regions. As 80 percent of the South Asian GDP is accounted for by India alone and it is the only South Asian country that is currently a part of the RCEP negotiations, we look at regional connectivity mainly between India and the rest of Asian region.

On the basis of connectivity statistics presented we concluded that East Asia has the best performance in port logistics management as a region. While countries like Singapore fare very high in logistics performance, most other countries in Southeast Asia fare much lower than East Asia on LPI. South Asia is seen to have improved more in comparison to East and Southeast Asia and this should help countries like India, Sri Lanka or Bangladesh reap the benefits if they are able to get into the value chains of products which require frequent passages through multiple ports in their different stages of production.

In terms of bilateral shipping connectivity, East Asia and Southeast Asia are well connected internally but the inter-region connectivity has shown slow progress and East Asia's connectivity with Southeast is a shade better than its connectivity with South Asia. This would imply that the maritime connectivity between the three regions do not vary significantly although there are vast differences in intra-regional connectivity. Hence, if businesses were to trade in parts and components between the three regions, challenges on the shipping front may be lesser than port clearances or port logistics.

A significant amount of investments have been made on building surface transport infrastructure. While we reviewed most of the initiatives, differences on various fronts have stalled the progress of multiple such projects from being finished in time. This is especially true for the South Asia- Southeast Asia connectivity. While the RCEP once negotiated would open the doors to easier trading, the lack of quality road and rail infrastructure coupled with hassles in border controls could be stumbling blocks for obtaining gains from trade. The BRI while lucrative may need to be watched closely and countries which would finance port and road infrastructure through soft loans from China may find it difficult to pay back later if trade potential is low.

Aviation connectivity becomes important for forming business links and for trade of sensitive, fragile or quickly perishable commodities. There is a lot of scope for improvement in South Asia's connectivity with East and Southeast Asia on this front. While aviation links are on the rise as business links increase this may be expected to increase complementarily.

Finally, digital connectivity has tremendous potential to improve business links especially between smaller businesses. All the Asian regions have shown increases in the usage of digital technology although East Asia is far ahead of its neighbours. Lowering costs of connecting digitally has immense potential to improve business links across regions. The incremental economic benefit would be high for South Asia on this front but increasing digital connectivity should be complemented with physical connectivity infrastructures like roads, railways and waterways.

In sum, the prospect of increasing trade and economic linkages across regions of Asia is tremendous but this can only be realised in a post-RCEP world if connectivity infrastructure is improved significantly. While efforts on improving port logistics would be most important in South Asia, road infrastructure connecting East, Southeast and South Asia would be required. Effective implementation of MVAs) with good highway and port infrastructure, and easier digital connectivity hold the key to reaping the true fruits of business opportunities facing the entire Asian region once a successful RCEP is implemented.

Notes

1 See "The Suez Canal-A Vital Shortcut for Global Commerce" World Shipping Council (www.worldshipping.org/pdf/suez-canal-presentation.pdf).
2 See "Master Plan on ASEAN Connectivity 2025" (http://asean.org/storage/2016/09/Master-Plan-on-ASEAN-Connectivity-20251.pdf).
3 See "Why Have Containers Boosted Trade So Much?" 22nd May, 2013. *The Economist*. (www.economist.com/the-economist-explains/2013/05/21/why-have-containers-boosted-trade-so-much).
4 See "India Starts Construction of INR1600 Crore Mizoram-Myanmar Kaladan Road" The Hindu Business Line, 17th April, 2017 (www.thehindubusinessline.com/news/india-starts-construction-of-1600-cr-mizoram-myanmar-kaladan-road/article23577107.ece).
5 See "ASEAN Summit: Connectivity Remains Challenge as Trilateral Highway through Myanmar and Thailand Remains Incomplete" Firstpost, 10th November, 2017 (www.firstpost.com/india/asean-summit-connectivity-remains-challenge-as-trilateral-highway-through-myanmar-and-thailand-remains-incomplete-4203223.html).
6 See www.bcimcarrally.com/.
7 See "BBIN Motor Vehicles Agreement Regains Momentum", 15th June, 2018, Press Information Bureau, Govt. of India (http://pib.nic.in/newsite/PrintRelease.aspx?relid=175638).
8 See "South Asian Countries Building Connections" 24th June, 2017, Prabir De, East Asia Forum (www.eastasiaforum.org/2017/06/24/bbin-countries-are-building-connections/).

9 See "About Belt and Road Initiative" (https://ie.enterprisesg.gov.sg/Venture-Overseas/Browse-By-Market/Asia-Pacific/China/About-OBOR).
10 See "How China got Sri Lanka to Cough Up a Port" 25th June 2018, *The New York Times* (https://mobile.nytimes.com/2018/06/25/world/asia/china-sri-lanka-port.html).
11 See "Greater Trade, Connectivity Key to ASEAN-India Ties: PM Lee" (www.straitstimes.com/asia/south-asia/greater-trade-connectivity-key-to-asean-india-ties-pm-lee).
12 See "National Civil Aviation Policy 2016" (www.civilaviation.gov.in/sites/default/files/Final_NCAP_2016_15-06-2016-2_1.pdf).
13 See "Digital Finance for All: Powering Inclusive Growth in Emerging Economies". Mckinsey Global Institute, September 2016 (www.mckinsey.com/~/media/McKinsey/Featured%20Insights/Employment%20and%20Growth/How%20digital%20finance%20could%20boost%20growth%20in%20emerging%20economies/MGI-Digital-Finance-For-All-Executive-summary-September-2016.ashx).
14 See "Southeast Asia's E-Commerce Market to Surpass US$25 Billion by 2020 Despite Market Challenges, Finds Frost & Sullivan."
15 See "How Technology Is Transforming the Lives of India's Farmers" 2nd October, 2017, *World Economic Forum* (www.weforum.org/agenda/2017/10/india-fourth-industrial-revolution-farming/).
16 See "MKRISHI Fisheries, A New Mobile App to Help Fishermen" 19th January, 2017, Firstpost (www.firstpost.com/tech/news-analysis/mkrishi-fisheries-a-new-app-to-help-fishermen-3696171.html).
17 See "Ecommerce Industry in India" India Brand Equity Foundation (www.ibef.org/industry/ecommerce.aspx).
18 See point 17 in Chairman's statement in the 14th ASEAN-India Summit, 8th September, 2016, Vientiene, Lao PDR (http://asean.org/storage/2016/09/Chairmans-Statement-of-the-14th-ASEAN-India-Summit-Final.pdf.pdf).

References

AIC. (2016). *ASEAN-India Air Connectivity Report.* New Delhi: ASEAN India Centre (AIC), RIS.
Cai, P. (2017). *Understanding China's Belt and Road Initiative.* Sydney: Lowy Institute for International Policy.
Fugazza, M. (2015). *Maritime Connectivity and Trade.* Geneva: Policy Issues in International Trade and Commodities Research Study Series No. 70, UNCTAD.
Hong, Y. (2017). *East Asia Connectivity for Regional Economic Integration.* Singapore: EAI Background Brief No. 1243, East Asia Institute, National University of Singapore.
Jouanjean, M.-A. (2017). *Digital Connectivity and Trade Logistics Chains: Getting it Shipped, Across the Border and Delivered.* OECD.
Kumar, N. (2015). Potential and Prospects of Strengthening Transport Connectivity for Regional Economic Integration in Southern Asia. *South Asia Economic Journal, 16*(2S), 39S–40S.
OECD, W. (2017). *Aid for Trade at a Glance 2017: Promoting Trade, Inclusiveness and Connectivity for Sustainable Development.* OECD, WTO.
UNCTAD. (2008). *Transport NEwsletter #38.* UNCTAD.

Part II

Selected issues in Asian economic integration

4 RCEP and Non-Tariff Barriers (NTBs)

Incidence, issues and the Indian perspective

Amitendu Palit

With the inception of the World Trade Organisation (WTO) in 1995, the agenda of free trade has moved ahead through reduction in import tariffs imposed by countries on movement of goods. The multilateral trade framework has contributed significantly to increasing access of exporters to various global markets by hastening the lowering, and in many cases, complete elimination of import tariffs. The WTO's efforts to cut tariffs has been complemented by those of various free trade agreements (FTAs) both regional as well as bilateral.

Non-tariff protectionism

The expansion of market access by lowering of tariffs has, interestingly been accompanied by A growth of protectionism in another form – non-tariff measures (NTMs). It's noticeable that while the WTO's multilateral framework and the proliferation of preferential trading arrangements like FTAs and RTAs have clipped national government proclivities to tax imports, market access for such imports, nonetheless, has been often reduced through NTMs. The latter often have as much trade-distorting impact as tariffs.

NTMs, by their very character, are more difficult to remove through trade agreements than tariffs. As 'on the border' trade restrictive measures, tariffs are visible and easier to identify and act upon. For countries imposing tariffs, cutting or removing them is not really cumbersome and can be done through simple executive actions. NTMs present much greater challenges in this respect. The most complicated aspect of NTMs, from a trade liberalisation perspective, is to distinguish between those that are necessary for achieving distinct social and economic outcomes in host countries, and those that while aiming to achieve these are actually regulated for restricting market access. Indeed, even those necessary for host country priorities might end up with trade-distorting effects making their rationalisation a more complicated endgame.

NTMs comprise a variety of regulations or domestic policies, other than customs duties, which '... can potentially have an economic effect on international trade in goods, changing quantities traded, or prices or both'.[1]

The UN classification of NTMs separates these technical and non-technical measures, which can affect imports into host countries. The former include sanitary and phytosanitary measures (SPS), technical barriers to trade (TBT) and pre-shipment inspection and formalities; the latter, however, includes a wide range of domestic policies that might directly or peripherally affect imports, such as rules of origin, competition policies, subsidies, intellectual property rules, investment regulations, finance measures, price control measures, quotas, government procurement rules and distribution restrictions.[2]

Many of the NTMs, as mentioned earlier, might have been introduced by host country governments for achieving important development objectives. Technical measures, such as SPS and TBT policies, are usually designed to achieve these objectives. SPS policies are meant for ensuring imports into countries comply with quality standards that the host country(s) considers essential for maintaining health and hygiene of its residents, as well as plants and animals. TBT policies try to achieve similar goals with respect to quality of habitat and primarily environment. However, both sets of policies, from a trade perspective, produce an identical dilemma: while countries are free to deploy them for protecting the qualities of animal, plant, human lives and the environment, how do global and regional trade policies ensure that these regulations are not 'unnecessary' and not meant for creating trade barriers? The WTO's SPS agreement admits that SPS measures might lead to 'restrictions on trade' and such restrictions, to some extent, might be necessary for ensuring the safety of food and animal and plant health. But a restriction '... not actually required for health reasons can be a very effective protectionist device and, because of its technical complexity, it can be a particularly deceptive and difficult barrier to challenge'.[3]

The distinction between NTMs necessary for achieving important public policy objectives such as in public health, and those that are introduced for distorting trade and protecting domestic industry and local producers, is not easy. This is where, conceptually, identifying NTBs that are unnecessary but intentional regulations maintained by countries on protective grounds, from other NTMs that have legitimate public policy goals, becomes difficult. Both generate trade costs; but while the latter can partly compensate these costs through welfare gains, the former has only trade-distorting and business-cost-enhancing characteristics (Ballingall and Pambudi 2016). It is this particular category of NTBs with which the trade community has been strongly engaged and whose elimination is sought through the ongoing programmes of multilateral and regional trade liberalisation.

Asia-Pacific, RCEP and NTBs

The Asian region, particularly the Asia-Pacific and Southeast Asia, has witnessed a dramatic reduction in import tariffs across a wide range of goods traded between countries. The reduction has been significantly precipitated by multiple FTAs in the region, the most significant among which are the FTAs entered into by ASEAN with countries in the neighbourhood of Southeast Asia. These include ASEAN's FTAs with Australia and New Zealand, China, India, Japan and Korea. Elaborate schedules of tariff commitments in these FTAs have contributed significantly to the decline in tariff barriers among countries, particularly on industrial and manufacturing commodities. The upcoming Regional Comprehensive Economic Partnership (RCEP) being negotiated between ASEAN and its FTA partners (Australia and New Zealand, China, Japan, India, Korea) is expected to continue the process of tariff elimination. There are expectations of the RCEP facilitating large-scale elimination of tariffs to the extent of making more than 90 percent of trade between its members tariff-free.[4]

The RCEP is just not another ASEAN+FTA, but is also representative of a greater regional integration architecture shaping within the Asia-Pacific with a prominently 'Asian' approach. Such an approach, characterised by the generous flexibility allowed to members in implementing market access liberalisation programmes through specific S&D (special & differential) provisions,[5] are in contrast to more rigorously structured US-style FTAs allowing limited deviations to members from common liberalisation agendas, such as the Comprehensive and Progressive Agreement for Trans-Pacific Partnership (CPTPP) (Palit 2014). More tariffs across the region are expected to fall because of RCEP, which is right now the largest mega-regional trade agreement being negotiated in the world, with its members accounting for one-third of global GDP, almost half of the world population and around a quarter of global merchandise and services trade.

But would the RCEP make a difference to NTBs? The question looms large given that the RCEP's success (or lack of it) in ameliorating trade-distorting NTBs would have significant implications for trade barriers in the region.

Several RCEP economies are Asia-Pacific Economic Cooperation (APEC) members as well. These include Australia, Brunei, China, Indonesia, Japan, Korea, Malaysia, New Zealand, Philippines, Singapore, Thailand and Vietnam.[6] Indeed, except the three small economies from ASEAN, that is Cambodia, Myanmar and Lao and India, the rest of RCEP is effectively a subgroup of APEC. It is therefore intuitively logical to assume that the RCEP's programme on NTBs would be reasonably close to that being implemented across most of the APEC, particularly its Asian members.

Empirical evidence on trade barriers in the region points to the high prevalence of NTMs in the Asia-Pacific. Ballingall and Pambudi (2016) note that the fall in tariffs has been accompanied by a rapid rise in NTMs across the region. They further note the number of NTMs in the region to have increased by 74 percent during the period 2004–2015. While recognising legitimate public policy goals behind some of the NTMs, they point to several being used intentionally for trade-distorting purposes, leading to high costs for firms and businesses across value chains.[7] These findings corroborate

results from other studies, such as by the United Nations Economic and Social Commission for Asia and the Pacific (UNESCAP, 2015), which points
to the alarming growth of trade-distorting new technical regulations across
the Asia-Pacific since the onset of the global financial slowdown in the last
decade.[8] Other studies from the region focusing across key industries like
agriculture and food, such as APEC Business Advisory Council (ABAC)
(2016), not only point to the high substitution of NTMs for tariffs by APEC
economies, but also the disturbing aspect of NTMs becoming more 'crea-
tive' for increasing their protectionist impact.[9] Indeed, the extent by which
NTMs have become instruments for creatively blocking imports is evident
in the current context of the US-China tariff war, with reports of Vietnam
working on the possibility of developing new NTMs for blocking Chinese
imports diverted from the US market.[10]

The growth of NTMs and their substitution of falling tariffs also applies to
RCEP economies. As mentioned variously earlier, notwithstanding the fact
that some NTMs are implemented on genuine grounds, many of these are
inherently protectionist. The latter largely manifest through SPS and TBTs
since SPS and TBTs are formally defendable on 'legitimate' public policy
grounds. Indeed, the high growth of SPS and TBTs across the world in recent years is probably the best example of the proliferation of NTBs. The
Asia-Pacific region and RCEP economies are not exceptions to this trend.
SPS and TBTs pertain to a wide range of mandatory technical regulations as
well as voluntary standards that have surfaced in the Asia-Pacific. The Asia-
Pacific region accounts for a significant chunk of new technical regulations –
as measured by SPS and TBTs – initiated by various countries across the
world since the early years of the millennium (UNESCAP 2015). Furthermore, led by China, and followed by Korea, Japan, Philippines and Thailand,
RCEP APEC economies are seen to have vigorously implemented new SPS
and TBTs since the onset of the global financial crisis and during the period
2008–2013 (UNESCAP 2015). Regular SPS measures in the Asia-Pacific region are seen to have increased particularly rapidly since 2010, while TBTs,
after having trended upwards during 2004–2008, and stabilised thereafter,
have spiked again in 2015 (Ballingall and Pambudi 2016). The noted trends
vindicate the larger tendency of most RCEP economies to have moved towards greater protectionism through new technical compliance issues. While
not being an APEC member, India, as a prominent RCEP member, has also
shown an increasing tendency to apply technical regulations to its imports, as
reflected by the high coverage ratio of TBTs for its trade (UNESCAP 2015).[11]

According to the notifications submitted to the WTO on SPS and TBT
measures implemented by individual members, there is considerable variation among RCEP economies (Table 4.1). SPS measures in force are more
than the TBTs. This is, however, not unexpected given the relatively rapidly
rising trend of SPSs in the current decade, as mentioned earlier and the fact
that SPSs account for around 60 percent of reported NTMs among APEC
members (ABAC 2016).

Table 4.1 SPS and TBT measures by RCEP members (as on November 2016)[12]

RCEP member	SPS	TBT
Australia	27	21
Brunei	0	0
Cambodia	0	1
China	119*	104*
Indonesia	44	23
India	28	1
Japan	23	59
Republic of Korea	34	77
Malaysia	6	16
Myanmar	0	1
New Zealand	88	8
Philippines	142	1
Singapore	17	17
Thailand	16	39
Vietnam	26	25
Grand Total	**570**	**393**

Source: Integrated Trade Intelligence Portal (https://i-tip.wto.org), WTO.
* Includes 2 SPS and 4 TBT measures reported by Hong Kong, China. Data on Lao PDR is not available. There are some difficulties in matching notifications with members on submissions made after November 2016, so the data is till November 2016.

China is one of the major users of both SPS and TBTs among RCEP economies, as seen from Table 4.1. While it is the second largest user of SPS after the Philippines, it is the highest TBT user among RCEP economies. But notwithstanding a greater number of SPSs than TBTs, studies point to imports to China encountering greater TBTs than SPSs on a per capita basis. Frequency index and coverage ratio for SPS and TBTs on imports to China are 27.4 percent and 20.1 percent for SPS, and 69 percent and 90 percent for TBTs,[13] underpinning the much greater impact of TBTs on imports to China. Among ASEAN members of RCEP, Indonesia is the next most prominent user of SPS after the Philippines though the number of SPS measures maintained by the Philippines is far more.[14] Indeed, more than 60 percent of the current SPS measures of RCEP economies are accounted for by the Philippines, China and New Zealand. On the other hand, smaller ASEAN economies like Brunei, Cambodia and Myanmar do not have any SPS measures in force. This is, in fact, an interesting reflection on the character of intra-ASEAN trade where these relatively smaller regional economies are vulnerable to NTBs imposed by larger Southeast Asian economies. Among non-ASEAN members of RCEP, China and New Zealand have a much higher incidence of use of SPSs compared with India, Australia, Japan and Korea. Studies on sector-specific use of SPSs point to animal products, food products and vegetable products,[15] inviting most of these, which is again obvious given that SPS measures are rationalised on the grounds of ensuring the safety of plants, animals and human health.

While being relatively less in number compared with SPSs, TBTs are still substantive among RCEP economies. China leads in TBT imposition, followed by Korea and Thailand, with the three accounting for more than 55 percent of existing TBTs among RCEP. The overall incidence of TBTs is much less among the ASEAN compared with SPSs. As noticed with SPSs earlier, smaller ASEAN economies like Brunei, Cambodia and Myanmar hardly use TBTs and are therefore vulnerable to their impacts from an intra-ASEAN, as well as future intra-RCEP trade perspective, assuming the current TBTs are retained by RCEP members over time. Studies point to electrical equipment, chemicals, metals and food products attracting largest TBTs in the Asia-Pacific region[16] and TBTs among RCEP economies are no exceptions in this regard. The further point to note in the context of TBTs is also the fact that businesses consider TBTs to have the highest negative impact among NTMs in time and costs (ABAC 2016) and even less TBT imposing nations like Malaysia having restrictions considered highly burdensome.[17]

NTBs: regional experience, harmonisation and challenges for RCEP

'Regulatory protectionism' has been on the rise in Asia-Pacific. This is line with the overall global trend of falling tariffs being accompanied by rising NTMs. The RCEP economies, as discussed earlier, are not an exception to this larger trend. While some NTMs certainly aim to achieve legitimate public health and social development goals, many others are clearly intended to serve protective objectives. Even the former with legitimate goals inflict significant costs for businesses. Rationalising NTMs and minimising NTBs therefore assume great importance in the RCEP perspective since persistence of these measures would not only negate the market access gains arising from falling tariffs, but would also keep adding to trade costs, thereby limiting the overall growth in regional trade that RCEP could achieve.

FTAs, particularly one as large and exhaustive as RCEP, can be an effective initiative for lowering NTBs. This is because of the simple reason that a mega-RTA like RCEP is a smaller platform than the WTO's multilateral forum and entails greater possibility of agreement among a smaller group of countries. Indeed, a constructive work programme towards elimination of NTBs from within RCEP can yield significant benefits, in terms of generation of higher trade, as found by empirical studies (Ratna and Huang 2016).[18] But for achieving such outcomes, RCEP must contain SPS and TBT provisions that don't just emphasise on 'intention' for removing NTBs, but also include provisions that can actually do so. Most ASEAN+1 FTAs prohibit maintenance of NTMs on imports and urge transparency of such measures, if imposed. But these are not sufficient for elimination of NTBs and controlling the growth of new restrictions. In order to do so, RCEP must delve deeper in domestic technical regulations and aim for harmonisation and mutual recognition of quality standards and conformity assessment procedures, which can have the most effective results in controlling trade costs of NTMs (Cadot and Gourdan 2015).

A common set of standards, either aligned to global benchmarks, or well-defined regional benchmarks, are expected to bring down trade costs for FTA members as producers from the latter don't have to comply with vastly different standards across the FTA territory anymore. Achieving such regulatory convergence could be a lengthy and complicated process. The easier option is to recognise the 'equivalence' of regulatory systems between partner countries in terms of they being different regulatory means for achieving the same quality ends. Thus, equivalence would achieve harmonisation among RTA members not by eliminating new standards, or by creating new ones, but by treating each other's standards as equivalent. Equivalence is reflected through 'mutual recognition' of standards, which imply FTA partners, while maintaining different domestic standards, can sell in other partner markets if their products conform to local standards. In practice though, this is difficult to achieve except among countries with largely similar economic conditions and institutional capacities, since there could always be the concern of lower standards of partners undermining the quality of products sold in domestic markets (Maur and Shepherd 2011).

Harmonisation of standards and conformity assessment in line with the ongoing regional work programmes of APEC and ASEAN economies can equip RCEP meaningfully for tackling NTBs (Ratna and Huang 2016). Most FTAs, however, find such equivalence difficult to impose due to large differences among member country standards in both SPS and TBT provisions. This is an issue with RCEP as the later discussion will reveal. As a result, RTAs go a notch lower by agreeing to mutually recognise conformity assessments. There are several multilateral and regional mutual recognition agreements (MRAs) for recognising results of testing and certification between member countries that RCEP members are parties to. Most of the APEC members of RCEP have been responding to the efforts of the APEC's Sub-Committee on Standards and Conformance (SCSC) for mutually recognising conformity assessment among APEC members. This is in line with the APEC's approach of achieving 'bottom up' harmonisation by allowing countries to voluntarily and gradually align national standards with international standards. This might eventually be the path that RCEP would have to walk. Before that, though, it is important to look at the regional experience with FTAs on harmonisation till now, beginning from CPTPP.

CPTPP and harmonisation

So far, the only Asia-Pacific FTA to have displayed substantive intent in this regard is the CPTPP. The CPTPP emphasises 'regulatory coherence'

(Chapter 25)[19] underpinning the intention of members to work closely for coordinating national regulations impacting external trade. As the provisions visualise, achieving regulatory coherence requires national regulatory agencies to work closely for developing good regulatory practices (GRPs) and conducting regulatory impact assessments (RIAs). The GRPs (addressed as 'core good regulatory practices' by CPTPP in Chapter 25) covers all categories of standards applicable to trade in goods, services and investments between members. In this respect, the coverage includes not just specific SPS and TBTs affecting goods, but also a broader range of regulations affecting cross-border flows that can be generally typified as NTMs. In line with a composite single-undertaking approach, CPTPP doesn't consider discrete development of regulations. Thus quality standards for products manifesting through SPS and TBTs are not to be regulated in isolation of standards for environment, labour and other regulatory issues covered by the agreement. In this regard, evolving quality standards in CPTPP member country markets, which include several RCEP members such as Australia, Brunei, Japan, Malaysia, New Zealand, Singapore and Vietnam, notified to WTO as new SPS or TBT measures need to be looked at in the light of their being products of composite GRPs. To what extent this might check the growth of ad hoc intentional protective measures needs to be seen over a period of time.

APEC economies have been working on implementing GRPs for quite some time now on the basis of the work agenda outlined in the APEC Leaders Meeting at Honolulu in November 2011 calling on APEC economies to work for 'building high quality regulatory environments' for 'promoting free and open trade and investment in the region'.[20] CPTPP member country ministers had issued a joint statement on the state of progress in negotiations after meeting on the sidelines of the occasion.[21] A considerable part of the regulatory coherence agenda of the CPTPP would build on the GRP work from the region as all members are APEC members as well. If the RCEP eventually aims to inculcate GRPs in its SPS and TBT provisions, then the APEC GRP programme is likely to be treated as a benchmark given the large number of APEC economies in RCEP as well.

The TBT chapter of CPTPP alludes to the use of GRPs for improving the 'efficiency and effectiveness of technical regulations, standards and conformity assessment procedures'.[22] In this regard, CPTPP members are expected to use APEC's MRAs for conformity assessment in telecommunication equipment and for equivalence in technical requirements.[23] In addition to telecom equipment, APEC also has MRAs for electrical and electronic equipment, which might become CPTPP's baseline norms for achieving specific technical standards. For items like food products where APEC economies are working on harmonisation of standards, CPTPP's product standards, at least to begin with, are expected to largely reflect those prevailing across the region.

RCEP issues

There are some variations among APEC economies in the extents by which their domestic conformity assessment rules reflect international standards and MRAs (Table 4.2). APEC economies belonging to CPTPP reflect greater degrees of domestic and international alignments, be it with ISO standards, or international accreditation MRAs (e.g. regional Asia-Pacific Laboratory Accreditation Corporation (APLAC), or the global International Laboratory Accreditation Cooperation (ILAC)). Some APEC economies not in CPTPP but in RCEP, such as China, the Philippines and Korea, also have domestic conformity assessments aligned with international standards, but by lesser extents. China's conformity assessment standards for several products are premised on International Organization for Standardization (ISO) and the International Electrotechnical Commission (IEC) standards, as are those in the Philippines.[24] As noted earlier, China and the Philippines have the largest SPSs among RCEP economies (Table 4.1), many of which might be cost-inducing NTBs even for RCEP Organisation for Economic Co-operation and Development members like Japan, Australia and New Zealand, given the qualitative differences in conformity assessment standards, and the procedural obstacles of complying with different standards. However, other APEC economies not in CPTPP, but in RCEP, like Thailand and Indonesia, which are also among the larger and prominent ASEAN economies, reflect much less alignment of domestic conformity with international benchmarks. Indonesia's domestic standardisation regulation follows international MRAs without mentioning specifics,

Table 4.2 International standards and domestic conformity assessment rules: APEC Members of CPTPP and RCEP

International standards	CPTPP member	RCEP member
ISO/IEC conformity assessment standards	Australia, Brunei, Canada, Chile, Japan, Malaysia, Mexico, New Zealand, Peru, Singapore, Vietnam	China, Philippines, Korea
International MRAs	Australia, Brunei, Canada, Chile, Malaysia, Mexico, New Zealand, Peru, Vietnam	China, Korea, Philippines
International schemes: International Electrotechnical Commission for conformity assessment schemes for electrotechnical equipment & components (IECEE[25])	Australia, Canada, Malaysia, Mexico, New Zealand, Singapore, USA, Vietnam	China, Korea

Source: 'Good Regulatory Practices for Conformity Assessment in APEC Member Economies', APEC#213-CT-01.11, October 2013, Sub-Committee on Standards and Conformance, APEC; http://publications.apec.org/publication-detail.php?pub_id=1473.

while Thailand specifies domestic conformity assessment with international standards only for specific medical products (e.g. condoms). These differences are a pointer to the difficulties RCEP is likely to experience in any efforts to standardise technical quality regulations among its members.

On GRPs and conformity assessment, CPTPP members comprise APEC economies, most of whom have aligned domestic standards to prevailing international standards. These are also economies accepting regional MRAs (e.g. APEC-TEL MRA). The RCEP presents a rather different picture in this respect in marked contrast to the CPTPP. On one hand, it has some members common with CPTPP – Australia, Brunei, Japan, Malaysia, New Zealand, Singapore, Vietnam – that have been imbibing international standards in domestic regulations. On the other, it has APEC members like China, the Philippines, Thailand and Indonesia that while belonging to APEC's work programme on standards and conformity assessment are less aligned with international standards and MRAs, in addition to regulatory variations among themselves. Except for Korea, which is expected to join the TPP in the next round, none of the non-TPP APEC members of RCEP are parties to multiple regional and bilateral MRAs.[26] The heterogeneity among APEC members of RCEP in aligning international standards with domestic quality benchmarks manifests in a larger contrast in the standardisation landscape of RCEP, given the additional presence of non-APEC members like Cambodia, Laos, Myanmar and India, who also have lesser alignment of domestic standards with international ones, compared with CPTPP countries.

The divergence among APEC members of RCEP also reflects existing differences within ASEAN in institutionalising GRPs. These are evident from the differences in coverage of standards, conformity assessment and MRAs in various ASEAN+1 FTAs. The ASEAN-India comprehensive economic cooperation agreement (CECA) has no provision for these measures. The ASEAN-People's Republic of China (PRC) CECA, while not including any provisions on standards and conformance in SPS, and mutual recognition, provides for strengthening cooperation in standards and conformity assessment in TBT without providing specific details. ASEAN's own FTA, mentions harmonisation of standards and reciprocal recognition of tests and certification for SPS and TBTs and has provisions of the MRA on electrical and electronic equipment including provisions on mandatory requirements, coverage, listing of testing laboratories and certifying bodies with specification of testing standards on ISO norms. In this context, it is important to note that standards and conformance provisions and MRAs figure in China's bilateral FTAs with Chile, Pakistan and New Zealand as well as in India's FTAs with Japan and Korea. But the provisions are largely of a general cooperative nature without mentioning specifics (Kawai and Wignaraja 2014).

ASEAN's FTAs with Australia and New Zealand (AANZFTA) and those with Japan and Korea are more exhaustive in institutionalising GRPs. The AANZFTA contains equivalence provisions for SPS and conformity assessment procedures with strong emphasis on exchange of information, cooperation and consultation. Efforts towards cooperation and mutual recognition of conformation assessments are also noted in ASEAN-Japan CECA though equivalence issues on SPS are not mentioned. Mutual recognition of product standards and SPS are absent from the ASEAN-Korea FTA too, though it focuses on extensive exchange of information on SPS and TBT measures through institutional mechanisms.

The difference in emphasis and coverage of MRAs between various ASEAN FTAs reflect the degree of success achieved by various ASEAN and APEC economies in aligning domestic standards to international norms and the extent by which they have been keen on achieving 'deep' liberalisation on regulating product standards in their FTAs. Among RCEP members, Australia, New Zealand, Japan and Korea have been active proponents of GRPs in their FTAs. This has reflected in greater alignment of their own domestic standards with international benchmarks. However, some other RCEP members like China, might not be highly enthusiastic in emphasising GRPs in RCEP talks. Indeed, from an ASEAN perspective it is difficult to discern a common view in this regard, simply because such a view does not exist, given the heterogeneities in regulations.

The Indian perspective

The implications for India need to be looked at from the negotiating outcomes resulting from interfaces between two prominent groups within RCEP: Countries that have taken major strides in aligning domestic standards with international benchmarks and are likely to emphasise such harmonisation in RCEP; and those that are yet to comprehensively align domestic standards with the global ones and are unsure of committing to a proactive agenda on harmonisation. The context poses several challenges for India. One of these, could arise from the alignment of the harmonisation agenda of the CPTPP with those of its common members in RCEP, manifesting in demand for imbibing high-quality scientific product standards among RCEP members. This could begin the process of establishment of new meta-standards on the lines of Hazard Analysis and Critical Control Point and Good Manufacturing Practices and progressive upgrading of quality benchmarks in member economies.[27] As a result India's challenges for upgrading its standards could be substantial.

As mentioned earlier, India, along with a few other RCEP economies, is neither a member of CPTPP, nor of APEC. The growth of new standards among some APEC members, who are in RCEP, could be challenging for India since the new standards could manifest through new SPS and TBT barriers. The 'protective' content of the new standards would depend on the extent by which they are influenced by other regulations, such as those on investment, labour or environment. The inter-dependence between regulations is an integral part of new 21st-century modern trade agreements such as CPTPP given their single-undertaking approach mentioned earlier. The inter-dependence can occasionally produce conflicting outcomes, like Australian consumer groups being concerned over whether tighter food labelling and product safety laws would provoke other CPTPP members to take recourse to remedies under the Investor-State Dispute Settlement rules.[28]

The growth of new high standards in APEC economies and their impact on RCEP negotiations would depend on the abilities of specific interest groups to keep lobbying effectively for institutionalising such standards. Several environmental groups in the US, for example, have expressed satisfaction over environment provisions in CPTPP, particularly efforts to protect trade in endangered species, prohibiting high fisheries subsidies and clamping illegal fishing.[29] While the US is no longer a part of CPTPP, these environment priorities in CPTPP might find their way into larger meta-standards that begin influencing product standards in APEC markets, including those of RCEP members. The protective manifestation of such influence is undeniable. For example, as major CPTPP members start cutting fisheries subsidies, they might wish to imbibe standards that make access to their markets more restrictive for countries that continue giving subsidies on fisheries. India is already experiencing some of these tendencies at the WTO negotiations on fisheries subsidies.[30]

Be it through new meta-standards, or otherwise, harmonisation of product standards across Asia-Pacific FTAs would establish a predictable set of quality benchmarks in some of India's major export markets such as the US, EU, Japan, Canada, Australia, Singapore and Malaysia. These 'core' standards would presumably be the ones that Indian exporters might be expected to adhere to down the line. The expectation would be accompanied by a gradual insistence on adoption of GRPs and harmonisation of standards in India's FTA negotiations that involve members from CPTPP. Apart from the RCEP, which has several CPTPP members, other FTA negotiations involving India which could be influenced by such insistence including those with Australia, Canada and New Zealand. Indeed, India might be urged to revisit some of its earlier FTAs, which either do not contain specific provisions on harmonisation of standards or are limited in this particular scope. This could include the FTAs with Japan, Korea, Singapore, Malaysia, or even the FTA with ASEAN. The insistence on harmonisation could imply signing MRAs on conformity assessment with national standard agencies of FTA partner countries. Till now, India is not a signatory to the various MRAs in the region, particularly those in the Asia-Pacific, such as the APEC-Telecommunications (TEL) MRA or the APEC-Electrical and Electronic Equipment (EE) MRA.

Notwithstanding these concerns and challenges, India's imperatives of obtaining greater market access in the Asia-Pacific at a time when lower tariffs are accompanied by rising NTBs, require it to work actively for making the RCEP an effective forum for rationalising NTBs. Mutual recognition of conformity assessments is an important step in this regard as such recognition, as argued earlier in the paper, can help in significant reduction of trade costs. Indian exporters have been traditionally unhappy with several of India's FTAs on the ground of these not having allowed Indian exports as much access in other markets compared with the access of the latter's exports in the Indian market. Apart from traditional issues of competitiveness, access of Indian exports in markets of RCEP members with whom it has bilateral FTAs, such as Japan, Korea, Singapore, Malaysia, Thailand and ASEAN, might well have been affected by NTBs. This needs to be acted upon through RCEP, as otherwise, concession on tariffs would not obtain reciprocal market access. The concern with respect to China is particularly high in this regard. As seen earlier, China is one of the largest imposers of NTBs in the Asia-Pacific. There is much consternation in India over granting China additional market access by lowering tariffs through RCEP. In order to effectively address this concern, India needs to act through RCEP, and also bilaterally with China, for getting around SPS and NTBs that are constraining market access for its important exports like pharmaceuticals. Obviously, India is not the only RCEP member encountering large NTBs in China since the latter are product-specific not country-specific. RCEP can therefore be an ideal forum where India can work with the rest of the members in persuading China to agree to a common set of standards that would ensure easy passage of its exports.

Final thoughts

RCEP is unlikely to result in a substantial increase of trade within its members unless it has strong provisions for rationalising NTBs maintained by members. This is a significant challenge for RCEP given the sharp increase in Asia-Pacific NTBs in recent years and the fact that several RCEP members are among the main users of new SPS and TBTs. While some of the latter could have been inspired by legitimate public policy objectives, most others have come up with protective intent. As the largest regional FTA covering almost half of the global population and about a third of world GDP, RCEP can be an effective group for tackling regional NTBs, if it can work out a meaningful programme of harmonisation of quality standards through mutual recognition of standards based on scientific parameters.

Given the large heterogeneity among its members on technical regulations and their alignment with global and regional standards, RCEP would find it difficult to insist on harmonisation. In this regard, it is likely to lag behind similar efforts that have been witnessed in the CPTPP. It would be unfortunate if standardisation efforts for tackling NTBs at RCEP remain as shallow as those in most ASEAN FTAs.

For India, in addition to negotiating at RCEP, it is important to note regional developments in standard-setting for being able to respond to the challenge of aligning its standards with international standards. It would be useful to explore the possibility of discussing bilaterally with some of the major RCEP members on conformity assessment collaboration in testing and certification. Greater engagement with regional standard-setting and certifying agencies in the Asia-Pacific could also be useful. The possibility of collaborating on upgrading national standards in the common search for their alignment with global standards can also be included as an agenda in future FTAs and RTAs that India might aim to negotiate such as those with Latin America and Africa.

Acknowledgements

An initial version containing some of the ideas in this paper was presented at the third National Standards Conclave, organised by the Ministry of Commerce, Government of India and the Confederation of Indian Industry at Delhi, India, on 23 and 24 June 2016. Later work on the paper has benefitted from the support provided by Korean Research Foundation. The author is grateful to Ananya Goyal of the National University of Singapore for research assistance.

Notes

1 UNCTAD (2015, page 1).
2 Ibid., page 3.
3 The WTO Agreements Series Sanitary and Phytosanitary measures, Page 10; World Trade Organization (WTO); www.wto.org/english/res_e/booksp_e/agrmntseries4_sps_e.pdf.
4 'RCEP talks: India 'unhappy' with revised services offers too', Business Standard, 5 February 2018. www.thehindubusinessline.com/economy/macro-economy/rcep-talks-india-unhappy/article22661235.ece.
5 'Guiding Principles and Objectives for Negotiating the Regional Comprehensive Economic Partnership' http://dfat.gov.au/trade/agreements/negotiations/rcep/Documents/guiding-principles-rcep.pdf.
6 Member Economies, APEC; https://apec.org/About-Us/About-APEC/Member-Economies.
7 Ballingall and Pambudi 2016, page i.
8 UNESCAP (2015), pages 4–7.
9 ABAC (2016), pages v–vii.
10 'Vietnam goes on the defense as China and US clash on trade', Bloomberg, 18 July 2018; www.bloomberg.com/news/articles/2018-07-17/vietnam-goes-on-the-defense-as-china-and-u-s-clash-over-trade.
11 UNESCAP (2015), Chapter 4, page 46, Table 4.1; Coverage ratio is value of trade affected by NTBs. The results in this study are for select ESCAP economies, out of which China and India are in RCEP.
12 The WTO database is regularly updated and fully synchronzesed with online notifications from various members. Our research revealed some reporting gaps in the data after mid-December 2016. As a result, we indicate these measures to be updated till November 2016.
13 UNESCAP (2015), Chapter 3, page 37, Table 3.1 and Chapter 4, page 46, Table 4.1.
14 Studies evaluating 'burdensomeness' for businesses with respect to SPS measures of various APEC economies point to Indonesia's SPSs being most burdensome with those of China, Malaysia, Korea and Thailand being a little

less. New Zealand and Philippines, interestingly, despite their higher SPSs, are considered less burdensome than these economies. See ABAC (2016), Page 26.
15 UNESCAP (2015), Chapter 3, Page 36.
16 UNESCAP (2015), Chapter 4, Page 45.
17 As mentioned in 14 earlier, Indonesia's TBTs are considered most burdensome, followed by those of China, Malaysia and Thailand. ABAC (2016), Page 26.
18 Removal of non-tariff trade costs can increase intra-RCEP exports by as much as 55% (Ratna and Huang, 2016).
19 The Legal Text: Comprehensive & Progressive Agreement for Trans-Pacific Partnership (CPTPP), released on February 21, 2018; Text published by Asian Trade Centre (ATC), Singapore.
20 'Annex D-Strengthening Implementation of Good Regulatory Practices', APEC Leaders' Declaration, Honolulu, Hawaii, United States, 13 November 2011; www.apec.org/Meeting-Papers/Leaders-Declarations/2011/2011_aelm/2011_aelm_annexD.aspx.
21 'Joint Statement from Trans-Pacific Partnership Ministers Meeting on Margins of APEC in Big Sky, Montana', Office of the United States Trade Representative, May 2011; https://ustr.gov/about-us/policy-offices/press-office/press-releases/2011/may/joint-statement-trans-pacific-partnership-ministers-me.
22 Article 8.9 (2) (a) (ii); The Legal Text: Comprehensive & Progressive Agreement for Trans-Pacific Partnership (CPTPP); Chapter 8, Technical Barriers to Trade, Pages 8–11.
23 Ibid. Annex 8-B, Section C, Pages 8–24.
24 Conformity Assessment rules in Philippines also reflect alignment with Codex standards.
25 IECEE is IEC System for Conformity Testing and Certification of Electrotechnical Equipment.
26 China and Philippines have not locked into APEC-TEL MRA.
27 The CPTPP, for example, emphasises on risk analysis as opposed to risk assessment that was used as a norm in the WTO's SPS Agreement.
28 'Food labelling and product safety laws in jeopardy under TPP says Choice', Esther Han, Sydney Morning Herald, The Sydney Morning Herald, 11 March 2016; www.smh.com.au/federal-politics/political-news/food-labelling-and-product-safety-laws-in-jeopardy-undertpp-says-choice-20160311-gnfss6.html.
29 Rohan Patel, 'What Environmental and Conservation Advocates are Saying About TPP's Environment Chapter', *theWhiteHouse*; November 6, 2015; www.whitehouse.gov/blog/2015/11/04/what-environmental-and-conservation-advocates-are-saying-about-tpps-environment.
30 Amiti Sen, 'India's fisheries subsidies may be targeted at WTO', Business Line, June 2, 2016; www.thehindubusinessline.com/economy/agri-business/indias-fisheries-subsidies-may-be-targeted-at-wto/article8682127.ece.

References

ABAC (2016), 'Non-Tariff Barriers in Agriculture and Food Trade in APEC: Business Perspectives on Impacts and Solutions', APEC Business Advisory Council, University of Southern California, Marshall School of Business. November; www2.abaconline.org/assets/2016/4%20Peru/Full%20Report%20-%20ABAC%20USC%20Marshall%20-%20Non-Tariff%20Barriers%20in%20Agriculture%20and%20Food%20Trade.pdf
Ballingall, John and Pambudi, Daniel (2016), Quantifying the costs of non-tariff measures in the Asia-Pacific region, New Zealand Institute for Economic Research

(NZIER), Working Paper 2016/4, November; https://nzier.org.nz/static/media/filer_public/ac/2d/ac2d99f1-ac0f-4f53-86d3-e1d3d65e096a/wp2016-4_non-tariff_measures_in_apec.pdf

Cadot, Olivier and Gourdon, Julien (2015). 'NTMs, Preferential Trade Agreements, and Prices: New Evidence'. Centre d'Etudes Prospectives et d'Informations Internationales, Working Paper No. 2015-01.

Kawai, Masahiro and Wignaraja, Ganeshan (2014), 'Policy challenges posed by Asian free trade agreements: A review of the evidence' in Richard Baldwin, Masahiro Kawai and Ganeshan Wignaraja (eds.). (2014), *A World Trade Organization for the 21st Century The Asian Perspective*; Asian Development Bank Institute (ADBI) and Edward Elgar (EE), UK.

Maur, Jean Christophe and Shepherd, Ben (2011), 'Product Standards', Chapter 10, in *Preferential Trade Agreement Policies for Development A Handbook*, edited by Jean Pierre Chauffour and Jean Christophe Maur. Washington DC: World Bank, pp. 197–216.

Palit, Amitendu (2014), *The Trans-Pacific Partnership, China and India*. New York and London: Routledge.

Ratna, Rajan Sudesh and Huang, Jing (2016), 'Regional Comprehensive Economic Partnership (RCEP) FTA: Reducing Trade Cost Through Removal of Non-Tariff Measures', *Korea and the World Economy*, Vol. 17, No. 2 (August 2016) 213–242.

UNCTAD (2015), International Classification of Non-Tariff Measures 2012 Version, UN, New York & Geneva. www.tradebarriers.org/docs/UNCTAD%20%20NTM%20classification%202012%20revised%20Version.pdf

UNESCAP (2015), Trade and Non-Tariff Measures : Impacts in the Asia-Pacific Region, Emerging Issues in Trade and Investment, Vol. 1, United Nations Economic and Social Commission for Asia and the Pacific; www.unescap.org/sites/default/files/NTM%20Flagship%20-%2025%20May.pdf

5 The legal issues of RCEP investment rules

A Sino-ASEAN perspective

Heng Wang

Introduction

Launched by the Association of Southeast Asian Nations (ASEAN) in 2012,[1] the Regional Comprehensive Economic Partnership (RCEP) has gone through 16 rounds of negotiations at the time of writing. Until December 2016, two chapters of the RCEP have been concluded in the latest two rounds: firstly, the chapter on Economic and Technical Cooperation and then the chapter on Small and Medium Enterprises (SMEs).[2] In the latest negotiations round of the RCEP at the time of writing, parallel meetings were held by the Working Groups on Investment, Intellectual Property, Competition, e-Commerce, and Legal and Institutional Issues.[3]

Despite the difficulties in negotiations, the RCEP would probably gain additional momentum with the setback to the Trans-Pacific Partnership (TPP). Although certain countries reportedly prefer to wait and see whether the TPP can "somehow regain traction" under the new US administration,[4] "[l]eaders from Australia, Malaysia, and other nations who had championed TPP quickly signalled … that they would shift their attention to the RCEP"[5] after the announcement of the US presidential election result. Meanwhile, China may want to conclude the RCEP as soon as possible and push harder than before.[6] In the RCEP negotiations, investment rules will be a major issue due to an enormous amount of investment within this free trade area. In the latest round of the RCEP negotiations, it is agreed to build on the outcomes to intensify negotiations, particularly in the core market access areas including that of investment.[7] All RCEP parties have submitted initial reservation lists for investment, and certain requests have been put in concerning initial reservation lists in investment.[8]

This article will explore the legal issues of the RCEP investment rules from a Sino-ASEAN perspective.[9] Due to the space constraint and a number of other reasons discussed below, this chapter will focus on the Investment Agreement between China and the ASEAN (Investment Agreement) and their implications for the RCEP, which is so far under-explored. Other pacts, including China's recent free trade agreements (FTAs) with Australia and Korea,[10] will be referred to when needed.

In this chapter, Part II will analyse the models of China's FTA investment rules, and in particular the uniqueness of the Investment Agreement for understanding the RCEP from the Sino-ASEAN perspective. Two key questions will then be explored in Parts III and IV respectively: what is the approach of the Investment Agreement? What are the major legal issues of the RCEP investment rules from the Sino-ASEAN perspective? Part V will present the concluding remarks.

The models of China's FTA investment rules and the uniqueness of the China-ASEAN investment agreement

Three models of China's FTA investment rules

A large number of China's FTAs incorporate investment chapters, including China's FTAs with the ASEAN, Australia, Chile, Costa Rica, Iceland, Korea, New Zealand, Pakistan, Peru, Singapore, and Switzerland. For the investment rules of China's FTAs that could potentially be relevant to the RCEP negotiations, there are at least three models.

The first model is the Investment Agreement. Signed in 2009, it contains relatively comprehensive but sometimes lenient investment rules. Axel Berger observes that China's FTAs with Pakistan, New Zealand, Peru and the ASEAN contain "comprehensive and genuine investment rules."[11] They basically fit into this category. That said, the investment rules in the China-ASEAN and China-New Zealand FTAs, for instance, are not the highest among China's trade pacts.

The second model is the China-Korea FTA. It incorporates comprehensive, detailed, and often strict provisions. One may argue that it generally includes the highest-level investment rules among China's FTAs, and largely follows the US treaty practice. The China-Korea FTA contains a number of provisions (including specific mandatory performance requirements,[12] the treatment granted to covered investment once admitted being no less favourable than that granted at the time of the original investment[13]) that are absent or less stringent in other FTAs, such as the Investment Agreement and the China-New Zealand FTA.

The third model is the China-Australia FTA (ChAFTA). As a work-in-progress type of pact, it contains short-form investment rules but focuses on Investor-state dispute settlement (ISDS).

In addition, it should be noted that there is a pattern in China's FTAs with Singapore and Costa Rica. They incorporate the Investment Agreement and reaffirm the commitments under the investment agreement between China and Costa Rica respectively.[14] Such a pattern is not likely to be adopted by the RCEP as the parties do not have an investment agreement within themselves.

The uniqueness of the China-ASEAN investment agreement

Other than the economic size of China and the ASEAN, the Investment Agreement is unique for analysing the issues of the RCEP investment chapter from the Sino-ASEAN perspective. First, the ASEAN is arguably the leader of RCEP negotiations, and China also plays an important role in the RCEP negotiations. The ASEAN plays a key role in the initiation and process of RCEP negotiations. Essentially, the RCEP was launched by the ASEAN and is being negotiated between the ASEAN and its FTA partners. RCEP membership is "based on ASEAN's FTA partners."[15] The ASEAN appears to play a leading role in the RCEP negotiations, which is supported by China.[16] The Investment Agreement is crucial to the understanding of the ASEAN's position in the bilateral economic relationship with China.

Second, the Investment Agreement per se is special for China. The Framework Agreement on Comprehensive Economic Co-operation between China and ASEAN (China-ASEAN Framework Agreement), which consists of the Investment Agreement, is unusual in the sense that it is the only FTA China concluded with more than one economy. One commentator even observes that the negotiations on the Investment Agreement are China's first ones over a multilateral investment agreement,[17] while another writer suggests that the Investment Agreement is "arguably an example of China's influence on rule-making on regional level."[18] As a mega FTA, the RCEP involves a significant number of countries including the ASEAN member countries. Therefore, the experience of the Investment Agreement should be of high relevance to China regarding the RCEP negotiations.

Last but not least, the Investment Agreement has wider implications than the investment rules of other Chinese FTAs. It is relevant not only to the RCEP and the China-ASEAN FTA, but also the China-Singapore FTA. On the one hand, the Investment Agreement, like other current agreements, will co-exist with the RCEP. The RCEP will not detract from the FTAs between or among negotiating parties,[19] and will cohabit with previous FTAs and investment treaties, including the Investment Agreement. On the other hand, the Investment Agreement not only governs the investment between China and the ASEAN under its FTA, but also applies to the investment between China and an ASEAN country under the China-Singapore FTA as it has been incorporated into the China-Singapore FTA.[20] Therefore, we should be acutely aware of the significance of the Investment Agreement in understanding the RCEP negotiations, and the approach of the Investment Agreement will be analysed to better understand possible issues in RCEP investment rules.

The approach of the China-ASEAN investment agreement

Flexibility

The Investment Agreement lends support to the argument that it shows some extra flexibility to China among its FTAs. It could lead to a growing consensus between China and the ASEAN, which helps to finalize the RCEP negotiations. Within a broader scenario, China was happy to sit down with all ten ASEAN countries at the outset of the FTA negotiations, which is contrary to the "divide and conquer" approach of Japan.[21] The China-ASEAN FTA appears to contain some special provisions among China's FTAs regarding investment. Nargiza Salidjanova pointed out that China "has only granted Pakistan and ASEAN full national treatment" regarding the post-establishment phase of investment.[22] Unlike recent treaty practice (such as the China-Korea FTA), the Investment Agreement incorporates special provisions for several ASEAN member countries on, among others, the scope of application and the denial of benefits. It is plain that they are made at the behest of ASEAN member countries and are not common in China's treaty practice. These stipulations indicate that China has taken a pragmatic approach to the ASEAN, which may continue to be the case in the RCEP. For the scope of application, the Investment Agreement only applies to investment that has been admitted in Thailand, and that has been specifically approved in writing for protection by the relevant authorities as per domestic law and policy.[23] In the provision on the denial of benefits, Thailand may deny foreign investors the benefits of investment treaty protection when the investor is controlled by a person of a non-party or the denying party.[24] It is easier to meet the conditions for the denial of benefits in the case of Thailand as they do not impose other requirements such as substantive business operations.[25] For the Philippines, it may deny foreign investors the benefits of the Agreement if the investment violates "The Anti-Dummy Law."[26] These provisions not only prevent treaty shopping as the case with other FTAs, but also take into account the relevant domestic rules of the ASEAN states. Other special provisions for certain ASEAN member countries can be found in the choice of the procedure in ISDS,[27] and the rate and payment of interest of compensation in the case of expropriation.[28]

The flexibility in Investment Agreement negotiations stems from and is highlighted in the China-ASEAN Framework Agreement.[29] The latter requires the negotiations on the Investment Agreement to (i) consider sensitive sectors and (ii) the special treatment and flexibility for the new ASEAN members.[30] One may argue that flexibility is a principle in the China-ASEAN FTA negotiation, particularly regarding the newer ASEAN member states as indicated in the preamble of the China-ASEAN Framework Agreement.

Why is there such flexibility? For one thing, flexibility is a salient feature of China's FTA practice. With certain exceptions (including investment liberalization), China often tends to follow and build on the proposals of the FTA partners. The Framework Agreement on ASEAN Investment Area (AIA Framework Agreement) was used as a template for the negotiations of the Investment Agreement.[31] The Investment Agreement reflects China's flexible approach to FTA negotiations since it largely mirrors the ASEAN Comprehensive Investment Agreement of 2009 except for the market access provisions.[32] At the same time, the flexibility in the Investment Agreement is presumably linked to the desire to complete the negotiation process of the China-ASEAN Free Trade Area. At that moment, although

China is only ranked as the eighth largest investor in the ASEAN, the signing of the Investment Agreement completed the negotiation process of the China-ASEAN Free Trade Area as the agreements of trade in goods and services had been signed.[33]

Less rigorous or developed rules

Overall, the Investment Agreement does not provide provisions that substantially go beyond China's commitments under previous bilateral investment treaties (BITs).[34] Rules in the Investment Agreement are usually less rigorous or more cautious than the counterpart of China's other trade and investment agreements and particularly the recent China-Korea FTA.

As for the scope of investment, the Investment Agreement has a seemingly narrower scope as it requires the investment to be made "in accordance with the relevant laws, regulations and policies" of the host country,[35] which excludes the investment that does not comply with domestic law and policy from the treaty coverage. This clause will help the host country government to exclude from ISDS investment that fails to meet this requirement. No such requirement exists in the China-Korea FTA. However, such a clause could be open to different interpretations by arbitration tribunals.[36] This definition seems to increase the obligations of the investors. Relating to this, it bears noting that a governmentally owned legal entity is protected as "juridical person of a Party" under the Investment Agreement,[37] which includes the state-owned enterprises (SOE). It fits China's interest to protect the investment by Chinese SOEs.

Investment treatment, as the main thrust of China's FTAs, is often weaker in the Investment Agreement than in the China-Korea FTA. As a key provision, the Investment Agreement provides for fair and equitable treatment (FET) and full protection and security (FPS).[38] However, it does not contain a reference to "customary international law" or "the customary international law minimum standard of treatment" to clarify FET and FPS as is the case with the China-Korea FTA.[39] Similar references are made in China's FTAs with New Zealand[40] and Peru,[41] although China's FTAs do not have a consistent standard of FET and FPS. Among them, FET in the Investment Agreement seems to impose less stringent requirement among these FTAs discussed here. In the Investment Agreement, FET is narrowly defined as prohibiting the denial of justice in legal or administrative proceedings. Under the FPS provision, the parties need to take measures that are "reasonably necessary" to ensure the protection and security of the investment,[42] which resembles its counterpart in the China-New Zealand FTA.[43] On a related note, the Investment Agreement uses the term "treatment of investment" and avoids the term "the minimum standard of treatment" that covers FET in the North American Free Trade Agreement, TPP, and China-Korea FTA.

Regarding expropriation, the Investment Agreement accepts some (e.g. a public purpose) but not all features of expropriation that are provided in other pacts. Concerning indirect expropriation, the Investment Agreement uses a related term "take other similar measures" in the clause on expropriation.[44] Moreover, the Investment Agreement recognizes that taxation measure may produce an effect equivalent to expropriation or nationalization, which is subject to arbitration if treaty parties could not determine whether the taxation measure has such effect.[45] However, the Investment Agreement does not lay down the criteria for situations that could constitute an indirect expropriation, as the case with the China-Korea FTA.[46] In contrast, indirect expropriation has been clarified in some of China's agreements signed before the Investment Agreement including the China-India BIT.[47]

For the conditions of expropriation, the Investment Agreement has more lenient requirements than the China-Korea FTA. It does not require "international standard of due process of law" as in the China-Korea FTA,[48] and instead defers to applicable domestic laws.[49] The Investment Agreement mandates the compensation "without unreasonable delay"[50] rather than "without delay."[51] Relating to this, China has not explicitly accepted the requirement of prompt, adequate, and effective compensation for expropriation, known as the Hull Rule or Hull Formula, which is adopted in the TPP[52] and some of ASEAN's investment agreements. It is observed that China's FTAs (including those with the ASEAN and New Zealand) have in fact adopted the Hull Formula.[53] Ultimately, these clauses will be interpreted by the arbitration tribunals if the treaty parties fail to provide the guidance.

Concerning non-conforming measures, the Investment Agreement does not include the standstill or ratchet mechanism, and instead allows new non-conforming measures. The former exists in the China-New Zealand[54] and China-Korea agreements.[55] The usual disclaimer for non-conforming measures is included. The most-favoured-nation (MFN) and national treatment do not apply to existing or new non-conforming measures adopted by the parties, which can be continued or amended.[56] It not only serves a grandfather clause exempting pre-existing law but also allows new non-conforming measures. It is worthy of note that the incorporation of the phrase 'new' non-conforming measures is "the first case."[57] As an exception to non-discriminatory treatment, it substantially restrains investment protection and gives a lot of room for regulators to adopt new measures that are not consistent with non-discriminatory treatment.

As another key component of investment agreements, ISDS is approached in a careful manner in the Investment Agreement. Compared with China's recent FTAs and particularly the ChAFTA, the Investment Agreement contains less developed or stringent ISDS rules. It is reflected in, among other things, the consolidation of claims, the limited scope of claims, and domestic administrative review. As an example of advanced procedural rules, the rule on the consolidation of claims is missing in the Investment Agreement, but occurs in China's trade agreements with New Zealand[58] and Australia.[59] The ISDS claims are limited to the violation of several provisions, which are non-discrimination treatment, the treatment of investment, expropriation, the compensation for losses, as well as the transfers and repatriation of profits.[60] Moreover, the breach of obligation should bring loss or damage to the investor concerning its investment regarding "the management, conduct, operation, or sale or other disposition of an investment,"[61] which in fact precludes the claims arising from the breach of pre-establishment MFN treatment. Similar to China's treaty practice, the Investment Agreement contains a two-step process for dispute resolution, which may require domestic administrative review.[62] However, the China-Korea FTA contains stricter rules than the Investment Agreement regarding, among others, the four-month time limit for domestic administrative review procedure, and the requirement for administrative review process being imposed "without delay."[63]

An incremental strategy

Taking the China-ASEAN FTA as a whole, it has taken a progressive approach towards investment rules: the Investment Agreement was signed separately and was near the end of the negotiation process of the China-ASEAN Free Trade Area. The ASEAN-China FTA adopts a step-by-step approach (first framework agreement and then specific agreements) rather than a single package in most of China's trade pacts. However, the scenario will be different in the RCEP as investment rules are to be a chapter of the RCEP rather than a separate agreement. The Investment Agreement also adopts an incremental strategy. It develops from previous BITs and has taken a step-by-step approach in its negotiations. The standards of investment protection under the Investment Agreement are higher than China's BITs with ASEAN countries before the year 2000 mainly regarding national treatment obligation, the extension of a priori consent to arbitration and the clarification of compensation standard.[64] As per the China-ASEAN Framework Agreement, the investment rule negotiations should aim to "progressively liberalise the investment regime."[65] Regarding the goals, the Investment Agreement has a similar clause and indicates that the deal works towards the creation of "a liberal, facilitative, transparent and competitive investment regime."[66] As an example of concrete obligations, the agreement requires the gradual removal of the non-conforming measures on a best-effort basis.[67]

More recently, the upgrade of the China-ASEAN FTA regarding investment rules is a typical example of the incremental approach. The Investment Agreement mainly deals with investment protection, which remains the same as the Upgrading Protocol of the China-ASEAN FTA. The Upgrading Protocol has kept the Investment Agreement mostly unchanged except for two upgraded clauses on investment promotion and facilitation. These upgrades do not bring substantial development. For the investment promotion, it adds, inter alia, the obligation to "encourage and create favourable conditions for investors and their investments" and the cooperation on industrial complementation and production networks.[68] Regarding the facilitation of investment, the upgraded version includes a best-endeavour clause to "further create stable, favourable and transparent conditions" to encourage greater investment within the free trade zone.[69] Regarding further development, the China-ASEAN FTA takes a forward-looking and progressive approach. Unless otherwise agreed, the treaty parties commit to conclude the discussions concerning investment liberalization and protection within three years after the Upgrading Protocol becomes operative,[70] which may bring more substantial development of investment rules.

The legal issues of the RCEP investment rules

Market access: moving towards investment liberalization?

The Investment Agreement has rarely dealt with investment liberalization, which contrasts with Japan's economic partnership agreements with individual ASEAN countries that highlight investment liberalization and protection.[71] Until recently China followed the traditional "European" approach in investment rules, underscoring investment protection but omitting concrete obligations on investment liberalization or market access.[72] Such an approach has been adopted in the Investment Agreement. More rules are devoted to the investment protection in the Investment Agreement, including MFN treatment, national treatment, FET, FPS, and the compensation in case of expropriation. The Investment Agreement also contains concise clauses on investment facilitation[73] and promotion,[74] both of which are upgraded recently.[75] Both upgraded provisions call for cooperation rather than imposing stringent requirements. In contrast, few rules deal with investment liberalization in this agreement.

Meanwhile, investment liberalization is not precluded from the Investment Agreement. However, investment liberalization is still in its early stage in the China-ASEAN FTA. It is reflected in the objectives and work plan rather than in the substantive obligations. The progressive liberalization of the investment regime is provided in the China-ASEAN Framework Agreement.[76] The Investment Agreement sets out the goal of "progressively liberalising the investment regimes of China and ASEAN,"[77] and the most recent China-ASEAN FTA Upgrading Protocol calls for "improved investment liberalization, protection, promotion, and facilitation."[78] Investment liberalization is to be taken into account in the subsequent negotiations of the China-ASEAN FTA. As noted elsewhere, the treaty parties agree to conclude the discussions concerning investment liberalization and protection within three years of the entry into force of the Upgrading Protocol.[79]

From the perspective of the ASEAN and China, it is possible that investment liberalization will be considered in the near future. Two-way investment between China and the ASEAN have grown nearly fourfold from $3.37 billion in 2003 to $12.2 billion in 2014.[80] In 2014, the ASEAN surpassed China and became the largest recipient of foreign direct investment in the developing world.[81] It is natural that investment rules assume increasing importance. Such a dramatic increase in investment presumably provides more incentives for both sides to pursue a more liberalized investment agreement. However, the parties need to assure themselves that they will benefit from this mega FTA.

The ASEAN is interested in investment liberalization and has adopted the rules on investment liberalization, including the pre-establishment national treatment clause in the ASEAN Comprehensive Investment Agreement.[82] Consistent with the global treaty practice, ASEAN countries utilized FTA negotiations to extend the market-access logic from trade in goods and services to investment, and incorporate pre-establishment national treatment provisions.[83] Looking at the negotiation history of the Investment Agreement, one author observes that the ASEAN "expects to have a greater emphasis on increased liberalization rather than a mere investment protection" partially due to the fact that some ASEAN member countries (e.g. Singapore and Malaysia) have comprehensive and advanced investment regimes and the free flow of investment is the aim of the AIA Framework Agreement.[84] For the ASEAN members, the absence of market-access provisions in the Investment Agreement is "a major deficiency" of the pact that needs to be addressed in future negotiations.[85]

China has been more positive about investment liberalization than before, which is reflected in the US-China BIT negotiations and Free Trade Zones (FTZs). The pre-establishment national treatment and the negative list approach in the scheduling of investment commitments have been agreed upon in the US-China BIT negotiations.[86] These developments have also been committed to in the recent China's FTAs,[87] and related efforts have been made in FTZs. For one thing, China is becoming a net capital exporter and has the desire for domestic reform to stimulate the economy. There is more incentive to take measures to protect and liberalize investment. Therefore, China may choose to accept pre-establishment national treatment and the negative-list approach in the RCEP negotiations, possibly envisaging the relevant further negotiations as is the case with its recent FTAs.

Turning to the RCEP, a vital issue is whether and how they will deal with investment liberalization. It is probably a key topic for debate in the ongoing RCEP talks. As noted above, the RCEP negotiations in the core market access areas of investment will be intensified after the submission of initial reservation lists for investment and of individual requests concerning these lists. An open issue is whether the RCEP will contain investment commitments scheduled on the negative-list approach and include the pre-establishment commitments based on national treatment for foreign investors and investments. The answer is probably negative due to the different positions of the parties. If the answer turns out to be positive, it will represent a significant shift in the approach to investment at the level of new mega FTA.

On the one hand, the RCEP investment negotiations seem to be quite ambitious, which will cover investment promotion, protection, facilitation, and liberalization.[88] It is observed that the ASEAN States and China have included market-access protections in recent agreements, which suggests the growing support for investment liberalization.[89] As China's FTAs only commit to this approach in the future, and at least to some extent it appears to depend on the progress of the US-China BIT negotiations, China may want to postpone it to a later stage as the case with China's FTAs with Australia and Korea.

On the other hand, there are considerable uncertainties and challenges in the negotiations. For the uncertainties, the possibility of investment liberalization may be affected by many factors such as the structure of the RCEP investment rules. It is yet to be seen whether the RCEP investment chapter will contain annexes that provide for country-specific obligations or provisions as in the TPP (e.g. "stability agreements" between Peru and covered investments or investors as part of an investment agreement,[90] Chile's reserved right to regulate for currency stability as per domestic law[91]). On a related note, an early signing of the RCEP does not necessarily involve all 16 states.[92] If this is the case and the country-specific carve-outs are available, it is more likely for the RCEP to take more stringent investment rules and provides for market access protections. Other considerations such as the geopolitical concerns may play a major role, which may lead to the preference for the early conclusion of a free-trade accord over the time-consuming negotiations on the thorny issue of investment liberalization. For the challenges, examples include whether and how the negative list will be negotiated, and whether the negative lists will be long or extensive. It is yet to be seen whether the RCEP would incorporate into investment chapter the latest liberalization efforts of each party. Investment liberalization obligations will be challenging given the different positions of parties, and it is reported that some RCEP parties are "potentially opposed to changing negative lists" on investment.[93] Therefore, these obligations will be worth watching closely.

Substantive provisions

There remain real questions about whether the RCEP could develop high-level investment rules, and whether there will be detailed clarifications of substantive obligations such as FET. Stronger investment protections may be provided in the RCEP, including the selective adaption of modern rules. In addition to investment protection and possible investment liberalization, investment facilitation and promotion could be further developed as the four pillars under the RCEP investment rules.[94] Among them, it is a principle of the RCEP negotiations to incorporate stipulations to facilitate investment.[95]

The Investment Agreement contains key elements of investment protection, including national treatment,[96] MFN treatment,[97] FET, FPS,[98] the free transfer of capital and profits,[99] expropriation,[100] the compensation for losses,[101] and the denial of benefits.[102] Open issues include carve-outs for the MFN treatment, and compensation standard for expropriation, to name a few.

For the non-discriminatory treatment, the provisions of the Investment Agreement may be adopted or modified in the RCEP as the treaty practice develops. From the Sino-ASEAN perspective, it is likely that the national treatment and MFN treatment will be incorporated in the RCEP. In the early stage of the Investment Agreement negotiations, China argued that the timing was not ripe to grant national treatment.[103] Eventually, national treatment has been incorporated into the Investment Agreement but only applies to the post-establishment stage. As discussed earlier, this situation will begin to change as China has agreed to pre-establishment national treatment in the US-China BIT negotiations and the future negotiations of China's agreements with Korea and Australia.[104] China will probably have a position on national treatment in the RCEP negotiations, which develops from that under the Investment Agreement.

It is yet to be seen how the RCEP may include carve-outs for the MFN treatment. The MFN obligation under the Investment Agreement does not extend to dispute resolution,[105] and this has been the case in the recent treaty practice of China including the ChAFTA and China-New Zealand FTA.[106] Such a provision is likely to be adopted in the RCEP to avoid "unexpected" change to ISDS rules faced by the host country. Similar to China's FTAs with New Zealand, Peru, Korea, and Australia, the Investment Agreement contains MFN treatment for pre-establishment activities.[107] However, there are carve-outs for such MFN treatment under the Investment Agreement, which exclude future and existing agreements.[108] Therefore, the MFN clause provides a rather weak protection here. Differing from the China-Korea FTA,[109] the latest ChAFTA removes the carve-out for future agreements in the MFN treatment.[110] As the consistent practice of China's treaty practice is lacking, it is interesting to see what position China may take in the RCEP.

Regarding FET and FPS, it is possible that the RCEP will clarify their scope by the reference to customary international law. The Investment Agreement has taken early efforts to confirm that the obligation of investment treatment is not violated by the mere breach of other provisions of the Investment Agreement or separate provisions in other international agreements.[111] However, the Investment Agreement does not refer to customary international law here. An increasing number of treaties of the ASEAN (including ASEAN's FTAs with Australia, New Zealand[112] and Korea[113]) and China (e.g. the China-Korea FTA[114]) have elucidated that the scope of the FET obligation is confined to protections available under customary international law minimum standard of treatment. China and the ASEAN have a similar position in limiting the scope of the FET obligations.[115] Both sides will probably agree that the RCEP should follow such practice and adopt similar rules that contain the reference to customary international law.

For the compensation standard for expropriation, the Investment Agreement has a similar clause with the ASEAN-Korea and ASEAN-Australia-New Zealand agreements regarding the fair market value of the expropriated investment.[116] However, it does not explicitly provide for prompt, adequate, and effective compensation for expropriation as the latter two pacts.[117] As reflected in China's investment treaty practice, China may continue to resist the explicit incorporation of the Hull Rule in the RCEP.

Concerning performance requirements, they may be included in the RCEP. The Investment Agreement neither prohibits specific mandatory performance requirements nor includes the treatment of foreigners in cases of civil strife. The latter is provided in the China-Korea FTA,[118] and more stringent obligation occurs in the TPP.[119] It remains open whether and how the provision on performance requirement will be incorporated, which is also a critical issue in the US-China BIT negotiations.[120]

Social clauses

Social clauses include environmental, transparency rules as well as provisions on taxation and prudential measures. It is in the public interest that these social or linkage provisions allow derogations from ordinary investment obligations. The Investment Agreement and other FTAs of China has a limited number of social clauses. Consistent with China's treaty practice, transparency is provided in the Investment Agreement that requires the public availability of investment-related laws and regulations.[121] It also includes a WTO-style general exception clause, which deals with health and public order.[122] Like China's trade agreements (including those with New Zealand, Peru, and Korea[123]), the Investment Agreement incorporates a provision on security exceptions.[124] Significantly, its term "including but not limited to" may lead to a broad interpretation of "essential security interests" to cover economic crisis.[125] Besides, it permits action to "protect critical public infrastructure from deliberate attempts intended to disable or degrade such infrastructure,"[126] which is absent in China's other trade pacts discussed above. For other issues, taxation measures are not subject to the Investment Agreement[127] and some of China's FTAs.[128]

A number of social clauses are missing in the Investment Agreement. They include the provision on the right to regulate in the public interest in environmental protection and currency stability, which exists in the TPP.[129] The provision on prudential measures is also absent in the Investment Agreement but is used in China's treaty practice.[130]

It is too early to tell which specific social clauses will be incorporated or to tell their wording. The RECP will probably include transparency rules. As a principle, the RCEP will incorporate stipulations to enhance the transparency in investment relations,[131] with the aim of "a liberal, facilitative, and competitive investment environment."[132] China has also started to accept deeper transparency obligations such as regulatory transparency in financial services.[133] Moreover, the RCEP may contain general and security exceptions clauses as the common practice of treaty practice. China may support more social provisions in the RCEP than in the Investment Agreement, since such a tendency is revealed in the recent treaty practice of China (including the China-Japan-Korea Investment Treaty and China-Korea FTA[134]). Meanwhile, China will probably prefer a soft law approach regarding sensitive issues (including that of environment). The China-Korea FTA accepts a provision to discourage the practice of attracting investment at the cost of weaker environment protection.[135] The China-Canada BIT further extends such provisions from environment to health and safety concerns.[136] Both agreements also provide that the measures to protect such public interests do not constitute indirect expropriation.[137] Environment measures are also covered by its general exceptions clause. As mentioned above, China will probably agree that taxation measures and prudential measures for the integrity and stability of the financial system should be exempted from investment disciplines.

ISDS

The relative unlikelihood of ISDS claims may contribute to the fact that the Investment Agreement does not contain sophisticated provisions as in the case of deep FTAs (including the specific safeguards for discouraging frivolous, abusive, and meritorious claims[138]). Containing short form ISDS rules, the Investment Agreement has less detailed ISDS rules in comparison with the China-New Zealand and China-Australia agreements. Some advanced procedural rules are missing in the Investment Agreement, including the transparency of ISDS, a public welfare notice, and the code of conduct for arbitrators, all of which could be found in the ChAFTA. The ChAFTA goes further by envisaging, within one year of the pact's entry into force, the consultations on the application of the United Nations Commission on International Trade Law (UNCITRAL) Rules on Transparency in Treaty-based Investor-State Arbitration to investor-state arbitration.[139]

The RCEP reportedly contains an ISDS mechanism.[140] The ISDS claims are more likely to arise under the RCEP than traditional bilateral agreements (including the Investment Agreement) as it involves more parties and covers more investment. This fact shows the need for advanced dispute resolution system. The key is how the ISDS rules are drafted and whether there will be enhancements regarding key aspects (e.g. a possible appeal system). The FTAs of China and ASEAN seem to converge regarding the incorporation of advanced ISDS rules and in particular transparency. A possible RCEP provision on enhanced transparency of ISDS procedures is an option to address public concern over opaque dispute resolution process, and could be supported by China and the ASEAN. The ASEAN Comprehensive Investment Agreement and the ASEAN-Australia-New Zealand FTA contain similar provisions on transparency of arbitral proceedings.[141] The ChAFTA investment chapter specifies that some arbitration documents (i.e. the request for consultations, the notice of arbitration, as well as tribunal's orders, awards, and decisions) are open and available to the public, and the others (including pleadings, memorials, briefs, and minutes or transcripts of hearings) may be made accessible to the public.[142]

Moreover, it could be helpful if the RCEP could provide guiding principles and rules regarding the interpretation of investment rules, which seem to be lacking in the Investment Agreement. Such a provision makes ISDS more consistent and predictable. On a related note, it is to be observed how the RCEP may allow the treaty party to participate in treaty interpretation in the ISDS procedure. The ChAFTA permits an investor's home country to present submissions to the arbitral tribunal on issues of treaty interpretation as per the non-disputing party submissions provision, which is similar to the TPP.[143]

Concluding remarks

The RCEP is likely to contain a number of provisions similar to the counterpart of the Investment Agreement, especially those that are widely accepted in the treaty practice. Examples may include the provision on subrogation, which allows insurance agency to be subrogated in the rights of the investor and trigger the investment protections under the pact.[144] Based on the analysis of the Investment Agreement and its implications for the RCEP, some observation could be made.

First, investment rules of China's FTAs vary with the partners but reflect a pragmatic approach. China's trade agreements do not have a consistent model for investment rules, and instead include divergent rules regarding fundamental issues (such as the standard of FET and FPS, and the carve-out of the MFN treatment). They often follow the proposals of the partners. Therefore, variability is the major feature of China's investment rules in FTAs. Notably, China is even more flexible in its investment agreement with the ASEAN. Moreover, the recent investment treaty practice of China indicates positions that are substantially compatible with the counterpart of the ASEAN.[145] Combing with such practice, the Investment Agreement could be a building block of the RCEP investment rules. All these contribute to the conclusion of the RCEP negotiations.

China may play a more active role in the RCEP negotiations than in the Investment Agreement. Although China will probably push for a lower standard RCEP, the possibility of selective high-level investment rules cannot be excluded. It is due to a number of factors. China has gained more experience and capacity through negotiations (including the BIT negotiations with the US and EU). It will probably highlight the protection of outbound investment, and endeavours to substantially contribute to the recalibration of international investment law.

Meanwhile, China will facilitate the early conclusion of the RCEP negotiations. More broadly, investment rules should be balanced with the rest of the rules of RCEP. Legal and economic considerations need to be combined with geopolitical ones. China's FTAs with the ASEAN and Singapore, for instance, were deemed to be mainly driven by geopolitical concerns.[146] For instance, it will not be surprising if the RCEP contains few obligations regarding host country review mechanisms, although it is a challenge to Chinese outbound investment.

Second, a large number of parties involved in the mega FTA bring considerable uncertainties and difficulties to the RCEP negotiations. RCEP parties have different positions on investment. Australia, for instance, is cautious regarding investor-state arbitration. India seems to be hesitant to incorporate investment chapter in the FTAs.[147] More recently, the Indian model BIT substantially deviates from the recent treaty practice. As a typical example, the Indian model BIT requires an investor to exhaust local remedies for at least a period of five years,[148] which is a substantial departure from the provisions on the exhaustion of local remedies in other investment treaties.[149] Moreover, it does not include the MFN clause, which contrasts with agreements such as the ChAFTA.

Other investment rules and particularly those concluded by the RCEP parties could exert influence over the negotiations of this larger pact. A prime example is that the RCEP negotiations may be affected by investment rules among the ASEAN member countries and by the agreements between the ASEAN and the ASEAN FTA partners. It is natural as the RCEP is being negotiated among the ASEAN and its partners. As the latest development, the investment chapter of the ASEAN-Japan Comprehensive Economic Partnership (AJCEP) Agreement has been finalized in the latter half of 2016,[150] although the AJCEP was signed in 2008. It indicates the difficulties of negotiating the investment chapter, and these latest developments may affect the RCEP negotiations. The RECP could also be affected by deep FTAs. Although the US has withdrawn from the TPP, the pattern of the TPP could be relevant (e.g. the tobacco carve-out, and the country-specific obligations) and several RCEP parties also negotiated the TPP.

There are many unanswered questions regarding key investment rules and in particular the standards of protection and liberalization: will the RCEP simply update, consolidate or streamline previous rules? Will the RCEP take short form and work-in-progress type rules, or move towards investment liberalization and stringent investment protections? Will the RCEP contribute to the convergence of international investment norms? From the Chinese perspective, it remains to be seen how flexible China will show in negotiations and what role it will play. It is possible that the RCEP investment rules will take a pragmatic, step-by-step approach, with low-level rules first followed by the future upgrade. In the beginning, the RCEP investment chapter may lean towards less ambitious rules given, inter alia, the different interests and positions of the parties, and the setback to deep FTAs. If properly managed, the RCEP can contribute to the development of investment law based on the reaffirmation of common ground on main issues.

Last but not least, the RCEP will carry enormous implications. The RCEP investment rules, while probably not be ground-breaking, will be significant, because they have a broad coverage regarding treaty parties and investment and build on the previous agreements, and possibly take into account current commitments of the parties. These developments of the RCEP will be worth watching closely to see whether the RCEP will contain innovative provisions, and what impact they might have on future negotiations on investment rules under other FTAs (including trade and investment agreements of the RCEP parties). In fact, the RCEP has been more innovative than China's recent FTAs with Australia and Korea in the sense of a separate chapter on SMEs, which is absent in China's recent trade pacts. Significantly, the RCEP could carry wider implications as it is deemed to be a potential pathway to a Free Trade Area of the Asia Pacific.[151] If properly managed, India and other RCEP countries could actively engage with China through the RCEP negotiation to explore a rule-based regional integration. The RCEP will substantially contribute to the convergence of international investment rules.

Notes

1 Jason Scott & Roman David, China Set to Push Asia Trade Deal Harder After Trump Win, Bloomberg (2016), available at www.bloomberg.com/news/articles/2016-11-15/trump-trade-snub-set-to-boost-china-s-bid-for-its-own-asia-pact.
2 *Sixteenth Round of Negotiations – 2-10 December 2016, Tangerang, Indonesia* (2016), available at http://dfat.gov.au/trade/agreements/rcep/news/Pages/sixteenth-round-of-negotiations.aspx.
3 *Sixteenth Round of Negotiations – 2-10 December 2016, Tangerang, Indonesia* (2016), available at http://dfat.gov.au/trade/agreements/rcep/news/Pages/sixteenth-round-of-negotiations.aspx.
4 Scott & David, China Set to Push Asia Trade Deal Harder After Trump Win. 2016.
5 *Why Trump's Withdrawal from the TPP is a Boon for China* (2017), available at www.scmp.com/news/world/united-states-canada/article/2064927/why-trumps-withdrawal-tpp-boon-china.
6 Scott & David, China Set to Push Asia Trade Deal Harder After Trump Win. 2016.
7 *Sixteenth Round of Negotiations – 2-10 December 2016, Tangerang, Indonesia* (2016), available at http://dfat.gov.au/trade/agreements/rcep/news/Pages/sixteenth-round-of-negotiations.aspx.
8 New Zealand Ministry of Foreign Affairs and Trade, *Regional Comprehensive Economic Partnership (RCEP)* (2017), available at www.mfat.govt.nz/en/trade/free-trade-agreements/agreements-under-negotiation/rcep/.
9 Due to space limit, it is a Sino-ASEAN perspective. But this is with all due respect for the roles of other RCEP parties in the shaping of the RCEP.

10 For the analysis of China's FTAs and the RCEP investment rule negotiations, see Heng Wang, *The RCEP and Its Investment Rules: Learning from Past Chinese FTAs*, 3 Chinese Journal of Global Governance, forthcoming (2017).
11 Axel Berger, *Investment Rules in Chinese Preferential Trade and Investment Agreements: Is China Following the Global Trend towards Comprehensive Agreements? at* www.die-gdi.de/uploads/media/DP_7.2013.pdf.
12 China-Korea FTA Article 12.7.2 (2015); China-New Zealand FTA Article 140.
13 China-Korea FTA Article 12.3.2. 2015.
14 China-Costa Rica FTA Article 89.
15 *State of the Region 2014–2015*, 36–37 (2014).
16 *Gao Hucheng: Support the ASEAN to Lead RCEP Negotiations* (2016), available at http://fta.mofcom.gov.cn/article/fzdongtai/201608/32899_1.html.
17 Huiping Chen, *China-ASEAN FTA: An Investment Perspective, in* CHINA-ASEAN RELATIONS: ECONOMIC AND LEGAL DIMENSIONS 141, (John Wong et al. eds., 2006).
18 Jun Xiao, The ASEAN-China Investment Agreement: A Regionalization of Chinese New BITs 20–21 (2010).
19 *Guiding Principles and Objectives for Negotiating the Regional Comprehensive Economic Partnership*, available at http://dfat.gov.au/trade/agreements/rcep/Documents/guiding-principles-rcep.pdf.
20 China-Singapore FTA Article 84.1 (2008).
21 Nargiza Salidjanova, *China's Trade Ambitions: Strategy and Objectives behind China's Pursuit of Free Trade Agreements*, U.S.-China Economic and Security Review Commission Staff Research Report, 16 (2015).
22 Id. at, 18.
23 China-ASEAN Investment Agreement Article 3.3.
24 Id. at, Article 15.2.
25 Id. at, Article 15.1(a).
26 Id. at, Article 15.3.
27 Id. at, Article 15.5.
28 Id. at, Article 8.3, footnote 6.
29 *China-ASEAN Framework Agreement*, Article 2(e).
30 *China-ASEAN Framework Agreement*, Article 8.3.
31 Chen, China-ASEAN FTA: An Investment Perspective 140. 2006.
32 Berger, *Investment Rules in Chinese Preferential Trade and Investment Agreements: Is China Following the Global Trend towards Comprehensive Agreements?* 23. 2013.
33 *China-ASEAN Investment Agreement Signed* (2009), available at http://news.xinhuanet.com/english/2009-08/15/content_11885891.htm.
34 Berger, *Investment Rules in Chinese Preferential Trade and Investment Agreements: Is China Following the Global Trend towards Comprehensive Agreements?* 22–23. 2013.
35 China-ASEAN Investment Agreement Article 1.1(d).
36 Karl P. Sauvant & Nolan Michael D., China's Outward Foreign Direct Investment and International Investment Law, 18 Journal of International Economic Law 893, 919, footnote 153 (2015).
37 China-ASEAN Investment Agreement Article 1(f).
38 Id. at, Article 7.1.
39 China-Korea FTA Article 12.5.1 (customary international law), 12.5.2 (the customary international law minimum standard of treatment). 2015.
40 China-New Zealand FTA Article 143.1("commonly accepted rules of international law").
41 China-Peru FTA Article 132.1 ("customary international law").
42 China-ASEAN Investment Agreement Article 7.2.

43 China-New Zealand FTA Article 143.3.
44 China-ASEAN Investment Agreement Article 8.1.
45 Id. at, Article 14.9, 14.10.
46 China-Korea FTA Annex 12-B, paragraph 3. 2015.
47 China-India BIT Protocol, Section III (2006).
48 China-Korea FTA Article 12.9.1(c). 2015.
49 China-ASEAN Investment Agreement Article 8.1(b).
50 Id. at, Article 8.3.
51 China-Korea FTA Article 12.9.3. 2015.
52 TPP Article 9.8.1(c).
53 Guiguo Wang, International Investment Law: A Chinese Perspective 456–457 (Routledge, 2015).
54 China-New Zealand FTA Article 141.1(c).
55 China-Korea FTA Article 12.3.2. 2015.
56 China-ASEAN Investment Agreement Article 6.1.
57 Xiao, The ASEAN-China Investment Agreement: A Regionalization of Chinese New BITs 9–10. 2010.
58 China-New Zealand FTA Article 156.
59 ChAFTA Article 9.21 (2015).
60 China-ASEAN Investment Agreement Article 14.1.
61 Id. at.
62 Id. at, Article 14.6(b).
63 China-Korea FTA Article 12.12.7. 2015.
64 Xiao, The ASEAN-China Investment Agreement: A Regionalization of Chinese New BITs 17. 2010.
65 *China-ASEAN Framework Agreement*, Article 5(a).
66 China-ASEAN Investment Agreement Article 2.
67 Id. at, Article 6.2.
68 China-ASEAN FTA Upgrading Protocol Chapter 3, Article 1 (2015).
69 Id. at, Chapter 3, Article 2.
70 Id. at, Chapter 5, paragraph 3.
71 Chaisse, 2015 #1107@615–616.
72 Wenhua Shan & Wang Lu, The China–EU BIT and the Emerging 'Global BIT 2.0', 30 ICSID Review 260, 261 (2015).
73 China-ASEAN Investment Agreement Article 21.
74 Id. at, Article 20.
75 China-ASEAN FTA Upgrading Protocol Chapter 3. 2015.
76 Article 5(a).
77 China-ASEAN Investment Agreement Article 2(a).
78 China-ASEAN FTA Upgrading Protocol recital 6 of the preamble 2015.
79 Id. at, Chapter 5, paragraph 3.
80 *China-ASEAN Free Trade Area Upgrade: High-Level Liberalization Commitments in Sectors of Finance, Telecommunication and Others* (2015), available at http://fta.mofcom.gov.cn/article/chinadm/chinadmgfguandian/201604/31477_1.html.
81 ASEAN Secretariat & UNCTAD, ASEAN Investment Report 2015: Infrastructure Investment and Connectivity(2015), available at http://unctad.org/en/PublicationsLibrary/unctad_asean_air2015d1.pdf.
82 ASEAN Comprehensive Investment Agreement Article 5 (2009).
83 Berger, Investment Rules in Chinese Preferential Trade and Investment Agreements: Is China Following the Global Trend towards Comprehensive Agreements? 31. 2013.
84 Chen, China-ASEAN FTA: An Investment Perspective 145. 2006.

85 Berger, Investment Rules in Chinese Preferential Trade and Investment Agreements: Is China Following the Global Trend towards Comprehensive Agreements? 23. 2013.
86 *MOFCOM spokesman Shen Danyang comments on China and US to promote energetically negotiations on bilateral investment agreement* (2013), available at http://english.mofcom.gov.cn/article/newsrelease/policyreleasing/201307/20130700200566.shtml.
87 See, e.g., ChAFTA Article 9.9.3(c). 2015.
88 *Guiding Principles and Objectives for Negotiating the Regional Comprehensive Economic Partnership*, available at http://dfat.gov.au/trade/agreements/rcep/Documents/guiding-principles-rcep.pdf.
89 Mark Feldman et al., The Role of Pacific Rim FTAs in the Harmonisation of International Investment Law: Towards a Free Trade Area of the Asia-Pacific. (2016).
90 TPP Annex 9-L, Section B, paragraph 1.
91 Id. at, Annex 9-E, paragraph 1.
92 *Why Trump's Withdrawal from the TPP Is a Boon for China* (2017), available at www.scmp.com/news/world/united-states-canada/article/2064927/why-trumps-withdrawal-tpp-boon-china.
93 Scott & David, China Set to Push Asia Trade Deal Harder After Trump Win. 2016.
94 *Guiding Principles and Objectives for Negotiating the Regional Comprehensive Economic Partnership*, available at http://dfat.gov.au/trade/agreements/rcep/Documents/guiding-principles-rcep.pdf.
95 Id. at, 1.
96 China-ASEAN Investment Agreement Article 4.
97 Id. at, Article 5.
98 Id. at, Article 7.
99 Id. at, Article 10.
100 Id. at, Article 8.
101 Id. at, Article 9.
102 Id. at, Article 15.
103 Chen, China-ASEAN FTA: An Investment Perspective 142. 2006.
104 CCTV, *50 Questions of the China-Korea FTA* (2015), available at http://m.news.cntv.cn/2015/06/01/ARTI1433136728385679.shtml; China FTA Network, *A Reading of the Free Trade Agreement between the Government of Australia and the Government of the People's Republic of China* (2016), available at http://fta.mofcom.gov.cn/article/chinaaustralia/chinaaustralianews/201506/22176_1.html.
105 China-ASEAN Investment Agreement Article 5.4.
106 ChAFTA Article 9.4.2. 2015; China-New Zealand FTA Article 139.2.
107 China-ASEAN Investment Agreement Article 5.1.
108 Id. at, Articles 5.2, 5.3(a).
109 China-Korea FTA Article 12.4.2. 2015.
110 ChAFTA Article 9.4. 2015.
111 China-ASEAN Investment Agreement Article 7.3.
112 ASEAN-Australia-New Zealand FTA Article 6.2(c).
113 ASEAN-Korea Investment Agreement Article 5.2(c) (2009).
114 China-Korea FTA Article 12.5.2. 2015.
115 Mark Feldman et al., The Role of Pacific Rim FTAs in the Harmonisation of International Investment Law: Towards a Free Trade Area of the Asia-Pacific, 10 (2016).
116 ASEAN-Korea Investment Agreement Article 12.2. 2009; ASEAN-Australia-New Zealand FTA Article 9.2(b).

117 ASEAN-Korea Investment Agreement Article 12.1(d). 2009; ASEAN-Australia-New Zealand FTA Article 9.1(c).
118 China-Korea FTA Article 12.5.4. 2015.
119 TPP Article 9.7.
120 Policy Considerations for Negotiating a U.S.-China Bilateral Investment Treaty. (2016).
121 China-ASEAN Investment Agreement Article 19.
122 China-ASEAN Investment Agreement Article 16.
123 See, e.g., China-New Zealand FTA Article 201; China-Peru FTA Article 194; China-Korea FTA Article 12.14. 2015.
124 China-ASEAN Investment Agreement Article 17(b).
125 Xiao, The ASEAN-China Investment Agreement: A Regionalization of Chinese New BITs 12. 2010.
126 China-ASEAN Investment Agreement Article 17.b(iii).
127 Id. at, Article 3.4(a).
128 See, e.g., China-New Zealand FTA Article 21.3; China-Korea FTA Article 12.14. 2015; ChAFTA Article 16.4.2. 2015.
129 See, e.g., TPP Annex 9-E, paragraph 1 (currency stability).
130 See, e.g., China-New Zealand FTA Article 9.5; China-Peru FTA Article 197; China-Korea FTA Article 12.14. 2015.
131 Guiding Principles and Objectives for Negotiating the Regional Comprehensive Economic Partnership 1.
132 Id. at, 2.
133 ChAFTA Annex 8-B, Article 5. 2015.
134 For the provisions on environment and investment, see e.g., China-Japan-Korea Investment Agreement Article 23 (2012); China-Korea FTA Article 12.16. 2015.
135 China-Korea FTA Article 12.16. 2015.
136 China-Canada BIT Article 18.3 (2014).
137 China-Canada BIT, Annex B.10, paragraph 3; China-Korea FTA Annex 12-B, paragraph 3(b).
138 See, e.g., TPP Article 9.23.4.
139 ChAFTA Side Letter on Transparency Rules Applicable to Investor-State Dispute Settlement. 2015.
140 Thuy Ong, *Multinationals Launch 50 Lawsuits Worth $31b Against Asian Nations* (2016), available at www.abc.net.au/news/2016-12-08/report-shows-hidden-costs-of-rcep-trade-deal/8103602.
141 ASEAN Comprehensive Investment Agreement Article 39. 2009; ASEAN-Australia-New Zealand FTA Article 26.
142 ChAFTA Article 9.17.2. 2015.
143 ChAFTA Article 9.16.2. 2015; TPP Article 9.23.2.
144 China-Korea FTA Article 12.11. 2015; China-ASEAN Investment Agreement Article 12.
145 Mark Feldman et al., The Role of Pacific Rim FTAs in the Harmonisation of International Investment Law: Towards a Free Trade Area of the Asia-Pacific. (2016).
146 Junji Nakagawa & Liang Wei, A Comparison of the FTA Strategies of Japan and China and Their Implications for Multilateralism 19 (2011).
147 Julien Chaisse, *The Shifting Tectonics of International Investment Law--Structure and Dynamics of Rules and Arbitration on Foreign Investment in the Asia-Pacific Region*, 47 George Washington International Law Review 563, 574, footnote 53 (2015).
148 2015 Indian Model BIT Article 15.2 (2015).
149 Grant Hanessian & Duggal Kabir, *The Final 2015 Indian Model BIT: Is This the Change the World Wishes to See?* 32 ICSID Review, 216–217 (2017).

150 *ASEAN, Japan Renew Commitment to Strengthen Cooperation*, (2016); *ASEAN, Japan to Take Partnership to New Heights* (2016), available at http://asean.org/asean-japan-to-take-partnership-to-new-heights/. (the investment chapters were being finalized as of June 2016).
151 *Factsheet: What You Need to Know about Regional Comprehensive Economic Partnership (RCEP)*, available at www.mti.gov.sg/MTIInsights/SiteAssets/Pages/FACTSHEET-WHAT-YOU-NEED-TO-KNOW-ABOUT/Factsheet%20 on%20RCEP%20(June%202014).pdf.

References

ASEAN-Australia-New Zealand FTA.
ASEAN Comprehensive Investment Agreement (2009).
ASEAN-Korea Investment Agreement (2009).
ASEAN Secretariat & UNCTAD, *ASEAN Investment Report 2015: Infrastructure Investment and Connectivity* (2015), available at http://unctad.org/en/Publication-sLibrary/unctad_asean_air2015d1.pdf.
Axel Berger, *Investment Rules in Chinese Preferential Trade and Investment Agreements: Is China Following the Global Trend towards Comprehensive Agreements?* available at www.die-gdi.de/uploads/media/DP_7.2013.pdf.
CCTV, *50 Questions of the China-Korea FTA* (2015), available at http://m.news.cntv.cn/2015/06/01/ARTI1433136728385679.shtml.
ChAFTA (2015).
China-ASEAN Framework Agreement.
China-ASEAN FTA Upgrading Protocol (2015).
China-ASEAN Investment Agreement.
China-Costa Rica FTA.
China-India BIT (2006).
China-Japan-Korea Investment Agreement (2012).
China-Korea FTA (2015).
China-New Zealand FTA.
China-Peru FTA.
China FTA Network, *A Reading of the Free Trade Agreement Between the Government of Australia and the Government of the People's Republic of China* (2016), available at http://fta.mofcom.gov.cn/article/chinaaustralia/chinaaustralianews/201506/22176_1.html.
Guiding Principles and Objectives for Negotiating the Regional Comprehensive Economic Partnership, available at http://dfat.gov.au/trade/agreements/rcep/Documents/guiding-principles-rcep.pdf.
Heng Wang, The RCEP and Its Investment Rules: Learning from Past Chinese FTAs. *The Chinese Journal of Global Governance (2017), 3: 160–181.*
Huiping Chen, China-ASEAN FTA: An Investment Perspective. In John Wong; Keyuan Zou; Huaqun Zeng (Eds.), *China-ASEAN Relations: Economic and Legal Dimensions* (2016). *Hackensack, NJ; London: World Scientific.*
Jason Scott & Roman David, *China Set to Push Asia Trade Deal Harder after Trump Win*. Bloomberg (2016), available at www.bloomberg.com/news/articles/2016-11-15/trump-trade-snub-set-to-boost-china-s-bid-for-its-own-asia-pact.
Julien Chaisse, *The Shifting Tectonics of International Investment Law-- Structure and Dynamics of Rules and Arbitration on Foreign Investment in the Asia-Pacific*

Region, 47 George Washington International Law Review 563 (2015). China-Singapore FTA (2008).

Jun Xiao, The ASEAN-China Investment Agreement: A Regionalization of Chinese New BITs. *Society of International* Economic Law. Second Biennial Global Conference, University of Barcelona, 8–10 July 2010, available at SSRN: https://ssrn.com/abstract=1629202 or http://dx.doi.org/10.2139/ssrn.1629202.

Junji Nakagawa & Liang Wei, *A Comparison of the FTA Strategies of Japan and China and Their Implications for Multilateralism,* Indiana University Research Center for Chinese Politics and Business (RCCPB) Working Paper #11 (2011), available at https://ssrn.com/abstract=2169361.

Karl P. Sauvant & Nolan Michael D., China's Outward Foreign Direct Investment and International Investment Law. *Journal of International Economic Law* (2015), 18: 893.

Mark Feldman et al., *The Role of Pacific Rim FTAs in the Harmonisation of International Investment Law: Towards a Free Trade Area of the Asia-Pacific, The E15 Initiative* (2016), available at http://e15initiative.org/publications/the-role-of-pacific-rim-ftas-in-the-harmonisation-of-international-investment-law-towards-a-free-trade-area-of-the-asia-pacific/.

Nargiza Salidjanova, *China's Trade Ambitions: Strategy and Objectives behind China's Pursuit of Free Trade Agreements*, U.S.-China Economic and Security Review Commission Staff Research Report (2015), available at http://origin.www.uscc.gov/sites/default/files/Research/China's%20Trade%20Ambitions%20-%20 05.28%2015.pdf.

New Zealand Ministry of Foreign Affairs and Trade, *Regional Comprehensive Economic Partnership (RCEP)* (2017), available at www.mfat.govt.nz/en/trade/free-trade-agreements/agreements-under-negotiation/rcep/.

Policy Considerations for Negotiating a U.S.-China Bilateral Investment Treaty (2016).

Sixteenth Round of Negotiations – 2–10 December 2016, Tangerang, Indonesia (2016), availableathttp://dfat.gov.au/trade/agreements/rcep/news/Pages/sixteenth-round-of-negotiations.aspx.

Thuy Ong, *Multinationals Launch 50 Lawsuits Worth $31b Against Asian Nations* (2016), available at www.abc.net.au/news/2016-12-08/report-shows-hidden-costs-of-rcep-trade-deal/8103602.

TPP.

Wenhua Shan & Wang Lu, *The China–EU BIT and the Emerging 'Global BIT 2.0'*, 30 ICSID Review 260 (2015).

2015 Indian Model BIT (2015).

6 Regional Comprehensive Economic Partnership

Facilitating intra-regional value chains through rules of origin

Rajan Sudesh Ratna

Introduction

The international trading system has undergone some major developments since the establishment of the World Trade Organisation (WTO) in 1995. The first one is a very slow progress in the WTO Doha Round negotiations which now appears to be heading towards its death, paving the way for a higher surge in regional trade agreements (RTAs). The second development relates to the emergence of international production networks (IPNs) which have led to fragmentation in production processes through the creation of value chains.

While studying the RTAs many studies have focused on rules of origin (RoO), mostly in terms of their restrictiveness and as a deterrent to regional trade. Only a few studies have discussed the development role that the preferential RoO play. With the OECD-WTO database on Trade in Value Added (TiVA) many researchers have focused now on the existence of regional and global value chains (GVCs). Most of these studies are linked to country case studies with a focus on global trade.

Very limited studies have focused on the linkages between the preferential RoO and the regional or global supply chains. Is it possible to promote regional value chain with the simplest RoO or is there a need for some onerous manufacturing obligations or the so-called restrictive RoO? This chapter analyses the RoO with regard to Regional Comprehensive Economic Partnership (RCEP) to examine whether the RoO will facilitate RCEP members to become part of regional value chains or not. Since the RoO of RCEP has not been finalised, this chapter relies on the various RoO criteria that RCEP members have agreed under the ASEAN + 1 FTAs and then looks at the likely RoO in RCEP, after which it evaluates which criteria can facilitate the intra-RCEP value chain. This chapter also analyses some of the sectors traded within RCEP and evaluates the criteria of RoO that will facilitate a higher integration through a regional value chain among RCEP members.

The chapter first updates the negotiations held in RCEP, then lays down the conceptual framework of RoO whereupon it highlights the findings of existing literature. The next section examines the trade structure of RCEP especially trade in raw material and intermediate products as well the intra-industry trade (IIT) and the domestic value-added content (using TiVA database) to examine the existence of IPN that exists among RCEP members. The study also examines various RoO criteria that are applied in ASEAN and ASEAN+1 agreements to explore the likely scenario of RCEP RoO. In that context, the chapter finally evaluates which criteria of RoO applied in RCEP will have a higher possibility of establishing intra-RCEP value chains.

RCEP

The RCEP is a comprehensive trade agreement that is being negotiated among 16 countries: the 10 members of ASEAN (Brunei, Cambodia, Indonesia, Laos, Malaysia, Myanmar, the Philippines, Singapore, Thailand, and Vietnam) and the six countries with which ASEAN has existing bilateral Free Trade Agreements (FTAs) under the ASEAN+1 arrangement – Australia, China, India, Japan, New Zealand and the Republic of Korea. The RCEP negotiations aim to achieve a modern, comprehensive, high-quality and mutually beneficial economic partnership agreement covering a wide range of trade-related issues. The RCEP market accounts for around 37 percent of world GDP, 48 percent of world population and 27 percent of the world's imports.[1] RCEP negotiations were launched by the leaders of the 16 participating countries in the margins of the East Asia Summit on 20 November 2012. If negotiated successfully, the RCEP would create the most extensive trading bloc in the world; and have significant implications as an ASEAN-centred regional free trade initiative.

Having trade in goods, services and investment as its three core areas, the RCEP negotiation encompasses other issues including economic and technical cooperation, intellectual property, competition and dispute settlement. Negotiations comprising 21 rounds have been held so far, the last being held in Yogyakarta, Indonesia, in February 2018, which also saw the first RCEP Summit meeting. On 14 November, 2017, in Manila, Philippines, the leaders instructed their Ministers and negotiators to intensify their efforts in 2018 to bring the RCEP negotiations to conclusion, and resolve to ensure they have the necessary support to achieve this outcome.[2] Discussions were continued on expanding the coverage of duty-free items and to bring 90 percent of the total national tariff lines in the tariff elimination list within a time frame of 15 years, while gradually reducing tariffs on the remaining 10 percent at a later date. It appears that RCEP chapters on economic and technical cooperation and small and medium-sized enterprises (SMEs) have been finalised,[3] however, on market access issues a lot of ground still needs to be covered. Liberalisation of service trade is also turning out to be a sensitive issue.

RoOs and value chains: conceptual framework

'RoOs' are an integral part of RTAs having objectives of promoting intra-regional trade and investment flows as well as preventing trade deflection, or simple trans-shipment from third parties. While the trade deflection is prevented through the substantial transformation clause; the intra-regional trade and investment flows are promoted through the provisions of cumulation. Substantial transformation in most of the RTAs is defined either in terms of a minimum value-added content or as a Change in Tariff Classification (CTC) between non-originating inputs and export product. This ensures that a higher processing happens in a country, which is beyond simple operations. The most common CTC is Change in Tariff Heading (CTH) which means that there shall be a change at the 4-digit Harmonized System (HS) level between non-originating inputs and export product. In many RTAs, a combination of these two criteria are used, which is treated as most stringent (Ratna, 2016).

The CTH test is a straightforward method, which is easy to implement. The adoption by most countries of the HS means that a similarly applied CTH test will normally lead to uniform determination of origin in such countries. This test is widely used in various preferential schemes, precisely because it can overcome many of the problems associated with the percentage criterion such as bias in favour of high-cost production and its susceptibility to changing world prices. However, this rule alone might not be sufficient for conferring originating status as the HS codes were devised primarily for the purposes of commodity classification and collection of statistical data, and not for origin determination purposes. It is generally realised that in the following two circumstances this rule might not serve its purpose. First, when the change in tariff heading is not sufficient to confer origin, in which case the application of certain specified processes or domestic/import content requirements become necessary. Second, when certain processing operations are sufficient enough by themselves to confer origin, even if the tariff heading of the final product does not change as compared to the tariff headings of its constituents. Another problem associated with this rule is in terms of the level of commodity classification/aggregation. In such a case, this rule should be applied such that any change in commodity code is treated as substantial transformation. In fact, many products at HS 4-digit level would not get the originating status if the CTH rule is applied alone. For instance, sweetened cocoa powder is classified as HS 1806.10 but all sweetened cocoa-based products are classified as HS 1806.2–1806.9. Therefore, in this case no change in tariff heading would occur at HS 4-digit level despite the fact that value addition takes place. Similarly, manufacturing coffee substitutes, fruit juices and transforming imported sodium nitrate into fertiliser cannot get originating status under the CTH rule if applied at HS 4-digit level.

As a general rule, under the percentage criterion, imported inputs (i.e., materials, parts and components) are considered to have undergone substantial transformation if a given percentage of value is added to the imported inputs which are used for the manufacture of the finished product. This requirement can be defined in the following two ways:

i   By providing the minimum percentage of the value of the product (on f.o.b. value or ex-factory price/cost) that must be added in the exporting country (direct method of calculation), or

ii By providing the maximum percentage of non-originating inputs to be used in manufacturing the exported product (indirect method of calculation).

In practice, the latter method of calculation is more commonly used in trade agreements. However, this method also has certain limitations as the value-added content would change depending on several factors, such as exchange rate fluctuations and inefficient manufacturing processes. For the calculation of value added, different agreements use different methods of treating the 'profit' of the local trader. While in some agreements this is taken into account, in other cases it is not. This issue has always been a bone of contention of various negotiations on RTAs.

Cumulation, on the other hand, is an instrument which allows producers to source raw materials and intermediate products from another RTA partner country without undermining the origin of the product. Establishing value chains among the RTA parties is easier due to reduced tariffs which ensures procurement of cheaper and/or higher quality intermediate inputs and the cumulation provision acts as a catalyst to this process. If the RTA parties are at different stages of economic development, the smaller partners can become a part of the value chain of the larger economy as its industries can be linked to the industries of a larger economy. Thus, RTA parties undergo an economic integration process which creates an enabling environment for establishing regional value chains through backward-forward linkages of industries which get stimulated by the cumulation provisions. There are different types of cumulation provisions which apply and hence a broad definition of these are given below:

BOX 6.1: CUMULATION PROVISIONS

Bilateral cumulation

Bilateral cumulation is the most basic form of cumulation as it operates between two parties and allows producers in either partner country to use materials and components originating in the other's country as if they originated in their own country.

Diagonal cumulation

Diagonal cumulation operates between more than two countries and allows producers to use materials and components *originating* in either country that is part of the agreement. In one form this is an extension of bilateral cumulation by extending it to the regional level.

Partial cumulation

Partial cumulation is the most common form of cumulation under which an input originating in one member of the preferential trade agreement (PTA) will be considered as the originating input in the other member country(ies) of PTA. In such a case the full value of the input/material is taken as originating and not the actual value content of processing in the intermediate PTA partner. On the other hand, if the input is not originating the value added in the intermediate PTA partner is totally disregarded as it does not meet the origin criteria. This is often termed as 'whole or nothing' approach.

Full cumulation

Full cumulation takes into account all operations conducted within the countries who are members of the PTA – even if they are carried out on non-originating material. Thus, there is no more restriction to only use originating materials and components for the final good. This concept allows more fragmentation of the production process among members of a trade agreement and increases economic linkages and trade in PTAs.

Unlike partial cumulation, in this type of cumulation even if the input sourced from an intermediate PTA partner is non-originating, the value-added component is added in the final export goods for determining origin cumulation. This is the highest order of cumulation as it recognises the processes done by the intermediate PTA partners.

(Source: Based on Das and Ratna, 2011)

It is therefore possible to establish IPN which establishes the regional value chain through cumulation provisions of preferential RoO.

Existing literature

In recent years, one of the major characteristics of international trade is the establishment of value chains with production process taking through multilayered, multiple countries and multiple firms establishing a complex web of the production process. Hummels (1998) observed, before the US-Canada Auto Agreement, that trade in auto parts between these two countries did not exist. After the agreement signed in 1965 which saw a reduction in the tariffs to zero, auto trade increased establishing auto supply chain between Canada and US, where 60 percent of US auto exports to Canada were engines and parts, while 75 percent of Canadian auto exports to the US were finished cars and trucks.

Palit (2010) observed that Indian SMEs must realise that the access to the global marketplace need not always be in the finished goods sector to be fruitful. Pointing out that while the India-ASEAN FTA provided Indian SMEs access to the Eastern markets and other FTAs were in the pipeline with Japan, Malaysia and Indonesia, he opined that there was immense scope for leveraging FTAs to engage with regional value chains. While examining the nexus between RoO and value chain in the ASEAN +1 agreements, Medalla (2011) noted that if the costs associated with compliance of RoO are up to or less than the margin of preference provided by the FTA, it would have a positive impact on the value chain.

Kimura and Obashi (2011) noted that the emergence of IPNs in East Asia was due to market-driven forces such as vertical specialisation and higher production costs in the home country and institutional factors such as FTAs. Banga (2013) observed that countries which are engaged in global value chains have shown enhanced access to regional and global economies, improved production techniques and greater capacity to generate employment. Nag and De (2011) observed that RoO play a significant role in promoting trade in low-value components and though tariff reduction is the most important tool for making a trade agreement work efficiently, through the regression analysis they established that a higher RoO restrictiveness index inhibits the positive growth of IIT. Estevadeoral et al. (2013) observed that the regional pattern of GVCs is largely determined by the existence of deeper RTAs, because they tend to incorporate disciplines like rules in investment policy, services, standards, intellectual property rights or the harmonisation of custom procedures etc.

Palit (2014) examined the opportunities for India to be a part of the regional supply chain in RCEP. While examining the characteristics of regional supply chains for a group of industries he observed that for India opportunities for both forward and backward participation exist in RCEP, which will, in the long run, make Indian producers part of regional production networks connecting to supply chains and markets beyond the RCEP. He also opined that the liberal RoO with lower Regional Value Content (RVC) would benefit the sectors of textiles and textile products, and leather and footwear to continue obtaining cumulation benefits.

Ratna (2016) observed that requirements relating to checking the import content or value addition have the potential for generating a higher degree of manufacturing operations among the RTA partners and these at times facilitate higher IIT. The presence of large SMEs and the fragmentation in production could create tremendous opportunities to get in these IPNs within the RTA members, which can then enhance chances of getting global markets as these enhance the technological skills as well as production of higher quality products. He pointed out that the intra-regional trade and investment flows could be influenced by the cumulation provision as it enhances the possibility of creating IPNs.

UNCTAD (2003) evaluated how the PTAs can influence the trade flows and investments decisions and thereby help countries aim for inclusive development. It observed that though the India-Sri Lanka FTA did not cover investment, it has stimulated new FDI for rubber-based products, ceramics, electrical and electronic items, wood-based products, agricultural commodities and consumer durables. Because of the agreement, 37 projects are now in operation, with a total investment of $145 million making India one of the top investors to Sri Lanka.

The impact of FTA on employment was studied by De Mel (2009) who estimated that as of 2007 end, some 6,747 individuals gained employment as a result of the Indian investment in 70 projects. De Mel also pointed that most of these projects appear to be in the services sector that is excluded by the Indo-Sri Lanka FTA, and therefore cannot be assumed to be jobs created because of the FTA, and in any case, the number of jobs is meagre in comparison to the quantum of investment. On the other hand, Kalegama and Karunaratne (2013) observed that within the first two years of the implementation of the Agreement, several sectors experienced over 100 percent growth, including industries such as chemical product manufacturing, cement manufacturing and pearl harvesting. Quoting that there is no valid data on employment, they stated that some 5,900 jobs were created due to Indian investment projects and in a few cases these related to relocation of labour from one company to another.

Given the limited scope of the agreement which has so far focused only on goods, the increased bilateral investment flows have made it possible for the two economies to integrate. The FTA not only facilitated the investment in the manufacturing sector, but also services sector.[4]

Methodology and limitations

To understand the nature of integration in RCEP, this study first examines the trade patterns of raw material and intermediate products. For this the classification of UN COMTRADE was used based on HS of Nomenclature. A higher share of trade in raw materials and intermediate products may mean that a higher level of integration through production networks or supply chains does exist.

An IIT index was calculated using the Grubel-Lloyd method, with the index ranging between 0 and 1. A higher IIT indicated an existence of IPN. The value indicates the extent of bilateral trade on similar products. A higher ratio (closer to 1) suggests that economies of scale and variety of sources of gains are being exploited. A comparison of the IIT of various sectors was done based on Standard International Trade Classification (SITC) and the intra RCEP IIT in these sectors was compared with the rest of world (RoW).

A higher intra-RCEP IIT would mean a better establishment of supply chain than the RoW. An increase in IIT has been observed in cases of increased value chains as each stage of production of a product is carried out in different countries. The fragmentation in production, which has led to value chains has also resulted in a higher IIT. A decline in the 'production depth' (value added over production) and a growing importance of trade in raw and intermediate products have resulted in manufacturing exports and imports of individual countries increasingly moving together. However, the IIT is also subject to an aggregate bias (towards unity), both in terms of sectors and regimes.

The TiVA data was used for the RCEP members to evaluate the extent of domestic value added content (DVAC) in the production of select sectors. The value addition was calculated using the formula that has been prescribed under RTAs by using the built-down method.[5]

Trade in raw materials and intermediate products

Theory suggests that the international fragmentation of production allows industries to reduce their production costs through sourcing of cheaper raw materials and intermediate products from such countries which can produce it relatively cheaper. Thus, one of the indicators used for establishment of IPNs or supply chains is sourcing of raw materials and intermediate products from trade partners. To understand the existence of supply chain linkages among RCEP members, an analysis of imports of raw materials and intermediate products was done. A high degree of supply chain will exist if the intra-RCEP imports have a higher share than what RCEP members source from the RoW (Figure 6.1).

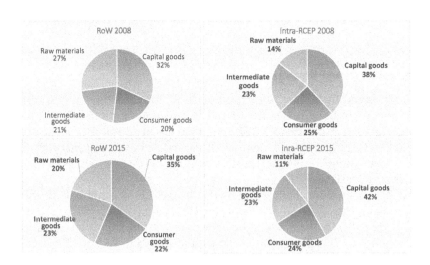

Figure 6.1 Import share of RCEP (2008 and 2015).
Source: Calculated on the basis of UNCOMTRADE database accessed through WITS.

From the figures above it appears clear that RCEP's imports of raw materials from 2008 to 2015 has seen a decline (both intra and from RoW). The intra-RCEP import share of intermediate products remained the same, but it increased for the RoW. In 2015 RCEP share of intermediate products was the same as RoW and RCEP. Therefore, there is no higher degree of supply chain among RCEP if one compares with RoW. Interestingly, intra-RCEP imports of capital goods are much higher and the possibility of an enhanced degree of transfer of technology and production efficiency is high. The technology infusion can be due to the inward flows of investments of multinational companies from the RCEP. This can enhance the opportunity of the establishment of value chain through trade in new raw materials and intermediate products through appropriate RoO of RCEP FTA.

IIT

Using the SITC Code for broad sectors an analysis of IIT was done for intra-RCEP and the World. It is clearly observed from the figure below that in all sectors the intra RCEP IIT is higher than that of the world and in all the sectors it is above 0.80 showing a high degree of existence of IPN. This gap is highest in the sectors of primary products, fuels and textiles which also indicates a better establishment of supply chain among RCEP members as these sectors represent raw materials or intermediate products (textiles, except apparel) (Figure 6.2).

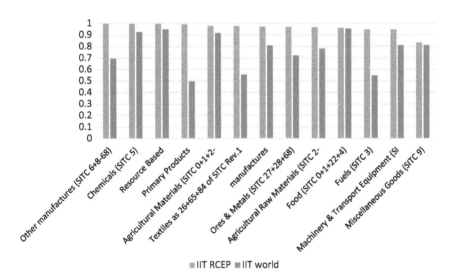

Figure 6.2 RCEP: intra-industry trade in select sectors (average of 2013–2016).
Source: Calculated on the basis of UNCOMTRADE database accessed through WITS.

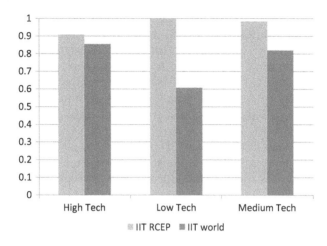

Figure 6.3 RCEP: intra-industry trade (average of 2013–2016).
Source: Calculated on the basis of UNCOMTRADE database accessed through WITS.

The COMTRADE database also classified the products in terms of technology. The IIT on low, medium and high technology products also show a higher intra-RCEP IIT than the world with the widest gap in low technology products (Figure 6.3).

RoO and TiVA

The OECD-WTO TiVA database provides disaggregated details on sources of value added by different countries in their gross exports of various industries. The database also provides the amount of domestic value-added that is generated by the export, throughout the production chain. In other words, any given export can be decomposed into value-added contributions from different domestic industries and different foreign industries.

RoO as practised by RCEP members

Before examining the domestic value-added in the gross exports as well as some sectors' exports, it would be important to understand the likely RoO that would emerge in RCEP. In recent years, ASEAN has concluded bilateral FTAs with its Dialogue Partners (Australia-New Zealand, China, India, Japan and Republic of Korea). All these FTAs have a different set of RoO. A summary of these RoO is given below (Box 6.2):

One would tend to expect that RCEP will negotiate a RoO which will evolve over ASEAN Trade in Goods Agreement (ATIGA) or ASEAN-1 FTA RoO. Looking at the above table it also appears that product-specific RoOs (PSRs) are likely to be adopted at 6-digit HS level of export products. In this case the preferred option from many RCEP members appears towards

---

BOX 6.2: SUMMARY OF ROO OF ASEAN + 1 FTAS

Agreement	*RoO Criteria*	*Additional Criteria*
ASEAN (ATIGA)	1 Wholly obtained 2 General Rules (co-equal): 40% RVCorCTC (change at 4-digit HS i.e. CTH)	There are more than 2,000 products from HS Chapters 1–26, 29–30, 33, 41–42, 44, 47–48, 50–63, 71–76, 78–81, 83–85, 87, 90–91, 94 and 96 listed in Annex 3 of the ASEAN Trade in Goods Agreement, which are subject to the product-specific rule specified therein and not to the "general rule" of "RVC of not less than 40% or CTC at the 4-digit level". Textiles: Separate processing rule
ASEAN ANZ	1 Wholly obtained 2 Co-equal rule/PSR: 40% RVCorCTC (change at 4-digit HS i.e. CTH)	
ASEAN China	1 Wholly obtained 2 General Rules - 40% RVC 3 PSRs	
ASEAN Japan	1 Wholly obtained 2 Co-equal rule/PSR: 40% RVCorCTC (change at 4-digit HS i.e. CTH)	
ASEAN RoK	1 Wholly obtained 2 Co – equal rule/PSR: 40% RVCorCTC (change at 4-digit HS i.e. CTH)	
ASEAN India	1 Wholly obtained 2 General Rule: 35% RVC + CTC (change at 4-digit HS i.e. CTH)	PSRs are under negotiation

Source: Collated by author from various sources.
ATIGA, ASEAN Trade in Goods Agreement; PSR, product-specific rule.

having PSRs with co-equal rules of CTH or 40 percent RVC in most cases. The co-equal rule allows an exporter to choose the most convenient criteria for determining the origin of the export products. The only likely opposition to this is expected to come from India which follows a simultaneous application of dual criteria of CTH + RVC (35–40 percent). Except in one case of ASEAN-India FTA where the RVC is 35 percent, in all other FTAs it is 40 percent. India has so far never accepted a single criterion on FTA RoOs. This has a historical background of its own experiences where despite the RoO criteria preferential imports happened by either circumventing the RoO provisions or merely because of the fact that they were too simple to be manipulated. India had several problems in imports of Vanaspati, copper wires, zinc oxide etc. from Nepal and Sri Lanka under its bilateral FTAs where the issues relating to the validity of RoO were questioned. Finally, import regimes on these items were changed to a tariff rate mechanism. Therefore, the Indian concern of not having a single criterion of CTH or 40 percent RVC is on account of its concerns on trade deflection and the fact that the CTH criteria are easy, since around 4,000 products at 6-digit HS level can undergo CTH even if they are produced from their penultimate stage only. At the same time, given a still high level of most-favoured-nation duty of India vis-à-vis ASEAN and other RCEP partners, the chances of circumvention still would exist. Whether these RCEP members can meet this 40 percent RVC criteria or not can be ascertained by the TiVA database, which has been discussed subsequently.

Similar to the criteria of RoO, different provisions relating to cumulation applies in these FTAs too. These provisions are also becoming now more and more complex and spreading like a 'noodle bowl' phenomena which so far was only limited to PTAs. The lack of uniformity in these rules is now becoming a major discussion point. The different cumulation provisions that apply in different PTAs in Asia and the Pacific are summarised below (Box 6.3):

BOX 6.3: CUMULATION PROVISIONS IN SOME OF THE AGREEMENTS

ATIGA

Article 30

1   Unless otherwise provided in this Agreement, goods originating in a Member State, which are used in another Member State as materials for finished goods eligible for preferential tariff treatment, shall be considered to be originating in the latter Member State where working or processing of the finished goods has taken place.
2   If the RVC of the material is less than 40 percent, the qualifying ASEAN Value Content to be cumulated using the RVC criterion shall be in direct proportion to the actual domestic content provided that it is equal to or more than 20 percent. The Implementing Guidelines are set out in Annex 6.

ANNEX 6

Implementing guidelines for partial cumulation under article 30(2): On ASEAN cumulative RoO

For the purposes of implementing paragraph 2 of Article 30 of this Agreement:

a   a good shall be deemed to be eligible for partial cumulation, if at least twenty percent (20%) of the Regional Value Content (RVC) of the good is originating in the Member State where working or processing of the good has taken place;

b   RVC of the good specified in paragraph (a) shall be calculated in accordance with the formula provided in Article 29 of this Agreement;

c   a good exported under this arrangement shall not be eligible for tariff preference accorded by the importing Member State under this Agreement;

d   a good exported under this arrangement shall be accompanied by a valid Certificate of Origin (Form D) duly and prominently marked "Partial Cumulation";

e   the relevant sections of the Annex 8 (Operational Certification Procedures), including Rule 18 (retroactive check) and 19 (verification visit), shall be applicable to Certificate(s) of Origin (Form D) issued for partial cumulation purposes.

ASEAN China

Article 5; ANNEX 3; Rule 5

Unless otherwise provided for, products which comply with origin requirements provided for in Rule 2 and which are used in the territory of a Party as materials for a finished product eligible for preferential treatment under the Agreement shall be considered as products originating in the territory of the Party where working or processing of the finished product has taken place provided that the aggregate ACFTA content (i.e. full cumulation, applicable among all Parties) on the final product is not less than 40%.

ASEAN India

Article 7; Annex 2; RULE 5

Unless otherwise provided for, products which comply with origin requirements provided for in Rule 2 and which are used in a Party as materials for a product which is eligible for preferential treatment under the Agreement shall be considered as products originating in that Party where working or processing of the product has taken place.

ASEAN RoK

Chapter 2; Article 2.1; ANNEX 3; Rule 7

Unless otherwise provided for in this Annex, a good originating in the territory of a Party, which is used in the territory of another Party as material for a finished good eligible for preferential tariff treatment, shall be considered to be originating in the territory of the latter Party where working or processing of the finished good has taken place.

ASEAN Japan

Chapter 3; Article 29

Originating materials of a Party used in the production of a good in another Party shall be considered as originating materials of that Party where the working or processing of the good has taken place.

ASEAN ANZ

Chapter 3; Article 6

For the purposes of Article 2 (Originating Goods), a good which complies with the origin requirements provided therein and which is used in another Party as a material in the production of another good shall be considered to originate in the Party where working or processing of the finished good has taken place.

Source: Collated by author from various sources

One important point that comes out clearly from the above tables is that different agreements have seen different RoO criteria and the cumulation provision, even though ASEAN remains as the fulcrum. Thus building a consensus on for a single approach will be a hard task for the negotiators. The Economic and Social Commission for Asia and the Pacific (2013) has observed this complexity in cumulation provision and has prescribed for having a more open and flexible cumulation provision which can really act as a catalyst to foster integration of economies forming RTAs. Baldwin and Kawai (2013) suggested for broader rules for cumulation so as to reduce the restrictiveness of regionalisation. The Asia-Pacific region, now has a share of 66 percent of the total global physical RTAs that are in force and have different sets of RoO. Menon (2013) noted that among the ASEAN+1 agreements there are 22 different types of RoO and for only 30 percent of the tariff lines share a common RoO. In each PTA there are several criteria that are used for determining the origin and therefore harmonising them is one of the most difficult tasks.

DVAC

The following section analyses the 'domestic value added content of gross and sectoral exports'. DVAC of gross exports includes the value added generated by the exporting industry during its production processes as well as any value added coming from upstream domestic suppliers that is embodied in the exports. The DVAC has been taken as a base to understand how much value added each RCEP member does at present. The present calculation of local/regional value addition in the FTAs in Asia and the Pacific is mostly based on the built-up method and the same criteria was applied in determining the DVAC of RCEP members in their gross exports as well as sectoral performances. In this regard, the sectors of textiles, textile products, leather and footwear; motor vehicles; and computer, electronics and optical equipment were selected for study. This was because these sectors are important export sectors of RCEP members and have a high intra-RCEP IIT.

The DVAC of gross exports of RCEP and select sectors are given at Figures 6.4–6.7 below. It would be seen that the RCEP member's DVAC for gross exports (to world) is higher than 50 percent, the highest being that of Brunei Darussalam and lowest being that of Singapore.

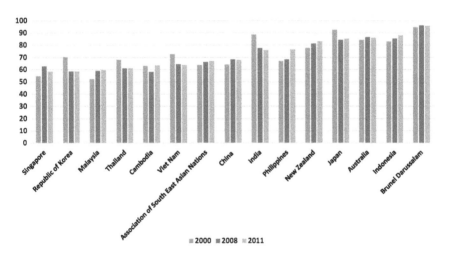

Figure 6.4 RCEP: overall DVAC of gross exports.
Source: Computed from the OECD-WTO Trade in Value Added (TIVA) Database (accessed in July 2017).

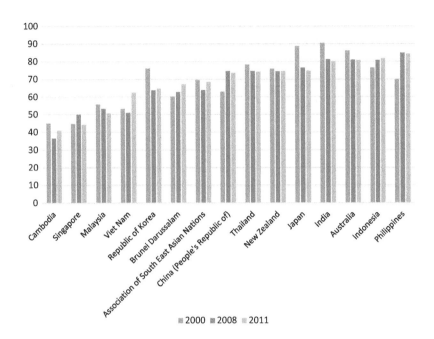

Figure 6.5 RCEP's DVAC in textiles, textile products, leather and footwear.
Source: Computed from the OECD-WTO Trade in Value Added (TIVA) Database (accessed in July 2017).

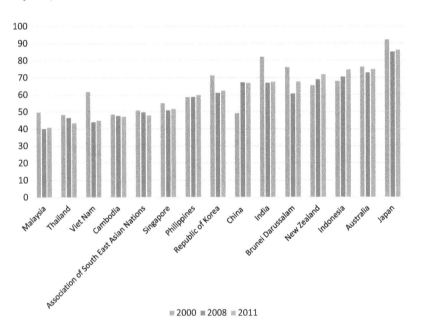

Figure 6.6 RCEP's DVAC in Motor vehicles.
Source: Computed from the OECD-WTO Trade in Value Added (TIVA) Database (accessed in July 2017).

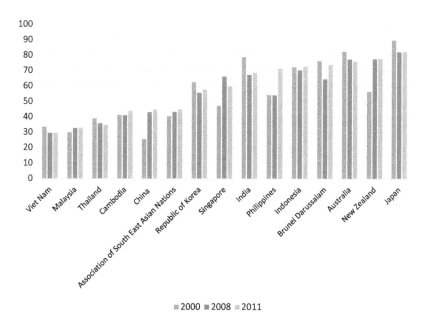

Figure 6.7 RCEP's DVAC in computer, electronic and optical equipments.
Source: Computed from the OECD-WTO Trade in Value Added (TIVA) Database (accessed in July 2017).

For periods 2000, 2008 and 2011 certain countries have illustrated a decline in their DVAC, however, for the rest it has seen an increase. However, this data covers a wide range of products exported and hence there could be sectoral variations in DVAC, for which the sectoral analysis has been carried out.

TiVA database covers textiles, textile products, leather and footwear in one sector and hence their separate value added determination is difficult. Yet, this sector is one of the important sectors for RCEP members. In this case, the lowest DVAC has been observed by Cambodia (40 percent), which is a major exporter of textile products. It is also worth noting that during the period of 2000–2011 Malaysia (50 percent); Republic of Korea (62 percent); Japan and Thailand; and, Australia and India (80 percent) have seen a decline in their DVAC, however their DVAC during 2008 and 2011 is more or less comparable. This may also mean that the global economic recession has pushed them towards lower value added activities (the exceptions being Brunei Darussalam, Cambodia and Vietnam) which might be due to the demand of foreign buyer to source raw materials from their own networks. Yet, this is the sector which has seen a minimum DVAC of 40 percent. Even one looks at ASEAN's DVAC as a group it shows a higher DVAC of around 67 percent in this sector. Thus if a better cumulation provision is introduced meeting a higher DVAC is not impossible in RCEP for this sector.

In the case of motor vehicles, Malaysia has shown the lowest DVAC of 40 percent and many RCEP members have seen the decline in the value-added content from 2000 to 2011. The highest DVAC in 2011 was shown by Japan (85 percent) though a decline from the year 2000. While Indonesia, the Philippines and New Zealand have shown a gradual increase in their DVAC, China showed the highest growth from 2000 to 2008.

Computer, electronic and optical equipment are another important sector for RCEP, however, in comparison with other sectors, this sector has shown a lesser DVAC (less than 40 percent) for some of the countries. In this sector the highest end is occupied by Japan (82 percent), New Zealand (78 percent), Australia (76 percent), Indonesia and the Philippines (72–73 percent). The lower end includes Vietnam (30 percent), Malaysia ((32 percent) and Thailand (35 percent). The ASEAN average is 45 percent in 2011. Many countries have also seen a decline in their DVAC during 2000–2011. Meeting the criteria of 40 percent value-added content as prescribed in the RoO for a single country, therefore will be difficult to achieve for some of the RCEP members. In such a situation, their preference will be for CTH criteria which will allow them to export under FTA even with a lower DVAC. However, if the indentation will be to establish an intra-RCEP value chain, then the provision of cumulation can be a good policy tool.

From the above sectoral analysis, it appears clear that meeting a standard RVC criteria of 40 percent prescribed in the ASEAN + 1 RoO is not difficult for many RCEP members. This, however, appears difficult in the sector of computer, electronic and optical equipment where Vietnam, Malaysia and Thailand may find difficult to achieve 40 percent RVC. It is in such a situation that cumulation provisions would push for a regional integration since these countries would need to source inputs from other RCEP members to meet 40 percent RVC. This, in lieu will promote intra-regional trade and thus facilitate the regional value chain.

Conclusion

The 'noodle-bowl' phenomenon has now reached a level which makes the exporter's life difficult, especially since the majority of them belong to vast SMEs. The Economic and Social Commission for Asia and the Pacific (2013) suggested that the RCEP should consolidate all the existing ASEAN+1 frameworks once implemented, which also was a topic of discussion during the 30th ASEAN Summit, whereby Heads of States express the importance of the RCEP to supersede existing FTAs rather than just an extension.[6]

Ratna (2016) observed that whether the RoO are in the form of meeting a local content requirement as a proportion of value-added, or CTH or a particular processing requirement, all of them have the potential to create greater economic activities among the RTA members. He further underscored that the value-added criteria would have greater potential to create regional value chains as it will promote generation of higher processing in the exporting country and will promote utilising the provisions of cumulation; while in case of CTH a product will qualify origin even if it composes 100 percent non-originating raw materials and thus may facilitate establishment of GVC. Therefore, in order to promote the regional value chain in RCEP, a RVC criteria alone with the cumulation provision will be preferred more.

Looking at various RoO criteria of ASEAN + 1 FTAs, the question that needs an answer is, will a co-equal rule of CTH or 40 percent RVC; or a simultaneous application of CTH and 40 percent RVC or 40 percent RVC alone promote intra-RCEP RVC? As illustrated in Box 6.2 and discussed thereafter, in most of ASEAN +1 FTAs since a co-equal rule has been agreed upon and that the CTH can happen in majority of products automatically (except where the parts and finished products are in the same heading, and in such cases the PSRs have generally been CTH), it is very unlikely that the dual criteria of CTH + RVC is going to be accepted by RCEP members. However, if RCEP members are serious in promoting intra-regional trade and thus establish RVC then the only option left to them is to drop the CTH criteria as a co-equal rule and adopt only the single criterion of RVC. In the case of RVC criteria, it would be important to know what should be the threshold criteria of value-added content. From the TiVA database it is clear that DVAC of gross exports of RCEP members are varied. Brunei Darussalam has the highest DVAC of around 95 percent and the lowest has been for 55 percent for Singapore. It is also pertinent to note that from 2000 to 2011 Japan, India, Republic of Korea, Thailand and Vietnam have seen a decline in their DVAC, while others have observed an increase. However, in none of the cases has it been less than 50 percent. Yet, for the Least Developed Countries members of RCEP, the majority of items they produce and export can fall in the wholly obtained or manufactured category. In the case of processed products which are sourced from non-originating inputs, meeting 40 percent of RVC may be a bit difficult. Therefore, for them a lower threshold of RVC will be a good step to provide them with the opportunity to fully integrate with RCEP members and become part of the value chain of more developed RCEP members. This will also be helpful in their efforts to double their exports, a goal that has been fixed by the 2030 agenda for sustainable development.

The opposition of India to a liberalised RoOs has been on the basis of its own experience of previous FTAs and thus it is following a cautious approach. However, for RCEP India faces a bigger pressure from other 15 partners and thus it might need to review its position. Given the fact that CTH criterion has its own limitations and in majority of items it happens even if processing or manufacturing will happen from the penultimate stage, it is in India's interest to go for a value-added content criteria if it needs to choose between the two. This will also augur well with the objective of promoting regional value chain within the RCEP members.

In order to give a further boost to promote regional value chains the cumulation provisions would also need to be fine-tuned. This will require looking at economic realities of all RCEP members. A full cumulation provision would be the best situation for the RCEP as the members are at various stages of value chains in the production network and this will acknowledge even a little value added or processing done in these countries in determining the origin of the final export product. This provision will also help the Least Developed Countries in the RCEP to get linked up to the larger economies of RCEP.

Notes

1 Source: World Bank.
2 Source: http://asean.org/storage/2017/11/RCEP-Summit_Leaders-Joint-Statement-FINAL1.pdf.
3 Source: www.ictsd.org/bridges-news/bridges/news/at-hanoi-meet-asia-pacific-ministers-debate-future-trade-integration-paths. Accessed on 25th May 2017.
4 The Economic Times (July 30 2013) available at http://articles.economictimes.indiatimes.com/2013-07-30/news/40895327_1_indo-lanka-free-trade-agreement-fta-sri-lanka.
5 The calculation of built down method is as below:

$$\text{Value added content} = \frac{\text{FOB Price} - \text{Value of Non-Originating Materials, Parts or Goods}}{\text{FOB Price}} \times 100\%$$

Value of Non-Originating Materials, Parts or Goods are calculated as:

i   The Cost, Insurance and Freight value at the time of importation of the goods or importation can be proven; or
ii The earliest ascertained price paid for the goods of undetermined origin in the territory of the party where the working or processing takes place;

6 Source: www.channelnewsasia.com/news/asiapacific/rcep-needs-to-be-substantial-for-it-to-be-worthwhile-pm-lee-8806018. Accessed on 23rd May 2017.

References

Baldwin, Richard, and Kawai, Masahiro (2013). Multilateralizing Asian Regionalism, *ADBI Working Paper Series No. 431* (August).
Banga, Rashmi (2013) "*Measuring Value in Global Value Chains*". UNCTAD Background Paper No. RVC-8.
Das, Ram Upendra, and Ratna, Rajan Sudesh (2011, April). *Perspectives on Rules of Origin: Analytical and Policy Insights from the Indian Experience*. London: Palgrave Macmillan.
De Mel, Deshal (2009, August & September). Indo-Lanka Trade Agreements: Performance and Prospects¡. *Economic Review*, Vol. 35, Nos. 5 & 6: 23–28.
Estevadeordal, Antoni; Blyde, Juan; Harris, Jeremy, and Volpe, Christian (2013). "*Global Value Chains and Rules of Origin*", available at http://e15initiative.org/wp-content/uploads/2013/08/Estevadeordal_E15-GVC_think-piece_26.08.13.pdf
Hummels, David, Rapoport, Dana, and Yi, Kei-Mu (1998). "*Vertical Specialization and the Changing Nature of World Trade*," Economic Policy Review, Federal Reserve Bank of New York.

Kelegama, Saman, and Karunaratne, Chandana (2013). "Experiences of Sri Lanka in the Sri Lanka – India FTA and the Sri Lanka – Pakistan FTA", background paper no. RVC-10, UNCTAD available at http://unctad.org/en/PublicationsLibrary/ecidc2013misc1_bp10.pdf

Kimura, Fukunari, and Obashi, Ayako (2011). *Production Networks in East Asia: What We Know So Far.* ADBI Working Paper 320. Tokyo: Asian Development Bank Institute. Available: www.adbi.org/working-paper/2011/11/11/4792.production.networks.east.asia/

Medalla, Erlinda M., and Rosellon, Maureen (2011). 'ROOs in ASEAN+1 FTAs and the Value Chain in East Asia', in Findlay, C. (ed.), *ASEAN+1 FTAs and Global Value Chains in East Asia*. ERIA Research Project Report 2010–29, Jakarta: ERIA. pp. 156–184.

Menon, Jayant. (2013). The challenge facing Asia's Regional Comprehensive Economic Partnership, East Asia Forum (23 June) available at www.eastasiaforum.org/2013/06/23/the-challenge-facing-asias-regional-comprehensive-economic-partnership/

Nag, Biswajit, and Debdeep, De (2011, May). Rules of Origin and Development of Regional Production Network in Asia: Case Studies of Selected Industries, *ART-NeT Working Paper Series, No. 101.*

Palit, Amitendu (2010). *FTAs can help SMEs to integrate with global supply chain.* The Hindu, 29 May 2010, available at www.thehindu.com/todays-paper/tp-national/tp-tamilnadu/FTAs-can-help-SMEs-to-integrate-with-global-supply-chain/article16042140.ece

Palit, Amitendu (2014). *Regional Supply Chains in Asia: Examining India's Presence and Possibilities in RCEP*, Working Paper No. CWS/WP/200/20, Centre for WTO Studies, New Delhi.

Ratna, Rajan Sudesh (2016). Preferential RoO: Facilitators of Regional and Global Value Chains. *Journal of International Trade*, Vol. 1: 29–46; New Delhi: Centre for WTO Studies.

United Nations Conference on Trade and Development (2003). *World Investment Report* available at http://unctad.org/en/Docs/wir2003light_en.pdf

United Nations, Economic and Social Commission for Asia and the Pacific (2013). *Asia-Pacific Trade and Investment Report 2013: Turning the Tide: Towards Inclusive Trade and Investment.* Sales No. E.14.II.F.2. Available from www.unescap.org/tid/ti_report2013/home.asp

Part III

Regional perspectives within Asia

India, ASEAN 5, CLMV and South Asia

7   India's integration in services with Asian FTA partners

Rupa Chanda and Sudeshna Ghosh

Introduction

Since the 1990s, when India adopted a Look East Policy, engagement with its Asian partners has been a critical element of India's economic and foreign policy. In the past decade, this policy has assumed a more pronounced strategic flavour, with the adoption of an "extended neighbourhood" policy[1] which includes not only the ASEAN region but also countries like Australia, New Zealand, Japan, China and South Korea through economic, political and institutional linkages and collaboration across a wide range of issues and sectors. India has signed several Free Trade Agreements (FTAs) with countries in this extended Asian neighbourhood. These agreements, unlike the first crop of India's agreements with its neighbouring countries in South Asia, are comprehensive, covering goods, services, investment and new issues such as e-commerce, R&D, and areas of non-economic and strategic cooperation. The India-Singapore Comprehensive Economic Cooperation Agreement signed in 2005, the India-Malaysia agreement signed in 2011, the ASEAN-India Trade in Services and Investment Agreement, the India-Japan and India-Korea comprehensive agreements are cases in point, while ongoing negotiations to sign comprehensive agreements with Australia, New Zealand, and Indonesia reflect India's continued thrust on broad-based regional integration. Reflecting the wider range of issues and strategic interests covered by India's FTAs in recent years, engagement modalities have also widened beyond state actors to include business councils, civil society, the research community, and regional and sub-regional organizations.

In this context, services and investment have become increasingly important in India's regional integration efforts. The prevailing view guiding the inclusion of services and investment in India is that while the country would have to concede more market access for goods than its partners given its relatively higher tariff levels, it can trade off these concessions by gaining greater market access for its services sectors and can leverage such comprehensive agreements for increased investment flows. Thus, gains in services and investment have been envisaged as potentially offsetting any perceived losses in goods.

At this juncture, more than a decade since India signed its first comprehensive agreement under its Look East Policy, it is important to ask to what extent India has been able to secure its interests in the areas of services and investment and whether the envisaged trade-off has indeed materialized. This chapter attempts to address this question by exploring the prospects and challenges of realizing India's interests in services through its comprehensive regional integration efforts in the Asian region. The chapter is structured as follows. Section 2 outlines the status of services in India and its existing and prospective FTA partner countries in Asia, in terms of the sector's contribution to value-added, trade, employment and investment flows, important sub-sectoral features and trends within the services sector, and bilateral relations in services, including linkages through value-added trade with its FTA partners in Asia. The discussion highlights the complementarities and overlaps in services between India and these countries and identifies potential areas of interest and concerns on both sides. Building on this overview of opportunities and challenges, Section 3 outlines the state of play in India's FTA negotiations with respect to services, including the status of commitments by India and its partner countries under various negotiated agreements and the implications for market access and other envisaged benefits in services and investment. The concluding section discusses the actual progress till date in realizing market access and other gains in services, the outcomes experienced, and the outlook for prospective agreements. It also outlines possible strategies for furthering services integration with India's FTA partners in Asia as well as ways to effectively leverage its agreements going forward.

Service sector overview

Prospects for services trade, investment and cooperation between India and its Asian partners rest on the strengths and weaknesses of the service sector and its role in respective economies. The existence of complementarities, overlapping interests, and areas of sensitivity and concern, which ultimately determine the extent and nature of integration between India and this region, are dependent on the competitiveness of this sector, on key trends and characteristics at the overall and sub-sectoral levels, and the regulatory environment in both India and its partner countries. This section outlines some of the salient features of the service sector which are pertinent to regional integration and motivates the case for the inclusion of services in India's FTA strategy with the Asian region.

Trends and characteristics in services output and trade

The service sector is the dominant sector in India and all its South East, East Asian, and Pacific partner economies. As shown in Figure 7.1, 40 percent or more of value added is accounted for by services in all the selected

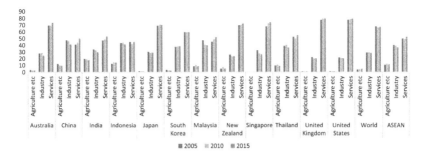

Figure 7.1 Sectoral contributions to value added (% of GDP).
Source: Compiled by the authors using UNCTAD Statistics http://unctadstat.unctad.org/wds/ReportFolders/reportFolders.aspx?sCS_ChosenLang=en (accessed April 3, 2018).
Note: Agriculture includes agriculture, hunting, forestry and fishing.

economies and for nearly 70 percent in case of the world. Its contribution to national and regional economies has grown over the past decade. India is comparable in this regard with its developing country Asian partners such as ASEAN, with services share of value added at a little over 50 percent, while the sector's share in India's developed country Asian partners such as Japan, Singapore and Korea is significantly higher at around 70 percent. What is noteworthy, however, is the lower and relatively greater decline in the share of industry in India's value added compared to other developing country FTA partners in Asia. This is not only indicative of India's premature shift towards services but also of its relative strength in services compared to industry, with implications for India's cross-sectoral negotiating strategy in FTAs.

At the sub-sectoral level, "other service activities", which include a wide range of services such as finance, insurance, communications, computer, R&D, and business services, account for the dominant share of the services sector. In this regard, India (along with China) has a much higher share of "other service activities" compared to other developing country Asian partners for which traditional sub-sectors such as transport and distribution play a greater role. What is again interesting to note is the relatively low and declining share of manufacturing in India, reflecting the basis for a manufacturing versus services trade-off in India's negotiating strategy in FTAs and its offensive interest in areas such as IT and business services (Figure 7.2).

Trends in trade reveal India's relatively stronger position in services as opposed to goods. As shown in Figure 7.3, India exhibits a much lower share of goods in total exports compared to its FTA partners in the Asia-Pacific region while its share of services in total exports at around 30 percent is much higher than in the ASEAN region or in individual ASEAN member countries. It is comparable to that in developed countries such as the US and the UK. In contrast, in the case of imports, India shows comparable shares

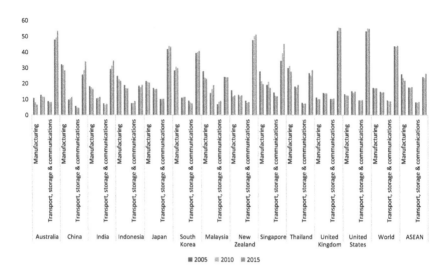

Figure 7.2 Contribution of services subsectors to value added (% of GDP).
Source: Compiled by the authors using UNCTAD Statistics http://unctadstat.unctad.org/
wds/ReportFolders/reportFolders.aspx?sCS_ChosenLang=en (accessed April 3, 2018).

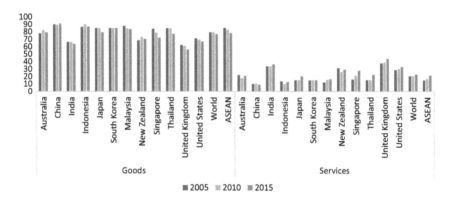

Figure 7.3 Share of total exports (%).
Source: Compiled by the authors using UNCTAD Statistics http://unctadstat.unctad.org/
wds/ReportFolders/reportFolders.aspx?sCS_ChosenLang=en (accessed April 3, 2018).

for both services and goods as other countries, at around 25 percent and
75 percent, respectively.

Revealed comparative advantage (RCA) indices reflect India's relative
strength in services more starkly, as shown in Figure 7.4. While India's RCA
index is lower than that of all its Asian FTA partner countries in the case of
goods, it is significantly higher in the case of services, even greater than in
service sector dominated economies such as Singapore and comparable to
that in developed economies like the UK and the US.

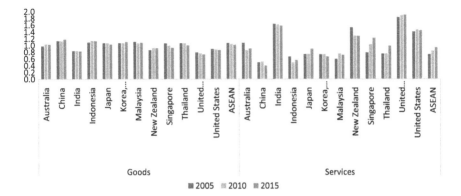

Figure 7.4 Revealed comparative advantage indices in goods and services.
Source: Compiled by the authors using UNCTAD Statistics http://unctadstat.unctad.org/wds/ReportFolders/reportFolders.aspx?sCS_ChosenLang=en (accessed April 3, 2018).

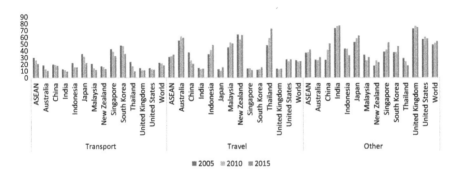

Figure 7.5 Share of total services exports (%).
Source: Compiled by the authors using UNCTAD Statistics http://unctadstat.unctad.org/wds/ReportFolders/reportFolders.aspx?sCS_ChosenLang=en (accessed April 3, 2018).

If one examines the export and import structure of the services baskets for India and its partners, then complementary interests are evident in modern and traditional services. The share of "other services" in total services exports is as high as 70 percent in India, compared to shares of 40 percent or less in most of the Asian partner countries, as shown in Figure 7.5. In contrast, traditional services such as travel and transport constitute a very small share of India's total services exports at less than 10 percent compared to shares of 20–30 percent in case of ASEAN and over 40 percent in segments like transport services for Singapore and South Korea. The structure of services imports reflects India's greater dependence on transport services imports compared to its Asian FTA partners and potential complementarities in this sub-sector given the higher contribution of this segment in some of the latter's exports. The significant share of "other services" imports across all the countries suggests scope for enhanced trade given the high contribution of this segment in India's services exports. Within this segment, disaggregated data reveal India's strength in computer and information services and other business services and the scope for increasing trade in these segments, given the growing imports of such services in the Asia-Pacific region. The trends in travel services similarly indicate untapped potential for increasing trade in this segment with several of India's Asian partners exhibiting a high share of travel services in their export baskets (Figure 7.6).

RCA indices for individual service subsectors likewise reflect these complementarities between India and key Asian FTA partners, in terms of India's relative strength being in "other services" as opposed to travel and transport services (Tables 7.1 and 7.2).[2]

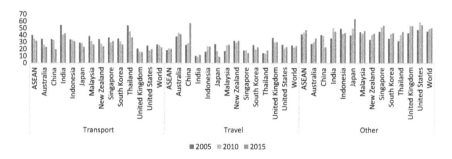

Figure 7.6 Share of total services imports (%).
Source: Compiled by the authors using UNCTAD Statistics http://unctadstat.unctad.org/wds/ReportFolders/reportFolders.aspx?sCS_ChosenLang=en (accessed April 3, 2018).

Table 7.1 RCA indices for services for selected countries and years

	Travel			Transport			Other commercial services		
	2000	2006	2012	2000	2006	2012	2000	2006	2012
India	0.66	0.47	0.50	0.52	0.50	0.60	1.45	1.53	1.39
Japan	0.16	0.28	0.40	1.62	1.47	1.37	1.29	1.18	1.14
Korea	0.69	0.39	0.51	1.91	2.07	1.82	0.73	0.84	0.93
Singapore	0.58	0.44	0.68	1.80	1.56	1.88	0.92	1.09	0.84
Thailand	1.72	2.09	2.71	1.03	1.00	0.60	0.50	0.46	0.36
ASEAN	1.24	1.21	1.49	1.23	1.24	1.19	0.73	0.81	0.72
USA	1.11	1.01	1.01	0.69	0.62	0.64	1.07	1.13	1.11
EU	0.96	0.91	0.80	1.01	1.00	1.00	1.03	1.06	1.11
China	1.70	1.41	1.04	0.53	1.04	1.01	0.77	0.80	1.00

Source: Compiled by the authors using UNCTAD Statistics http://unctadstat.unctad.org/wds/ReportFolders/reportFolders.aspx?sCS_ChosenLang=en (accessed April 3, 2018).

Table 7.2 RCA indices for selected other commercial services

	Computer and information			Other business services		
	2000	2006	2012	2000	2006	2012
India	8.08	6.92	5.65	–	1.52	1.25
Japan	0.75	0.19	0.16	1.19	1.10	1.01
Korea	0.01	0.10	0.07	1.07	0.78	0.81
Singapore	0.29	0.30	–	1.35	1.56	0.85
Thailand	–	0.01	0.01	0.88	0.82	0.60
ASEAN	0.29	0.28	0.44	1.09	1.12	0.89
USA	0.80	0.54	–	0.74	0.76	0.78
EU	1.17	1.24	1.24	1.11	1.09	1.13
CHINA	0.39	0.73	1.27	1.18	1.32	1.37

Source: Compiled by the authors using UNCTAD Statistics http://unctadstat.unctad.org/wds/ReportFolders/reportFolders.aspx?sCS_ChosenLang=en (accessed April 3, 2018).

Thus, if one juxtaposes trends in India's service sector output, trade and competitiveness with those in its manufacturing sector and with trends in its FTA partners, several areas of complementarity emerge. A comparative overview of India's global presence in services exports and imports, including at the sub-sectoral level with that of its existing and prospective South East, East Asian and Pacific FTA partners similarly suggests the potential for enhancing trade in services between India and this region.

Bilateral relations in services trade and investment

Bilateral data on exports and imports of manufacturing and services indicate that India's exports to the Asia-Pacific region have increased for both manufactures and services. As shown in Figure 7.7, India's contribution to manufacturing and services imports by countries in this region has grown, though the share remains low. The increase in import sourcing from India has, however, been much greater in services than in manufacturing, especially in the case of ASEAN.

Data provided by the Reserve Bank of India on the direction of India's trade in services indicate that individual Asian FTA partner countries, excepting Singapore and Japan account for less than 1 percent of India's services exports while the US and the UK remain its main markets, together accounting for over half of its services exports. In some services such as computer and information services, the US and the UK account for over 80 percent of India's exports while this region constitutes less than 5 percent of its IT services exports. Similarly, this region accounts for a very small share in India's services imports, except for Singapore whose significance in India's services import basket has grown over time and spans a variety of segments, including finance, insurance, other business services, computer and information, travel and transport services.

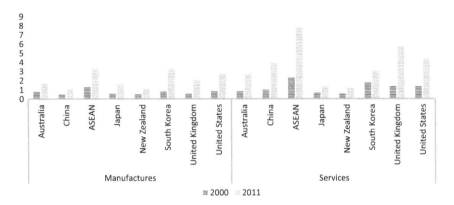

Figure 7.7 Manufactures and services imports from India, (%)*.
Source: Compiled by the authors using OECD Statistics http://stats.oecd.org/ (accessed March 7, 2018).
*: of total manufactures and services imports, respectively.

The engagement between India and this region in terms of value-added trade is also revealing. India's overall participation rates in Global Value Chains, both backward and forward,[3] are low compared to those of its FTA partner countries in Asia. However, its backward participation has more than doubled over the 2000s particularly in manufacturing, while its forward participation has barely increased, both for manufacturing and services. Hence, at the global level, there appears to be scope to both increase India's imports and exports of services in the value chain at home and abroad, respectively. In the context of the concerned Asia-Pacific FTA partners, the growth in bilateral value-added trade between India and these partner countries is noteworthy. In both manufacturing and services, there is a shift in India's backward Global Value Chain participation from traditional partners such as the US towards Asian partners such as ASEAN, China and Australia, and especially China. On the other hand, India has also grown in importance as a source of value-added in manufacturing and services for the ASEAN region, though its contribution remains much lower than that of other Asian countries, especially China. Once again reflecting India's relative competitiveness in services, the increase in India's value-added forward contribution to ASEAN is much greater for services than for manufacturing, rising from less than 5 percent to close to 15 percent between 2000 and 2011. Figures 7.8 and 7.9, respectively, highlight the origin of value-added for India and from India for selected Asia-Pacific FTA partners and other benchmark economies.

Deeper engagement in services between India and its Asian partner countries may also be realized through investment flows. Comprehensive agreements which cover investment and involve preferential treatment of partner country investors through either more favourable foreign direct investment (FDI) regulations or tax treatment can help stimulate FDI flows

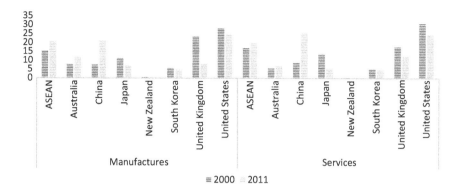

Figure 7.8 India's origin of value added in gross exports.
Note: Source industry: Total.
Source: Compiled by the authors using OECD Statistics http://stats.oecd.org/ (accessed February 22, 2018).

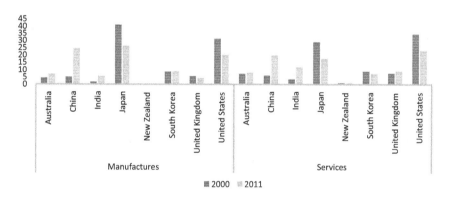

Figure 7.9 ASEAN's origin of value added in gross exports.
Source: Compiled by the authors using OECD Statistics http://stats.oecd.org/ (accessed February 22, 2018).
Note: Source industry: Total.

between partner countries, including in services. However, as highlighted in Tables 7.3 and 7.4, the investment potential between India and its Asian FTA partner countries as well as the ASEAN bloc remains untapped and skewed towards a few countries. Cumulative FDI data provided by the Department of Industrial Policy Promotion by partner country for the post-2000 period shows that only Singapore and Japan contribute in any significant way to India's total FDI inflows while other Asian partners account for less than 0.5 percent of India's FDI inflows.

Data provided by the ASEAN Secretariat shows India's growing importance as an investment source for ASEAN countries. It features among the top 15 non-ASEAN investment sources, accounting for $14.4 billion in

Table 7.3 Share of FTA and selected non-FTA partners in India's FDI inflows (%)

FY	2006–2007	2010–2011	2013–2014
China	0.00	0.00	0.34
Japan	0.37	4.48	4.72
Malaysia	0.02	0.12	0.24
Singapore	2.53	4.89	16.44
South Korea	0.31	0.38	0.48
Thailand	0.02	0.02	0.17
UK	8.23	2.17	8.83
USA	3.75	3.36	2.22

Source: DIPP country fact sheets.

Table 7.4 Bilateral FDI between India and ASEAN

Economy	ASEAN to India (April 2000–June 2017)		India to ASEAN (April 1996–March 2017)	
	FDI inflow	Share in India's FDI inflow	FDI outflow	Share in India's FDI outflow
Brunei	0.18	–	2.3	0.003
Cambodia	0.05	–	27.9	0.04
Indonesia	626.88	1.1	1220.5	1.74
Laos	0	–	16.1	0.02
Malaysia	859.12	1.4	1383.4	1.98
Myanmar	8.97	0.01	230.6	0.33
Philippines	225.28	0.4	249.5	0.36
Singapore	57600.41	96.6	65783.6	93.96
Thailand	324.69	0.5	570.6	0.81
Vietnam	4.76	0.008	529.2	0.76
ASEAN	50650.34	100	70013.9	100
Memo item:				
Total share of ASEAN in India's inward and outward FDI	17.4		22.9	

Source: Based on EXIM Bank Report (2018).

cumulative investment or 1.8 percent of total inflows into ASEAN during the 2010–2016 period.[4] However, as shown in Table 7.4, although ASEAN accounted for a significant 22.9 percent of India's outward FDI flows for the 2000–2017 period, Singapore alone attracted 94 percent of India's FDI in ASEAN, while others received very marginal shares of this investment.

In terms of the sectoral composition of this FDI, the service sector is an important destination sector for inflows from Asian partner countries, and its share has grown over the years. Around 50 percent of FDI inflows from these countries to India is constituted by services, mainly sub-sectors such as telecommunications, other services, finance and computer and information services. In the case of some partner countries like Singapore, there has been a significant increase in country share from less than 3 percent in the mid-2000s to over 16 percent in 2012–2013 and a noteworthy shift towards financial, real estate and infrastructure services.[5] Examination of data on company-specific FDI from these partner countries similarly reveals the growing importance of several services in investment inflows from this region to India, especially in real estate, finance, construction and software and data processing. ASEAN's investments in India have mainly been in real estate services followed by transportation, logistics and Information and Communication Technology.

Services also feature importantly in India's outward FDI to its Asian partners. Over the 2005–2015 period, 62 percent of India's FDI outflows to ASEAN was in services, the key segments being professional, IT, financial, trade and distribution services, as highlighted in Table 7.5. IT, financial, business and transportation services constituted 25 percent of India's FDI in the region. Further, in several services segments, ASEAN as a destination accounted for a very high share (30 percent and more) for all investing firms, indicating the strategic role of investment in India's bilateral relations with ASEAN.

Overall, the bilateral trends in services trade and in investment flows justify India's 'Look East/Act East' policy and its focus on services under its FTAs. The low shares of most of the countries in this region in India's services trade basket, in both gross and value-added terms, alongside the recent growth in sourcing of services from India indicate the scope to expand bilateral services trade, in traditional and emerging services. Gains to India on the import side could arise in transport services, financial and insurance services and construction services, and in IT-ITeS and business services on the export side. In travel and other business services, there is a two- way scope for enhancing trade. In terms of modalities, all four modes are important in bilateral relations given the range of services of interest on both sides. On the investment front, the importance of services in bilateral FDI inflows and outflows combined with the current low level of presence in each

Table 7.5 Indian services investment in ASEAN by firms, 2005–2015

Industry	Investment	No. of investing firms	ASEAN share (%)
Communication	14586	42	36.2
Construction	4342	64	31.8
Financial, insurance	1278	99	12.6
IT, ITeS (including software publishing)	1629	223	12.0
Professional, scientific, technical activities	1637	38	69.8
Transportation, storage	3736	54	41.6
Total	33253	983	28.2

Source: Based on ASEAN Investment Report, 2017.

other's markets, excepting the case of Singapore, highlights the unrealized potential in bilateral investment relations in services. These low shares are indicative of regulatory and other barriers that impede bilateral relations. Hence, the structure of the FTAs signed with these countries, the provisions in their services and chapters and the breadth and depth of services commitments on both sides can influence the realization of these opportunities and collaboration prospects, as discussed next.

Status of India's FTA negotiations and commitments in Asia-Pacific

India has always been a supporter of multilateralism. But with the slow-down in multilateral negotiations, India, like other countries, has increasingly turned towards signing bilateral and regional trade agreements. These agreements have shifted their geographic focus from neighbouring countries in SAARC to the ASEAN region and to individual countries in South and South-East Asia and the Pacific. Cumulatively, India had 16 agreements in 2018 The trend towards signing more broad-based agreements which include services commenced in 2005 with the entry into force of the India-Singapore Comprehensive Economic Cooperation Agreement. (CECA) followed by several comprehensive bilateral agreements in succession with Korea in 2010 and with Japan and Malaysia in 2011, and the expansion of the existing ASEAN-India FTA to include services and investment in 2015. Negotiations for comprehensive agreements are ongoing with several other countries in the Asia-Pacific region. Figure 7.10 shows the evolution of India's FTAs over the 1948–2018 period while Table 7.6 shows the specifics of notified Indian FTAs which are currently in force.

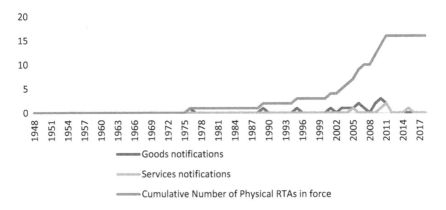

Figure 7.10 India: Evolution of FTAs, 1948–2018.
Note: Physical RTA count goods and services together.
Source: Compiled by the authors using RTA statistics from WTO https://rtais.wto.org/UI/charts.aspx Accessed: 3–5–18.

Table 7.6 In force trade agreements of India (notified to WTO)

Name of the agreement	Partner countries	Signed	Entry into force	Type of agreement
Association of Southeast Asian Nations (ASEAN) – India Free Trade agreement	Brunei Darussalam; Myanmar; Cambodia; Indonesia; Lao People's Democratic Republic; Malaysia; Philippines; Singapore; Viet Nam; Thailand	13-Aug-09 (Goods) 13-Nov-14 (Services)	01-Jan-10 (Goods) 01-07-2015 (Services)	Goods, services & investment
Asia Pacific Trade Agreement (APTA) Partial scope agreement	Bangladesh; China; Korea, Republic of; Lao People's Democratic Republic; Sri Lanka	31-Jul-75	17-Jun-76	Goods
Chile – India Partial Scope Agreement	Chile	08-Mar-06	17-Aug-07	Goods
Global System of Trade Preferences among developing countries (GSTP) partial scope agreement	Algeria; Argentina; Bangladesh; Benin; Bolivia, Pluri-national State of; Brazil; Cameroon; Chile; Colombia; Cuba; Ecuador; Egypt; Ghana; Guinea; Guyana; Indonesia; Iran; Iraq; Korea, Democratic People's Republic of; Korea, Republic of; Libya; Malaysia; Mexico; Morocco; Mozambique; Myanmar; Nicaragua; Nigeria; Pakistan; Peru; Philippines; Singapore; Sri Lanka; Sudan; Tanzania; Thailand; The former Yugoslav Republic of Macedonia; Trinidad and Tobago; Tunisia; Venezuela, Bolivarian Republic of; Viet Nam; Zimbabwe	13-Apr-88	19-Apr-89	Goods
India – Afghanistan partial scope agreement	Afghanistan	06-Mar-03	13-May-03	Goods
India – Bhutan free trade agreement	Bhutan	28-Jul-06	29-Jul-06	Goods

(*Continued*)

Name of the agreement	Partner countries	Signed	Entry into force	Type of agreement
India – Japan free trade agreement & economic integration agreement	Japan	16-Feb-11	01-Aug-11	Goods & services
India – Malaysia free trade agreement & economic integration agreement	Malaysia	18-Feb-11	01-Jul-11	Goods & services
India – Nepal partial scope agreement	Nepal	27-Oct-09	27-Oct-09	Goods
India – Singapore free trade agreement & economic integration agreement	Singapore	29-Jun-05	01-Aug-05	Goods & services
India – Sri Lanka free trade agreement	Sri Lanka	28-Dec-98	15-Dec-01	Goods
Republic of Korea – India free trade agreement & economic integration agreement	Republic of Korea	07-Aug-09	01-Jan-10	Goods & services
MERCOSUR – India partial scope agreement	Argentina; Brazil; Paraguay; Uruguay	25-Jan-04	01-Jun-09	Goods
South Asian Free Trade Agreement (SAFTA) Free trade agreement	Bangladesh; Bhutan; Maldives; Nepal; Pakistan; Sri Lanka	06-Jan-04	01-Jan-06	Goods
South Asian Preferential Trade Arrangement (SAPTA) partial scope agreement	Bangladesh; Bhutan; Maldives; Nepal; Pakistan; Sri Lanka	11-Apr-93	07-Dec-95	Goods

Source: Compiled by the authors from Regional Trade Agreements Database of WTO: http://rtais.wto.org/UI/PublicSearchByMemberResult.aspx?MemberCode=356&lang=1&redirect=1 Accessed: 3-5-18.

As shown in Table 7.6, all of India's FTAs which cover services are with Asian countries, starting with the India-Singapore CECA, which set the template for its subsequent comprehensive agreements. The Agreement on Trade in Services under the Framework Agreement on Comprehensive Economic Cooperation between India and ASEAN was India's first such comprehensive agreement with a major regional bloc. Several other such comprehensive agreements are currently under negotiation, including the Regional Comprehensive Economic Partnership (RCEP). A positive list approach has been taken in these FTAs, that is, services that have been committed for liberalization, have been scheduled, with compensatory adjustments in case of withdrawal or modification of commitments.

Scope and depth of commitments

An examination of the sectoral coverage of commitments shows that both India and its partners have either bound the status quo or have taken the General Agreement on Trade in Services (GATS) plus commitments in terms of the number of services sectors and subsectors scheduled. Some schedules go beyond the offers made in the Doha round request-offer process. The following tables summarize the scope and nature of these commitments made by India and its partners to highlight the nature and extent of liberalization undertaken, how they compare with those under the GATS and other FTAs, and what kind of orientation and sensitivities they reflect on either side.

Table 7.7 shows that while India committed only six sectors under the GATS, it committed eight sectors in the India-Singapore CECA and eleven sectors in the India-Japan and the India-Korea agreements. While partner countries such as Singapore, Korea and Japan have committed six, eight and eleven sectors, respectively, under the GATS, they have committed twelve, ten and eleven sectors, respectively, in their FTAs with India. Thus, both sides have increased the sectoral scope of their services commitments.

In the case of ASEAN, the approach has varied across member states. India had requested an ASEAN-Australia-New Zealand plus offer but has instead received different commitments from each of the ASEAN member states. On its part, it has scheduled one set of commitments for eight ASEAN members, and one each for Indonesia and the Philippines. It has scheduled relatively fewer services in this FTA (though more than under the GATS) and has been more conservative (for some services GATS minus) in case of the Philippines.[6] ASEAN members have likewise varied in the sectoral scope of their commitments as shown in Table 7.8, with countries like Singapore making extensive commitments under the India-ASEAN first package and others such as the Philippines, Lao, Malaysia and Thailand scheduling fewer sectors, possibly reflecting sensitivities and overlapping interests with India in certain services (health, education, financial) and Least Developed Country concerns with liberalizing market access in the case of Lao.

Table 7.7 Sectoral coverage of commitments by India and selected partners under various FTAs

	India's commitments under the GATS and various FTAs						Singapore's commitments		Korea's commitments		Japan's commitments
	GATS India	India-Korea	India-Singapore	India-ASEAN*	India to Indonesia	India to Philippines	GATS Singapore	India-Singapore	GATS Korea	India-Korea	Japan
Business services	✓	✓	✓	✓	✓	✓	✓	✓	✓	✓	✓
Communication services	✓	✓	✓	✓	✓	✓	✓	✓	✓	✓	✓
Construction & related engineering services	✓	✓	✓	✓	✓		✓	✓	✓	✓	✓
Distribution services	✓	✓	✓					✓	✓	✓	✓
Educational services	✓	✓						✓		✓	✓
Environmental services	✓	✓						✓	✓	✓	✓
Financial services	✓	✓	✓	✓	✓	✓	✓	✓	✓	✓	✓
Health related & social services	✓	✓	✓	✓	✓	✓	✓	✓			✓
Tourism & travel related services	✓	✓	✓	✓	✓	✓	✓	✓	✓		✓
Recreational cultural & sporting services	✓	✓	✓				✓	✓	✓	✓	✓
Transport services	✓	✓	✓	✓	✓		✓	✓	✓	✓	✓
Other services not included elsewhere								✓			

Source: Authors' construction based on schedules of services commitments under selected FTAs and Chanda (2014) and Chanda (November 2014).

Note:
* India to nine ASEAN countries, except Philippines.
* For India to Philippines, among these seven sectors, construction & related engineering services & transport Services are not present.

Table 7.8 Scheduling of services by ASEAN member countries

India-ASEAN first Package

	Brunei	Cambodia	Indonesia	Lao	Malaysia	Myanmar	Philippines	Singapore	Thailand	Vietnam
Business services	✓	✓	✓	✓	✓	✓	✓	✓	✓	✓
Communication services	✓	✓	✓	✓	✓	✓		✓	✓	✓
Construction & related engineering services	✓	✓	✓	✓	✓	✓		✓	✓	✓
Distribution services	✓	✓		✓			✓	✓	✓	✓
Educational services	✓	✓	✓	✓			✓	✓		✓
Environmental services	✓	✓		✓			✓	✓		✓
Financial services	✓	✓			✓			✓		✓
Health related & social services	✓		✓				✓	✓	✓	
Tourism & travel related services	✓	✓		✓	✓	✓		✓	✓	✓
Recreational cultural & sporting services		✓				✓	✓			
Transport services	✓	✓	✓		✓	✓		✓	✓	✓
other services not included elsewhere										

Source: Authors' construction based on ASEAN schedules of services commitments in the India-ASEAN FTA.

Note: GATS plus: ▓ GATS minus: ░ .

It is interesting to note that several ASEAN countries have made more extensive commitments in their FTA with China compared with their commitments to India. Services such as health, education, financial, distribution and environmental services typically feature among the less scheduled sectors for both India and these partners, indicating that social, employment and regulatory concerns have influenced the scope of commitments.

In addition to examining the overall sectoral coverage, it is also important to look at the scope of the commitments within each service sector by assessing the number of sub-sectors committed. Such a sub-sectoral examination is important as simply committing many services may not be meaningful if the number of sub-sectors committed is limited. Tables 7.9 and 7.10 provide such details for India's FTAs with ASEAN and non-ASEAN partners, respectively.

It is evident that India and its partners have by and large committed a larger number of sub-sectors within the services they have scheduled in their FTAs than under the GATS. This is especially so in the case of business and communication services. Some services such as distribution or education services, which have not been scheduled under the GATS by many of the countries, have been scheduled under these FTAs, indicating increased willingness to offer market access under the agreements. However, the approach varies across partners. India has committed fewer subsectors for the Philippines, especially in business services, though its sub-sectoral coverage is GATS plus overall. The Philippines and the Lao have scheduled very few sub-sectors and several ASEAN countries, including Indonesia, Thailand, Malaysia and the Philippines show GATS sub-sectoral coverage. In contrast, several ASEAN members such as the Philippines, Malaysia, Thailand and Indonesia have scheduled significantly more sub-sectors under their FTAs with other countries like China and New Zealand compared to what they have committed in their FTA with India.

Another dimension is the actual content of these commitments in terms of the nature of limitations maintained as well their modal distribution. The latter is indicative of whether India and its partner countries exhibit similar willingness to liberalize across the four modes of supply in their FTAs compared to their stance under the GATS. The modal comparison reveals that India has improved the depth of its commitments, with a significant increase in the share of unrestricted commitments across modes 1, 2 and 3 for all the selected services except communication services. The improvement is greatest for business services and for modes 1 and 2; limitations have mainly been inscribed for mode 3, taking the form of local incorporation requirements, FDI ceiling limits of 49 percent or 51 percent or 74 percent and requirement of authorization and licenses from concerned regulatory authorities. Mode 4 remains unbound. Several services which were not scheduled under the GATS, such as education, transport and environmental services have been committed under these FTAs, with 100 percent unrestricted commitments across modes 1–3.

Table 7.9 Number of subsectors committed in selected FTAs by India and its partner countries

	GATS					India-Korea		India-Japan		India-Singapore		India-Malaysia	
	India	Korea	Japan	Singapore	Malaysia	India	Korea	India	Japan	India	Singapore	India	Malaysia
Business services	8	34	36	21	21	33	50	32	61	39	55	27	47
Communication services	11	12	11	7	6	16	19	15	21	9	12	15	19
Construction & related engineering services	1	7	5	1	5	1	1	5	6	5	8	5	8
distribution services	0	4	4	0	0	2	4	4	8	2	11	2	2
Educational services	0	0	4	0	0	1	2	1	5	0	4	1	1
Environmental services	0	4	7	0	0	2	4	2	7	0	3	2	4
Financial services	10	15	9	17	14	17	12	14	2	12	17	0	0
Health related & social services	1	0	1	0	1	1	0	1	1	1	7	1	5
Tourism & travel related services	2	3	4	4	2	3	3	3	3	2	7	2	4
Recreational cultural & sporting services	0	0	4	1	2	2	2	2	4	3	8	2	2
Transport services	0	15	17	3	3	11	21	11	23	9	31	8	10
Other services not included elsewhere	0	0	0	0	1	0	0	0	0	0	3	0	1
Total	33	94	102	54	55	89	118	90	141	82	166	65	103

Source: Authors' construction based on schedules of services commitments under the GATS and selected FTAs, Chanda (2014) and Chanda (November 2014).

Table 7.10 Number of subsectors committed in the ASEAN-India FTA by India and its partner countries

	India-ASEAN first package												
	India except Indonesia, Philippines	*India to Indonesia*	*India to Philippines*	*Brunei*	*Cambodia*	*Indonesia*	*Lao*	*Malaysia*	*Myanmar*	*Philippines*	*Singapore*	*Thailand*	*Vietnam*
Business services	12	10	2	9	25	16	8	22	24	2	37	21	24
Communication services	15	15	15	10	16	15	10	3	9	0	23	1	30
Construction & related engineering services	1	1	0	0	5	9	8	7	1	0	5	2	5
Distribution services	0	0	0	0	12	0	0	0	0	0	6	1	4
Educational services	0	0	0	1	3	4	4	1	10	0	5	0	4
Environmental services	0	0	0	0	7	0	6	0	0	1	3	0	4
Financial services	16	16	16	6	16	14	4	0	0	26	17	0	24
Health related & social services	1	1	1	1	1	0	0	0	2	0	6	1	2
Tourism & travel related services	2	2	2	5	4	2	4	5	2	3	5	4	2
Recreational cultural & sporting services	0	0	0	0	1	0	0	0	2	0	5	3	2
Transport services	1	1	0	4	11	3	0	6	7	16	12	4	18
Other services not included elsewhere	0	0	0	0	0	1	0	0	0	0	3	0	0
Total	48	46	36	36	101	64	44	44	57	48	127	37	119

Source: Authors' construction based on schedules of services commitments under the India-ASEAN FTA.

Note: GATS plus: [dark shading], GATS minus: [light shading].

In the context of the ASEAN-India FTA, a content analysis of India's commitments shows that India's commitments are generally shallower than those under its FTAs with other Asian partners. While India's commitments to the majority of ASEAN member states are largely similar in depth and scope to its GATS commitments, in the case of the Philippines the commitments are less liberal, with many unbound entries across all four modes. The lack of commitment in modes 3 and 1 is particularly striking. Mode 1, where committed, is often subject to authorization, commercial presence and other technological requirements, while mode 3, where committed, is subject to a range of conditions such as local incorporation, approval, licensing and prior collaboration requirements. Market access has been withheld in segments like computer and related services, health services, maritime and tourism services specifically for the Philippines and Indonesia. In general, one finds that there is customization of commitments across the ASEAN member states. Where there are overlapping competitive interests such as in professional services, as with the Philippines, the commitments are both shallow and narrow in scope.

On the other side, commitments made by partners such as Korea and Japan show a mix of improvement and backtracking on the GATS. While the number of services these countries have committed may be larger, the extent of liberalization is not necessarily greater, especially in professional services where limitations in the form of commercial presence and qualification requirements, residency and nationality conditions have been inscribed. In many cases, the commitments are more restrictive than those they have made in the GATS. Added to these are barriers arising from cultural and linguistic differences, which affect India's professional and business services exports to some of these markets. Under the ASEAN-India FTA, the liberalization stance varies across the member states. While countries like Indonesia, Malaysia and Singapore have made more liberal commitments compared to those made under the GATS, by introducing partial commitments in some sub-sectors and converting some unbound entries into partial commitments, others like the Philippines have introduced limitations such as commercial presence and FDI ceiling requirements and have made some of their partial GATS commitments into unbound entries.

Table 7.11 summarizes the mode-wise degree of liberalization undertaken by ASEAN in its FTAs with India and other countries in the region, clearly highlighting that ASEAN has maintained more restrictions vis-à-vis India across most modes compared to that under its other FTAs. While the commitment is most restrictive in the case of mode 4 and is comparable to that offered by ASEAN to China, the difference in the degree of market access granted to India vis-à-vis other partner countries, as reflected by the much lower commitment index scores for modes 1–3, is striking. The latter is likely to reflect the reciprocation of India's shallow commitments under the ASEAN-India FTA, apart from the fact that competing interests between

Table 7.11 Liberalization in ASEAN FTAs

	ASEAN-China	ASEAN-ANZ	ASEAN-South Korea	ASEAN-Japan	ASEAN-India
Modes 1 & 2: Cross-border trade in services					
Simple average	0.457	0.420	0.531	0.081	0.109
Mode 3: Investment					
Simple average	0.354	0.538	0.502	0.120	0.120
Mode 4: Movement of people					
Simple average	0.046	0.277	0.123	0.046	0.046
Total averages	0.286	0.412	0.386	0.083	0.092

Source: Based on Appendix Tables in Cornish and Findlay (2011).

India and certain ASEAN countries in areas such as professional and business services and service provider mobility have led to weaker commitments in general under this FTA.

Overall, none of these agreements significantly enhance the scope or depth of market access in services for either side vis-à-vis the GATS. They also do not go beyond the status quo in terms of existing national policies. Across sectors, some of the most important services, namely, business services, financial (banking), communication and transport services are subject to the most limitations on both sides.

Rules and provisions

In addition to the nature of commitments, the broad architecture of the FTAs and provisions of these FTAs are also indicative of the areas of negotiating interest. The architecture and key provisions in India's comprehensive agreements are similar to those under GATS. There is not much progress on rule-making and provisions, on key issues like domestic regulation, mutual recognition, subsidies and business practices. However, on the issue of movement of natural persons (MNP), these agreements do extend the GATS disciplines in that they provide greater detail on the scope of the MNP provisions, explicitly noting the different categories of natural persons and what they cover, and by linking MNP to other regulatory issues by including additional provisions within the MNP chapter. This contrasts with the GATS Annex on MNP which is quite ambiguous. These FTAs outline in detail the definition of the different categories of natural persons, that is, contractual service suppliers, business visitors, independent professionals and intra-corporate transferees, specify the terms and conditions for entry and stay of these different categories, such as the period for which entry would be granted for a single visit and the maximum period of stay allowed, exempting natural persons from making social security contributions in the other country, specifying the documentation and administrative requirements for different kinds of natural persons, and even outlining the conditions applicable to spouses and dependents. Some of these agreements contain occupation lists of service providers for whom mode 4 access is to be liberalized and for which mutual recognition of qualifications is to be facilitated through discussions between regulatory authorities from both sides. The India–Korea agreement, for example, lists 163 occupations under the professional category which are covered by the MNP provisions under this agreement.[7] Hence, the mode 4 chapters of these agreements are GATS plus in terms of rule-making, reflecting India's interest in accessing partner country markets through this mode.

Review of the evidence and outlook

The preceding discussion indicates that there is considerable scope for gains through enhanced trade and investment flows in services. There are bilateral trade and investment prospects across a variety of services, including professional, business, tourism, transport, construction, logistics, urban infrastructure and financial services. Although there are competing interests with some of these countries, there is also sufficient complementarity in services trade structure and competitiveness. There is also scope to collaborate in areas of common interest and to leverage bilateral expertise in sectors such as health, education, telecom and IT.

To what extent have the expected gains materialized for India? The prevailing view and available evidence suggest that these agreements have not benefited India's services sector for several reasons. First, as seen earlier, the commitments remain subject to limitations. For instance, opportunities in professional services under mode 1 have been limited by commercial presence requirements. Mode 4 remains largely unbound and mode 3 is also restricted, especially in the case of ASEAN. Second, where liberalization has been granted, this has not necessarily translated into effective market access due to the continued presence of behind-the-border regulatory barriers and the introduction of national policies, which are often discriminatory. Third, India itself may not be in a position to leverage these agreements in terms of attracting more investments or expanding services and investment exports due to issues of competitiveness, standards, its business environment and regulatory preparedness.

The mobility of professionals which was a key interest for India in these agreements remains undermined by recognition and qualification barriers, failure to conclude Mutual Recognition Agreements with these countries in selected professional services, employment laws and discriminatory practices. For instance, although occupation lists have been included in these FTAs, discussions among regulatory authorities have not taken off. The only case where some progress has been made is with Singapore, with the recognition of four Indian nursing institutions to facilitate the practice of Indian nurses in Singapore. Changes in national employment policies and immigration laws, such as the 'Employment Pass Framework' introduced in 2010 in Singapore, which aims to reduce the foreign share of the total workforce of companies located in Singapore to around one-third, has had adverse implications for Indian service suppliers. Further, Singapore restricted the movement of skilled professionals from India by giving preference to Singapore citizens in jobs and putting Indian IT firms under its fair consideration framework watch list, although the India-Singapore CECA was expected to facilitate the mobility of intra-corporate transferees and not put restrictions on their mobility.[8] In the case of Japan, despite prospects for enhancing bilateral relations in health services through the mobility of nurses, caregivers and doctors, lack of recognition of Indian medical qualifications continues to restrict opportunities in modes 4 and 1.[9] Regulatory requirements in other modes also undermine market access. For example, Singapore has required much higher capital adequacy norms for Indian banks, prescribing an Asset Management Ratio of 70 percent for SBI and ICICI, compared to 35 percent for other foreign banks.[10] In addition to these restrictions, surveys reveal that differences in culture, language and organizational practices impede relations with these countries.

Reviews of some of these agreements also reveal the lack of meaningful gains for India. The oldest among these FTAs, the India-Singapore CECA, has undergone two reviews. The first review concluded in 2007 and the second was concluded recently. While the asset maintenance ratio issue for both SBI and ICICI bank has been resolved and most Indian IT companies have now been taken out of the fair consideration framework watch list, a permanent solution on both these issues is still pending. One positive step has been the recognition of three more Indian nursing institutions in Singapore and the proposal to review another 17 for future recognition.[11]

Although it is premature to discuss the impact of the ASEAN-India agreement in services as it is much more recent and its enforcement was delayed due to non-ratification by the Philippines legislature (given the direct competition between India and the Philippines in services), the general view is that India has not reaped the expected benefits.[12] Some critics have commented that India has got a raw deal in both goods and services and the expectation that gains in services would offset any disadvantages India has in goods vis-à-vis ASEAN, will not be realized. ASEAN countries have themselves not been able to meet the target dates for removing restrictions on services trade within the bloc and there remain large regulatory differences with slow progress on issues such as mutual recognition among the member states. There is also no commitment to address the behind-the-border issues under the ASEAN-India Services Agreement. Moreover, overlapping and competing interests are likely to make progress in key sectors and modes difficult to achieve. Thus, though there is much potential, the prospects for ASEAN-India gains in services are plagued by challenges.

Given these experiences under other FTAs, what then is the outlook under the prospective RCEP agreement? This mega agreement which includes trade in goods, trade in services, investment, economic and technical cooperation, intellectual property, competition, dispute settlement, e-commerce, small and medium enterprises and other issues,[13] as with India's other comprehensive agreements, is expected to give rise to gains in services for India, compensating for its lack of competitiveness in goods trade. However, it is increasingly being realized that these gains will depend on the extent of effective market access India gets from RCEP partners. Although India had wanted at least the provisions on mode 4 agreed upon in the ASEAN-New Zealand FTA, that is, the facilitation of movement of service providers engaged in trade and investment activities and the establishment of streamlined and transparent procedures for temporary entry related applications, to be included in the RCEP, ASEAN has not agreed.[14] India is unhappy with the offers made in services by other RCEP countries, especially in mode 4. There appears to be an imbalance in negotiations between goods and services which has raised concerns about RCEP in India. Experience suggests that mode 4 gains are unlikely, while in mode 3, to what extent India can gain beyond the case of IT and IT-enabled services is unclear.

If indeed India is to realize its services trade and investment interests with its partners in East and South East Asia, it will need to secure market access in key modes of services supply and sectors. But in addition, it will have to negotiate for greater transparency and easing of behind-the-border regulatory barriers. It must be forward-looking, exploiting synergies that exist across modes and across sectors, such as those between manufacturing industries like IT hardware, electronics, automotive on one hand and IT and IT-enabled services on the other, between outward FDI in IT-enabled services on one hand and related mode 1 and 4 based professional services exports on the other. In the case of ASEAN, it should align its strategies with the ASEAN Economic Community Blueprint 2025 and other efforts in the region to access the regional production network using its own strengths in services. Finally, it must continue with its domestic reform agenda and boost its own competitiveness, upgrade domestic standards, and improve the business environment if it is to successfully leverage these agreements through exports and investments.

Notes

1 Bhatia (January 2016).
2 Revealed Comparative Advantage or RCA is the ratio of a country's exports of a sector/product to its total exports to the world's exports of the same sector/product to the world's total exports.
3 Backward participation refers to the use of foreign inputs in a country's exports. Forward participation refers to the use of a country's inputs in another country's exports.
4 The ASEAN Secretariat (2017).
5 DIPP (various years).
6 See Tables 7.8 and 7.10.
7 See Seshadri (2015).

 8 Mishra (2018).
 9 See Seshadri (2016).
10 Ibid., 8. See also Seshadri (2017).
11 Ibid., 8.
12 Saraswat, Priya and Ghosh (May 2018), https://economictimes.indiatimes.com/news/economy/foreign-trade/view-india-must-tread-carefully-on-free-trade-agreements/articleshow/64055496.cms and Srivastava (2014), https://indianexpress.com/article/business/business-others/asean-fta-review-shows-india-got-almost-nothing/.
13 http://asean.org/?static_post=rcep-regional-comprehensive-economic-partnership.
14 Sen (Feb 2018), www.thehindubusinessline.com/economy/macro-economy/rcep-talks-india-unhappy/article22661235.ece.

References

Bhatia, R., 'Act East Policy – Emerging Contours', 13 January 2016, www.orfonline.org/research/act-east-policy-emerging-contours-2/ (accessed: 11-4-18)

Chanda, R., "Mapping the Universe of Services Disciplines in Asian PTAs", in *The Preferential Liberalization of Trade in Services: Comparative Regionalism* (eds.) P. Sauve and A. Shingal, Edward Elgar Publishers, 2014, pp. 224–293.

Chanda, R., "Impact Analysis of India's Free Trade Agreements", for Department of Economic Affairs, Ministry of Finance, Government of India, New Delhi, November 2014.

Cornish, M., and C. Findlay, "Services Liberalization in the 'ASEAN Plus' Free Trade Agreements, in Findlay, C. (ed.), *ASEAN+1 FTAs and Global Value Chains in East Asia*, ERIA Research Project Report 2010–29, Jakarta: ERIA, 2011, pp. 132–155.

Department of Industrial Policy & Promotion, Government of India. Country Fact-sheets, various years.

Export-Import Bank of India, New Delhi in association with the Indian Mission to ASEAN, Jakarta. 2018. *Strengthening ASEAN-India Partnership: Trends and Future Prospects.*

Mishra, A.R., 'India, Singapore conclude second review of trade pact', 27 June 2018, www.livemint.com/Politics/nLYauYcmQzG4JIXFY1UNjK/India-Singapore-conclude-second-review-of-trade-pact.html (accessed: 2-7-18)

Saraswat, V.K., P. Priya and A. Ghosh, 'India must tread carefully on free trade agreements', 07 May 2018, https://economictimes.indiatimes.com/news/economy/foreign-trade/view-india-must-tread-carefully-on-free-trade-agreements/articleshow/64055496.cms (accessed: 2-7-18)

Sen, A., "RCEP Talks: India "unhappy" with revised service offers too", Feb 5, 2018, www.thehindubusinessline.com/economy/macro-economy/rcep-talks-india-unhappy/article22661235.ece

Seshadri, V.S., 2015. *India-Korea CEPA: An appraisal of progress.* ASEAN-India Centre at Research and Information System for Developing Countries: New Delhi.

Seshadri, V.S., 2016. *India-Japan CEPA: An appraisal.* ASEAN-India Centre at Research and Information System for Developing Countries: New Delhi.

Seshadri, V.S., 2017. *India-Singapore CECA: An appraisal of progress.* ASEAN-India Centre at Research and Information System for Developing Countries: New Delhi.

Srivastava, S., "ASEAN FTA review shows India got almost nothing", Indian Express, October 3, 2014, https://indianexpress.com/article/business/business-others/asean-fta-review-shows-india-got-almost-nothing/

The ASEAN Secretariat, Jakarta and United Nations Conference on Trade and Development, Geneva. 2017. *ASEAN Investment Report 2017: Foreign Direct Investment and Economic Zones in ASEAN.*

Data sources

http://asean.org/?static_post=rcep-regional-comprehensive-economic-partnership
https://rtais.wto.org/UI/charts.aspx
http://stats.oecd.org/
http://unctadstat.unctad.org/wds/ReportFolders/reportFolders.aspx?sCS_ChosenLang=en

8 ASEAN-5 and its RCEP priorities

Challenges and the way forward

Sanchita Basu Das

Introduction

The Association of Southeast Asian Nations, or simply known as ASEAN, has been leading the negotiation of the Regional Comprehensive Economic Partnership (RCEP) since 2012. It is bringing together ten of its own members and another six big economies of the Asia-Pacific region. The latter group includes Australia, China, India, Japan, New Zealand and South Korea. If negotiated successfully, RCEP is estimated to cover 30 percent of world's Gross Domestic Product (GDP), 50 percent of the world population and 30 percent of global trade. Given its sheer size, RCEP is often termed as mega-regional.

From the beginning, ASEAN made it distinctly clear what it expects to achieve with RCEP. In the framework document, that was signed in 2011 to provide a guideline for subsequent negotiation, ASEAN promised to deliver on 'a comprehensive and mutually beneficial' agreement that would cover 'broader and deeper engagement with significant improvements over existing ASEAN FTAs/CEP with Dialogue Partners'. It further stated that the agreement will also address new issues that may emerge in the future. Besides outlining features like high transparency upon signing of the agreement, availability of economic and technical cooperation for implementation and focus on trade facilitation, the framework document provided flexibilities in terms of negotiation process, that is, sequential manner or single undertaking and future accession, both for the ASEAN free trade agreement (FTA) partners who may decide not to participate at the outset or new members and special and differential treatment for less developed ASEAN members (ASEAN Secretariat 2011). Looking at these, one may quickly extrapolate that while ASEAN wanted an institutionalized trade regime that would improve upon its existing trade agreements, thereby strengthening trade and investment in the region, it was mindful about the complexity of negotiation and the development status of some of its participating members. This made many wonder whether RCEP can truly manage to introduce a new paradigm in ASEAN's international trade regime.

The Guiding Principles for negotiating RCEP was issued in August 2012. In addition to reiterating the fact that RCEP is meant to achieve a 'modern, comprehensive, high-quality and mutually beneficial' deal, the guiding principles stated the coverage as trade in goods, trade in services, investment, intellectual property, competition, dispute settlement and any other issue that will be mutually agreed upon during the course of negotiation (ASEAN Secretariat 2012). The issues later were extended to e-commerce and government procurement.

Sixteen countries commenced the negotiation in 2013 and have completed 20 rounds of negotiation at the time of the writing of the chapter in December 2017. With immense challenges still unresolved, there is yet no concrete sign of conclusion anytime soon. In the past five years, new economic and geo-strategic issues have evolved and some have even changed their course of action. One such key issue is another mega-regional, the Trans-Pacific Partnership (TPP), once led by the United States and publicized as its key strategy to 'pivot to Asia'. The TPP was launched in 2011 and marketed as a 21st-century trade agreement that will address issues much beyond what is currently discussed under the World Trade Organization (WTO). Although the 12 participating members concluded negotiations and signed the deal in early 2016, the agreement fell through the cracks of the US election. In early 2017, as the new US administration, led by President Donald Trump, assumed office, it pulled the US out of the trade pact, leaving policymakers of the other 11 countries to come up with an accommodating arrangement of Comprehensive and Progressive Trans-Pacific Partnership (CPTPP) in November 2017.

Given the background, this chapter looks at ASEAN's rationale for joining RCEP negotiations. It pays attention to both economic and strategic interests of the ASEAN countries that they expect to be served by participating in the mega-regional. As negotiation is a multiparty game, it is bound to face challenges and hiccups. RCEP is not immune from that. The chapter discusses some of the contentious issues during RCEP negotiation. Finally, the key points of the chapter are put together to provide a conclusion. The chapter provides an RCEP account from a perspective of ASEAN-5 countries, that is, Indonesia, Malaysia, the Philippines, Singapore, and Thailand, as these are the countries that are more profoundly commercially linked to the bigger RCEP economies, like China, Japan, South Korea and India. As Vietnam is fast catching up with other advanced ASEAN countries, the chapter takes Vietnam under consideration where felt necessary.

RCEP serves economic priorities

The section explains various economic rationales for the ASEAN countries to undertake the RCEP negotiation. These include, the importance of trade and Foreign Direct Investment (FDI) in their economies, participation in East Asia production network, improve trade facilitation environment and multilateralising the existing ASEAN+1 FTAs.

Trade and investment are crucial for ASEAN economies

ASEAN countries' trade, particularly the merchandise one, has increased from US$1,237 billion in 2005 to US$2,172 billion in 2016, reflecting an average annual growth rate of 5.3 percent. As against this, merchandise trade of several of the non-ASEAN RCEP countries, such as, Japan, China and South Korea rose at a rate of 1.1 percent, 9 percent and 4.7 percent, respectively over the same period (Table 8.1).

Merchandise trade been an important component of ASEAN countries' GDP for long (Table 8.2). In fact, for most of the ASEAN-6 countries, merchandise trade share as percent of GDP is more than 100 percent, and much higher when compared to non-ASEAN RCEP participants. For most of the ASEAN-6

Table 8.1 Merchandise trade performance, 2005–2016

	2005	2010	2016	Average annual growth rate (2005–2016)
Indonesia	163	293	280	5.1
Malaysia	256	363	358	3.1
Philippines	91	110	143	4.2
Singapore	430	663	630	3.5
Thailand	229	376	410	5.4
Vietnam	69	157	351	15.9
ASEAN-6	1,237	1,963	2,172	5.2
Australia	231	414	387	4.8
China	1,422	2,974	3,686	9.0
India	242	577	624	9.0
Japan	1,111	1,464	1,253	1.1
South Korea	546	892	902	4.7
New Zealand	48	62	70	3.5

Source: WTO Trade Statistics, author's calculation.

Table 8.2 Merchandise trade (% Share of GDP)

	1980	1985	1990	1995	2000	2005	2010	2015	2016
Indonesia	32.9	27.0	34.4	35.2	60.7	52.3	38.8	34.0	30.0
Malaysia	89.8	82.1	126.0	158.9	178.9	172.7	142.4	126.6	120.7
Philippines	38.8	29.7	43.0	55.8	92.7	88.0	55.1	44.1	46.8
Singapore	359.3	264.6	292.0	276.3	284.1	337.2	280.3	216.8	206.3
Thailand	47.0	40.8	63.4	75.1	103.6	121.0	110.3	104.5	100.7
Vietnam	6.1	17.3	80.3	65.4	96.5	120.0	139.3	171.6	174.3
Australia	27.2	27.8	25.2	30.1	33.9	31.5	33.2	32.2	30.7
China	12.4	22.3	28.9	38.1	39.0	61.6	19.0	35.2	32.9
India	12.4	10.6	12.7	17.8	19.7	29.1	33.7	31.6	27.6
Japan	24.7	22.0	16.6	14.3	17.6	23.4	25.7	29.0	25.3
New Zealand	48.4	52.0	41.3	44.4	50.2	42.3	42.7	40.9	38.4
South Korea	61.0	61.2	48.3	46.8	59.2	60.8	81.5	69.7	63.9

Source: WTO Trade Database, author's calculation.

countries merchandise trade as percent of GDP has gone up. Besides Singapore, which is a free port since its independence in 1965, countries like Malaysia, the Philippines, Thailand and Vietnam, have a sizable proportion of merchandise trade. The ASEAN countries, as a whole, has increased their share in global exports over this time. While in the early 1980s, Japan dominated the trade share in the broader Asian region at 6.6 percent, it changed drastically by the early 1990s. By 2015/2016, the ASEAN countries accounted for 6.7 percent of total global trade compared to 3.9 percent of Japan (Table 8.3).

Hence, for the ASEAN policymakers RCEP is an important initiative that will support the importance of trade in these economies further.

Similar to trade, FDI has long played a crucial role in the development strategy of the ASEAN countries. The Japanese FDI, in particular, has been active in catalysing the growth of ASEAN manufacturing exports, explained by the 'flying geese' model of shifting comparative advantage (Sally and Sen 2005). However, with the advent of the 1997–1998 financial crisis and Japan's prolonged period of economic recession, the ASEAN countries experienced a significant slowdown in FDI inflows. At the same time economic surge of China and, to a certain extent, of India, as competing destinations for FDI, also saw ASEAN countries suffer from a slowdown in FDI inflows (Table 8.4). In 1990, while the ASEAN countries attracted most of the FDI flows among the developing economies, the share went down in 1995 and 2000. China gained prominence as a key FDI destination by the late 1990s. It was only in the 2000s when the ASEAN countries paid attention to economic integration to provide economies of scale and streamlined cross-border flows, that the share of FDI flows again picked up some momentum. By 2014, the share of ASEAN is at par with the Chinese share of investment flows in the country. Hence, economic integration in a bigger geography via RCEP is viewed positively for FDI flows among the ASEAN policymakers.

Table 8.3 Merchandise trade (% share of world trade)

	1980	1985	1990	1995	2000	2005	2010	2015	2016
Indonesia	0.8	0.7	0.7	0.8	0.8	0.8	1.0	0.9	0.9
Malaysia	0.6	0.7	0.8	1.5	1.4	1.2	1.2	1.1	1.1
Philippines	0.3	0.3	0.3	0.4	0.6	0.4	0.4	0.4	0.4
Singapore	1.1	1.2	1.6	2.3	2.1	2.0	2.2	1.9	1.9
Thailand	0.4	0.4	0.8	1.2	1.0	1.1	1.2	1.3	1.3
Vietnam	0.0	0.1	0.1	0.1	0.2	0.3	0.5	1.0	1.1
ASEAN	**3.2**	**3.4**	**4.3**	**6.4**	**6.1**	**5.8**	**6.4**	**6.6**	**6.7**
Australia	1.1	1.2	1.2	1.1	1.0	1.1	1.3	1.2	1.2
China	**0.9**	**1.8**	**1.6**	**2.7**	**3.6**	**6.7**	**9.7**	**11.9**	**11.5**
India	0.6	0.6	0.6	0.6	0.7	1.1	1.9	2.0	1.9
Japan	**6.6**	**7.8**	**7.4**	**7.5**	**6.5**	**5.2**	**4.8**	**3.8**	**3.9**
New Zealand	0.3	0.3	0.3	0.3	0.2	0.2	0.2	0.2	0.2
South Korea	1.0	1.5	1.9	2.5	2.5	2.6	2.9	2.9	2.8

Source: WTO Trade Database, author's calculation.

Table 8.4 FDI Inflows in ASEAN, China and India (US$ billion)

Year	ASEAN	China	India	Developing economies
1990	12.8 (37%)	3.5 (10.1%)	0.2 (0.7%)	34.6
1995	28.6 (24.3%)	37.5 (31.9%)	2.2 (1.8%)	117.8
2000	22.5 (9.7%)	40.7 (17.5%)	3.6 (1.5%)	232.2
2005	43.2 (13.1%)	72.4 (21.9%)	7.6 (2.3%)	330.2
2010	105.1 (18.1%)	114.7 (19.8%)	27.4 (4.7%)	579.9
2014	132.8 (19.5)	128.5 (18.9%)	34.4 (5.1%)	681.4
2015	126.6 (16.8%)	135.6 (18.0%)	44.1 (5.8%)	752.3
2016	101.1 (15.6%)	133.7 (20.7%)	44.5 (6.9%)	646.0

Source: UNCTAD (various issues), author's calculation.

Note: Figures in parentheses denotes share of FDI flows to total flows to developing countries.

RCEP strengthens ASEAN countries participation in East Asia production network

Strengthening participation in the regional production network, thereby increasing trade volume, is also an important consideration for ASEAN countries to become part of the RCEP deal. The ASEAN countries are part of a larger East Asian regional production network process since the beginning of the 1990s. There are three key characteristics of this East Asia's engagement in production networks (mentioned as network trade), as described by Athukorala (2013). First, development of production network in the Asian region can be traced back to 1968, when the US MNCs set up their operations in Singapore and later relocated their production facilities to Malaysia, Thailand and the Philippines, to take advantage of lower cost. However, the phenomenon picked up steam when China emerged as a 'global factory' in the early 1990s. China's performance as a destination of final assembly, based on imported parts and components (P&C) from neighbouring countries, assumes importance in this respect. More recently, the production networks saw gradual expansion to Vietnam. Over time, the development of production network led to a new form of division of labour among countries in East Asia, especially on the basis of their skill differences, relative wages and communication and transport infrastructure.

Second, the share of East Asia in world network trade increased from 32 percent in the early 1990s to more than 40 percent more recently, implying that the region is an active participant in this new form of production. Within East Asia, China has been a major driving force in network trade. The shares of advanced ASEAN countries also went up during this period, except for Singapore. The decline in Singapore's share reflects on its changing role in production network: from assembly and testing activities to managerial functions, product design and technology-intensive augment of production (Athukorala 2008).

Third, the P&C account for a much larger share in network trade across all countries in the region. Except for China and Thailand, P&C account for

Table 8.5 Intra- and extra-ASEAN Trade (% of total trade)

	Indon	Mal	Php	Sing	Thai	Viet	A-5	Aus	China	India	Japan	N. Z.	S. K
Indon	–	5.5	1.6	10.5	4.6	2.0	**24.2**	2.9	15.2	4.9	10.7	0.4	5.5
Mal	4.1	–	1.3	13.0	5.9	2.5	**26.8**	3.1	15.8	3.2	8.7	0.5	3.8
Php	2.9	3.5	–	6.6	5.2	1.6	**19.8**	1.0	13.9	1.3	14.9	0.3	5.5
Sing	6.6	11.0	1.7	–	3.3	2.4	**25.0**	2.3	14.0	2.5	5.3	0.4	5.1
Thai	3.4	5.3	2.0	3.8	–	3.1	**17.6**	3.3	15.6	1.9	12.3	0.5	2.7
Viet	1.7	2.4	0.9	2.8	3.5	–	**11.3**	1.5	20.1	1.6	8.6	0.2	11.1

Source: The ASEAN Secretariat Statistical Publication and author's calculation.

more than 50 percent of total network export. The P&C share is particularly high for ASEAN countries. Moreover, the share of P&C is higher in imports vis-à-vis exports, implying that although the East Asian countries depend on their neighbours as markets for P&C, they rely on the rest of the world as a market for the final products.

All these reflect that a key reason for ASEAN countries to negotiate RCEP derives from its intention to participate effectively in the regional production networks. This implies that for the ASEAN countries, economic integration is important not only among each other but also with broader Asian region (Table 8.5). For example, Indonesia's intra-ASEAN-5 trade share is 24 percent, while that with Japan, China and South Korea put together is 31.5 percent. Similarly, Thailand's trade within the ASEAN-5 countries is 18 percent, vis-à-vis 30 percent with the Northeast Asian countries.

RCEP- a tool to lower non-tariff barriers (NTBs) in the region

Other than tariffs, NTBs both at the border and beyond the border impede trade flows. Literature suggests the importance of strong institutions in lowering trade costs through higher transparency, simplification of trade procedures and greater predictability (Helble, Shepherd, and Wilson 2009). Therefore, in addition to lowering border tariffs, it is crucial to eliminate or streamline the NTBs that are discriminating in nature and cover issues like diverse product standards, lack of transparency in trade procedures, weak enforcement of government regulations and the logistics gaps among the economies. Although removal of NTBs is promised in several of the ASEAN initiatives, there seems to be lack of political will to implement such commitments. Hence, NTBs are mentioned as the most difficult impediments for cross-border movement of goods (Intal et al. 2014; World Bank and ASEAN Secretariat 2013).

The prevalence of NTBs can also be observed in the latest data provided by the World Economic Forum (2016) *Enabling Trade Report. The data* compares the quality of institutions, policies and services that facilitate the cross-border flow across 136 countries. It can be observed that among the ASEAN-6 countries, Singapore has the most liberalized trading environment, with transparency in cross-border procedures. International trade

Table 8.6 Enabling trade index rankings, 2016

Ranking out of 136 countries	Enabling trade index 2016 ranking	Market access sub-index		Border administration sub-index	Transport infrastructure sub-index	Operating environment sub-index
		Domestic market access	Foreign market access			
Indonesia	70	30	92	79	64	64
Malaysia	37	43	107	47	17	26
Philippines	82	22	39	93	116	104
Singapore	1	2	84	1	3	2
Thailand	63	88	96	44	35	83
Vietnam	73	77	79	86	66	77
Australia	26	15	127	32	20	21
China	61	101	124	52	12	42
India	102	135	117	75	28	76
Japan	16	47	133	11	5	14
New Zealand	18	6	111	23	41	8
S. Korea	27	85	105	28	11	47

Source: World Economic Forum (2016).

is also well-supported by a strong infrastructure and business-operating environment in the city-state. Malaysia is also fairly perceived in terms of its institutional quality for facilitating trade with an overall ranking of 37. Among the four sub-indices, it is found that Vietnam and Thailand perform poorly with respect to allowing domestic market access. In terms of efficiency and transparency of border administration, most of the ASEAN-6 members, with an exception of Singapore, perform poorly. The same could be said for infrastructure and business-operating environment in the region (Table 8.6).

Among the non-ASEAN RCEP countries, apart from China and India, most of the countries rank decently in the overall enabling trade index. China and India, the two largest markets as RCEP members, particularly perform poorly in terms of domestic market access. In relative terms, India ranks the lowest for border administration and general operating environment for international commerce.

The ASEAN countries expect RCEP to address the issue of NTBs that exist both at the border and beyond the border among the participating members.

RCEP helps to multilateralise the existing ASEAN FTAs

Since the early 1990s, the ASEAN countries have been working on many bilateral and regional FTAs. The countries started on their idea of ASEAN FTA in 1993, which they subsequently widened to include services sector liberalization through ASEAN Framework Agreement on

Services (AFAS) in 1995 and investment liberalization through ASEAN Investment Area (AIA) in 1998. AFTA, AFAS and AIA later got subsumed under ASEAN's overarching vision of an ASEAN Economic Community (AEC).

Since 2000, the ten ASEAN countries have been together pursuing FTAs with Australia-New Zealand, China, India, Japan and South Korea. They have also been signing bilateral FTAs individually with distant partners like the US, India, the Middle East and the Australia-New Zealand markets. Among the ASEAN member countries, Singapore has the largest number of FTAs that are in effect currently. This is followed by Malaysia and Thailand, who have enacted 12 FTAs each.

Despite starting the process 20 years back, the economic integration in ASEAN is said to be limited. The final users felt that ASEAN integration is yet to provide an arrangement of seamless movement of goods and services. While tariffs have been reduced, NTBs are prevalent in the region. Services sector liberalization has been restricted by challenges in market access and movement of people. Further issues evolved from uneven implementation of AEC commitments.

As for the ASEAN+1 FTAs, they differ from each other, depending on a country's interest. Japan may look for trade and investment liberalization and facilitation as such measures would provide free, transparent and stable business environment for Japanese firms that participate in production networks of Asia. While Singapore, Japan and Korea may push for intellectual property rights, developing countries of ASEAN, China and India may have less interest in the protection system. India could be keener on liberalizing services trade, for example, IT software, legal, financial and medical services, compared to opening up its goods sector. This leads to significant differences between the ASEAN+1 FTAs. The ASEAN+1 FTAs are signed and negotiated over different points of time. Each ASEAN+1 FTA differs in terms of way of negotiation and economic coverage.

Following the issues with ASEAN integration and ASEAN+1 FTAs, it was found that the utilization rate of such initiatives by the private sector remained low. In a survey of 841 export-oriented firms by the Asian Development Bank Institute (ADBI), it was found that while Chinese firms have relatively higher usage rate at 45 percent, Japanese and Korean firms are at 29 percent and 21 percent, respectively. Among the ASEAN countries, fewer firms make use of the FTAs – Thailand (25 percent), the Philippines (20 percent) and Singapore (17 percent). Companies reported that the reasons for not using FTAs were lack of information, low margin of preference, prevalence of NTBs, exclusion list, multiple Rules of origin (RoOs) derived from numerous FTAs in the region and administrative costs (Kawai and Wignaraja 2011).

RCEP is expected to address the issue of multiple FTAs in the region as also their multiple RoOs. By multilateralising the trade agreement, RCEP is said to minimize the business cost on the region.

RCEP serves strategic priorities[1]

Besides economics, RCEP serves several strategic imperatives for the ASEAN countries. This section elaborates on three such strategic rationales of RCEP.

RCEP combines ASEAN+3 and ASEAN+6 configurations

Since 2001, the East Asian countries have been thinking of a region-wide FTA. A high-level policy group, called the East Asia Vision Group (EAVG), suggested an association of ASEAN+3 countries (also known as East Asia FTA (EAFTA)), comprising of the ten ASEAN members and China, Japan and South Korea. In 2004, a feasibility study was undertaken under Beijing's leadership, which later concluded that economic benefits from East Asian FTA (EAFTA) would exceed AFTA, any ASEAN+1 FTA or other bilateral and sub-regional arrangements.[2] The report recommended that an EAFTA should be comprehensive in nature and should be of high standard. It should be negotiated and implemented as a single undertaking. The report further recommended that an EAFTA, once formed among the ASEAN+3 countries, can be extended to other countries in the region. Although the EAVG urged East Asian leaders to start the process of forming an EAFTA soon, there was not much subsequent discussion after that.

In 2009, as the world economy felt the 2008 global economic crisis and the regional economies witnessed limited benefits from proliferation of FTAs, South Korea took a lead to conduct the second phase of EAFTA study. The study recommended that EAFTA would help enhance the resilience of the East Asian regional economy against external shocks and sustain regional economic growth. It could also help overcome the problems caused by the proliferation of FTAs with differing RoOs and overlapping agreements that have resulted in increasing transaction costs for intra-regional trade and raising production costs for production networks in East Asia. It further recommended that EAFTA should follow a gradual and realistic strategy and must begin with the consolidation of the existing three ASEAN+1 FTAs. The report attached importance on the concrete trade and investment facilitation measures which could help all participating economies to fully realize the benefits of an EAFTA.[3]

In the meantime, in 2006, Japan proposed an alternative approach, the Comprehensive Economic Partnership of East Asia (CEPEA), based on the ASEAN+6 framework with India, Australia and New Zealand as additional members. A study group was set up in 2007 to prepare a report of recommendations for the ASEAN+6 Economic Ministers. The report, presented in 2008, argued that a wider regional economic partnership that included India, Australia and New Zealand would create larger gains than any other regional FTA.[4] The study sets out CEPEA's objectives as deepening economic integration, narrowing development gaps, and achieving sustainable development through the three pillars of economic cooperation, facilitation of trade and investment, and liberalization of trade and investment as well as institutional developments.[5]

Following these studies, during the Fourth East Asia Summit in October 2009, officials were tasked to consider the recommendations of both EAFTA and CEPEA studies. In August 2011, East Asia Summit Economic Ministers welcomed a Chinese and Japanese joint 'Initiative on Speeding up the Establishment of EAFTA and CEPEA'. To end the discussion around different ASEAN+3 and ASEAN+6 regional architecture, in November 2011, ASEAN proposed its own model for an ASEAN-centric regional FTA, called the RCEP.

RCEP was created in reaction to TPP

Besides the debate over EAFTA and CEPEA, ASEAN also felt external pressure through another Asia-Pacific trade arrangement, namely TPP. In 2011, the agreement was led by the US and was announced as a 'gold standard' FTA. The grand promotion of the agreement on its potential benefits and real opportunity costs of trade liberalization seemed to have cornered ASEAN states. It seemed to have swept away the ASEAN-centred pattern of 'plus' diplomacy that had underpinned Asian regionalism for long (ASEAN+1, ASEAN+3 or ASEAN+6 and later +8). Moreover, it was felt that the US was not interested in promoting regional trade integration with ASEAN countries as a group. While China, India, Australia-New Zealand, Japan and Korea have enacted FTAs with ASEAN and the EU has been proposing an FTA with ASEAN as well, the US has not discussed the possibility of a US-ASEAN FTA. Instead, the US went for bilateral FTAs with Singapore and other selected ASEAN countries under the framework of TPP. This reflects US' interests over high-level FTAs with comprehensive coverage and its view on the lack of preparedness of some ASEAN countries to participate in such FTAs. Even the older forum of APEC that was supported by the US and connected the US to Asia includes only seven ASEAN members – Brunei, Indonesia, Malaysia, the Philippines, Singapore, Thailand and Vietnam.[6]

RCEP strengthens ASEAN's unity and centrality

RCEP showcases ASEAN's principle of 'all for one and one for all', as a key component of its foreign economic relations. The flexibility principle in the RCEP, such as 'the agreement can be accomplished in a sequential manner or single undertaking or through any other agreed modality' and 'the agreement shall provide for special and differential treatment to the ASEAN Member States'[7] provides a more generous consideration of each state's development needs. The political leaders believe that ASEAN needs to forge closer ties, forming common positions on numerous issues, in order to negotiate with bigger economic partners or other regional groupings. Hence, through RCEP, ASEAN is able to further entrench its centrality, which is an idea that the regional architecture is led by ASEAN and the region's relations with the wider world are conducted keeping in mind the interest of the ASEAN community. This aspect was severely challenged amid the rapid pace of regional economic cooperation arrangements evolving in the region. The RCEP, once concluded, is expected to demonstrate ASEAN's capability to bring together its own ten members and external partners for economic growth, development and harmonization.

Contentious issues in RCEP negotiation

The RCEP negotiation has been going on for the past five years and this itself portrays the underlying challenges in the trade deal. From the beginning it was clear that RCEP is the first of its kind and has no other precedent to emulate. It primarily engages developing countries and involves three different dynamics among its participating members. These are – the ten ASEAN members, ASEAN and its FTA partners and the six FTA partners. While the ten ASEAN members have been working together on economic integration since the 1990s, ASEAN, as a region and as individual countries, has been working with the FTA partners since 2000. It is the six FTA partners that may not have existing trade agreements with one another and this has become a critical problem for negotiation between China and India. The following points below provides some of the challenges in RCEP negotiation.

Coverage under Trade in Goods – In most FTA negotiations, issues related to coverage, that is, the proportion of products that will be included in the agreement, pose a substantive challenge. While all participating members agree with the benefits of market access liberalization measures, they also face domestic pressure to limit competition in their home markets (Chandra 2008; Milner 1997). While the RCEP comprises a country like Singapore, which is least concerned with liberalization, it also includes countries like Indonesia and India, which are likely to make market access negotiations difficult. Hence, although RCEP negotiations are happening under immense confidentiality, there are murmurings that for trade in goods anything between 80 percent and 92 percent seems plausible.[8] ASEAN is proposing for 92 percent, but there is resistance from participating countries that have growing trade deficits with China. There are also industries like sugar, steel and textile that some countries desire to protect from competition.

Mismatch in economic interest – It has been well-documented for long that trade brings benefit by permitting countries to export goods that they have as their comparative advantage. Trade may suffer if the countries have competing interest. RCEP negotiation suffers from such mismatch of interests. While for a large proportion of ASEAN countries comparative advantage lies in manufacturing activities, India's strength is in services. For India, trade in goods is limited as manufacturing and agriculture sectors are less competitive and the domestic market is considered as enough to generate income. Most regularly, it was felt that liberalizing merchandise trade results in a larger jump in imports versus exports, leading to trade deficit at least in the short-run.[9] Alternatively, India has a comparative advantage in information technology, telecom services, financial and tourism services. In 2015, it ran a services trade surplus of US$33 billion with the world, compared to US$2.2 billion surplus of ASEAN countries. This mismatch in priorities leads to difficulties in trade deals between ASEAN and India. It took six long years to negotiate ASEAN-India Trade in Goods Agreement and services and investment negotiations were concluded much later. Till now, most of the ASEAN's trade agreements focused on goods and paid limited attention to services. Trade in services, in particular, is vulnerable to international competition and involves many regulatory barriers.

Issue of Development Gap – RCEP participating members show a significant degree of development gap. These gaps are not only observed in terms of differences in GDP per capita, but also in terms of human development indicators such as life expectancy, literacy, public expenditure on health and education and poverty. In terms of per capita income, the difference is particularly pronounced between the less developed ASEAN member countries and mature economies like Korea, Australia, Singapore, New Zealand and Japan. Vo (2005) has raised concerns that any kind of deeper economic integration could lead to huge social costs incurred by the less developed economies of ASEAN. This could be due to structural adjustments and the risks of falling into a low-cost labour trap. Hence, there is pressure from the less developed ASEAN countries to give due consideration to their development stages. Appropriate resources should also be allocated to these economies to build soft and hard infrastructure. Although RCEP mentions a flexibility clause from the beginning to take into account such differences, the clause itself cannot be an excuse for a low-quality trade agreement. The act of having to balance a high-quality agreement with some degree of flexibility for less developed members prolongs the negotiation.

Other Issues – The investment chapter remains controversial over the issue of investor-state dispute settlement (ISDS), where the private sector gets to file lawsuits against the state. It has been reported that there are currently 50 lawsuits worth US$31 billion at international arbitration tribunals against the governments participating in RCEP negotiation.[10] Countries like India, Indonesia and Australia would like to reconsider the ISDS mechanism before RCEP strengthens the rights of investors.

The Intellectual Property Rights (IPR) chapter is contentious as it is said to be demanding for data exclusivity, which is likely to delay regulatory approval for medicines that go off patent.[11] A provision like this goes beyond the WTO agreement on Trade-Related Aspects of IPR. This is problematic for less developed countries who are highly dependent on accessibility of

affordable medicines. This also adversely affects countries that are producers of generic medicines.

RCEP negotiations have also been criticized over import of TPP text
into the agreement. This is possible as seven of the RCEP members are also
part of the TPP deal. A leaked draft of RCEP text has shown an extensive
similarity between TPP and RCEP over ISDS, telecommunication chapter,
e-commerce and IPR.[12] It is feared that as all RCEP members are developing
economies, it is difficult for them to comply with rules similar to TPP. In addition, it is unfair to make RCEP an incubator for WTO-plus commitments.

Conclusion

ASEAN has been negotiating RCEP since 2013. The main idea was to ad-
vance the five different ASEAN FTAs with Australia-New Zealand, China,
India, South Korea and Japan under a single framework. The objective was
to craft a multilateral trade deal that is both high quality and comprehensive in nature. However, like other ASEAN FTAs, RCEP started with the
resolution of giving due consideration to the development stage of participating members. This includes flexibility principle and capacity building
clause for less developed ASEAN members.

For ASEAN countries, trade agreement like RCEP, is of immense importance. In fact, for most of the ASEAN-6 countries, merchandise trade share
as percent of GDP is more than 100 percent, and much higher when compared to non-ASEAN RCEP participants. FDI is crucial for the economic
development of these countries. Related to trade and investment, ASEAN's
interest in RCEP derives from the countries' participation in the production network that is spread across the broader Asia-Pacific region. For these
countries', economic integration among themselves is as important as their
integration in the broader region.

RCEP is also important to address the NTBs that exist both at the border and beyond the border among the participating members. These NTBs
are discriminating in nature and are the most difficult impediments for
cross-border trade and investment. Although removal of NTBs is mentioned
in several ASEAN FTAs, there is lack of political will to comply with such
commitments. Finally, RCEP is expected to address the issue of multiple
FTAs in the region that is discouraging the private sector from using them.
The private sector not only has to spend resources to understand the characteristics of the FTAs, but also has to comply with their different rules and
regulations. This raises the business cost, thereby going against the primary
function of trade agreements.

In addition to the economic rationale, RCEP serves several strategic imperatives of the ASEAN countries. The mega-deal combines the discussion
of trade architecture around ASEAN+3 and ASEAN+6 and strengthens
ASEAN's unity and centrality. It also positions an Asia-centric deal, show-
casing the economic weight of the region in the global economy. This seemed

to be under threat when TPP was introduced as a high-quality agreement connecting the US to Asia.

Despite its importance to ASEAN economies, there are several challenges to be addressed before the final negotiation outcome. These can be observed across several issues – trade in goods and services, investment, intellectual property rights and many others. The issues emerge because of the development gap among RCEP participating members and lack of bilateral trade agreements among the non-ASEAN RCEP members.

There is immense pressure on countries to conclude RCEP negotiation in 2018. This is more so as RCEP is meant to symbolize that Asia is keen on trade and is open for business. It also indicates that despite the discussion of creeping protectionism in the West, the RCEP participating countries continue to see trade as a tool to increase competition, transfer technology and upgrade skills for their higher productivity.

In the end, time will only tell how and when RCEP will be eventually formulated. While the countries need to understand the long-term importance of the trade pact in their domestic economies and accordingly make compromises during negotiation, they should also be clear in their mind that it is the implementation integrity eventually that will materialize the potential benefits of RCEP.

Notes

1 This section draws from Basu Das (2014).
2 Joint Expert Group for Feasibility Study on EAFTA, Towards an East Asian FTA: Modality and Roadmap, 2006 (www.thaifta.com/thaifta/Portals/0/eafta_report.pdf).
3 Joint Expert Group on EAFTA Phase II Study, Desirable and Feasible Option for an East Asia FTA: A Report, Monograph, 2009 (www.thaifta.com/thaifta/Portals/0/eafta_phase2.pdf).
4 According to the Global Trade Analysis Project (GTAP) model, EAFTA would result in a 1.93 percent increase of gross domestic product, while CEPEA would result in a 2.05 percent increase in gross domestic product (CEPEA Track Two Study Group 2009).
5 Phase II Report of the Track Two Study Group on Comprehensive Economic Partnership in East Asia, 2009. (www.dfat.gov.au/asean/eas/cepea-phase-2-report.pdf).
6 When APEC was established in 1989, ASEAN comprised of only five members – Indonesia, Malaysia, The Philippines, Singapore and Thailand. Brunei became a member in 1984, Vietnam in 1995, Laos and Myanmar in 1997 and Cambodia in 1999.
7 ASEAN Framework for Regional Comprehensive Economic Partnership (ASEAN Secretariat, 2011).
8 www.bworldonline.com/content.php?section=Economy&title=rcep-countries-seek-free-trade-in-up-to-92%25-of-all-product-types&id=137426.
9 In case of ASEAN-India, in the post FTA era of 2010, India's trade deficit with ASEAN went up from US$7.6 billion in 2009/10 to US$14.8 billion in 2015/16. ASEAN's share in India's total trade deficit has gone up from 7 percent to 12 percent during this time.

10 www.tni.org/en/publication/the-hidden-costs-of-rcep-and-corporate-trade-deals-in-asia.
11 www.bilaterals.org/?the-indian-government-needs-to.
12 http://m.themalaymailonline.com/what-you-think/article/tpp-rules-in-rcep-must-be-rejected-civil-society-organisations.

References

ASEAN Secretariat (2011). 'ASEAN Framework for Regional Comprehensive Economic Partnership' (http://asean.org/?static_post=asean-framework-for-regional-comprehensive-economic-partnership

ASEAN Secretariat (2012). 'Guiding Principles and Objectives for Negotiating the Regional Comprehensive Economic Partnership' (http://asean.org/storage/2012/05/RCEP-Guiding-Principles-public-copy.pdf)

ASEAN Secretariat and World Bank (2013). *ASEAN Integration Monitoring Report (AIMR)*, Jakarta and Washington.

Athukorala, P.-C. (2013). 'Global Production Sharing and Trade Patterns in East Asia', *Working Papers in Trade and Development No. 2013/10*, Crawford School of Public Policy, ANU College of Asia and the Pacific, June.

Athukorala, P.C. (2008), 'Singapore and ASEAN in the New Regional Division of Labour'. *Singapore Economic Review,* 53(3): 479–508.

Basu Das, S. (2014). *The Political Economy of the Regional Comprehensive Economic Partnership (RCEP) and the Transpacific Partnership (TPP) Agreements: An ASEAN Perspective.* ISEAS Trends 2014 #2, Singapore: Institute of Southeast Asian Studies.

Chandra, A.C. (2008). *Indonesia and ASEAN Free Trade Agreement: nationalist and regional integration strategy*, Lanham: Lexington Books.

Helble, M., Shepherd, B., and Wilson, J.S. (2009). 'Transparency and regional integration in the Asia-Pacific'. *World Economy,* 32(3), 479–508.

Intal, P., Fukunaga, Y., Kimura, F., Han, P., Dee, P., Narjoko, D., and Oum, S. (2014). *ASEAN Rising: ASEAN and AEC Beyond 2015*, Jakarta: Economic Research Institute for ASEAN and East Asia (ERIA).

Kawai, M., and Wignaraja, G. (2011). 'Main Findings and Policy Recommendations' in M. Kawai and G. Wignaraja (Eds.), *Asia's Free Trade Agreements: How is Business Responding?* Asian Development Bank, ADBI and Edward Elgar, Cheltenham, UK & Northampton, MA, USA. pp. 33–75.

Milner, H.V. (1997). *Interests, Institutions and Information: Domestic Politics and International relations.* Princeton, NJ: Princeton University Press.

Sally, R., and Sen, R. (2005). 'Whither Trade Policies in Southeast Asia? The Wider Asian and Global Context'. *ASEAN Economic Bulletin,* 22(1): 92–115.

World Economic Forum (2016), *The Global Enabling Trade Report.* Geneva: The World Economic Forum.

9 Regional Comprehensive Economic Partnership

Prospects and implications for CLMV

Vo Tri Thanh

Introduction

During the past five decades, the Association of South East Asian Nations (ASEAN) has made significant progress in regional integration. First, ASEAN has radically transformed itself from a set of countries in Southeast Asia to one "inspired by and united under One Vision, One Identity and One Caring and Sharing Community" (ASEAN Charter). Second, ASEAN moved progressively from a less developed region to a much more prosperous and a most dynamic region and a "hub" for global trade and investment. As noted by Economic Research Institute for ASEAN and East Asia (ERIA 2014: 5), "CLMV growth story is one ASEAN success story with lessons... on the potential benefits of economic integration". Third, from "divided" stances, ASEAN has gradually become a community which is internationally recognized with the role of "centrality" in initiating and developing regional architectures. This process has also been arguably inclusive, with increasing engagement of and shared benefits for less developed members such as Cambodia, Laos, Myanmar, and Vietnam (CLMV). In return, efforts to promote ASEAN integration also contributed to narrowing the development gap in the region, which has for long been another pillar of regional integration.

The declared establishment of ASEAN Community at the end of 2015 marks no end to ASEAN integration process. Upon deepening its mandate and contribution, ASEAN still encounters several major challenges. Adhering to its vision by 2025[1] may be less than fully accommodated, even impeded, by major international trends, such as a multipolar world and geopolitical pressure, aging population, technological revolution, clashes of mega-FTAs, and the emergence of Asian powerhouses, etc. Boosting the development of CLMV to catch up more swiftly with more advanced ASEAN members poses another challenge, as this process cannot preclude competition that comes as a consequence of further trade and investment liberalization.

In this context, the Regional Comprehensive Economic Partnership (RCEP) might add another substance to the evolvement of ASEAN. Depending on its structure and timeline for implementation, in particular,

RCEP may alter the development prospects of CLMV – those with arguably less capacity to mitigate adverse impacts from economic integration. This chapter thus looks into the potential impacts and prospect of RCEP and its associated implications to CLMV.

The remainder of this chapter is structured as follows. Section 2 briefs the evolutions and arrangement of RCEP. Section 3 discusses the potential impacts of RCEP on the CLMV. Section 4 elaborates on the major issues and challenges to the CLMV. Section 5 contains the concluding remarks.

RCEP: evolutions and potential arrangement

Evolutions

RCEP is an ambitious project which aims to achieve a comprehensive economic partnership between ASEAN and the six traditional partners, namely, China, Japan, Korea, Australia, New Zealand, and India. The negotiation process of RCEP was formally kicked off in 2012. The proposed RCEP area will be the largest in terms of population, with a combined GDP of around USD 19 trillion.

RCEP is a new regional free trade agreement (FTA), yet the underlying idea of this arrangement is not new. In fact, it reflects an upgradation of the idea toward liberalization under the East Asian framework, either in the form of ASEAN + 3 or Comprehensive Economic Partnership in East Asia (CEPEA). Besides, RCEP is also in line with the proposal of East Asian Community, whereby a continuation of Centric Circle Strategy is made from ASEAN integration to ASEAN-plus process.

ASEAN-centered and driven RCEP

In all ASEAN member countries, both the poverty rate and income gap have been decreasing sharply. At the same time, the share of the middle-income class is rising. The relatively more impressive growth performance of the CLMV countries has led to a narrower development gap between the CLMV and the ASEAN-6 (Brunei Darussalam, Indonesia, Malaysia, the Philippines, Singapore, and Thailand) during the past decade (Table 9.1). This observation is even more meaningful as the average economic growth rate of the ASEAN-6 has been respectable during the 1996–2011 period. As a reflection, the growth process in the ASEAN region and within each member state has been inclusive. More importantly, there remains ample room for the CLMV to further strengthen its efforts.

ASEAN's GDP growth performance is explained partly – but significantly – by the modality and template of ASEAN's integration itself. Specifically, the realization process of the AEC has several fundamental elements. The progressive and transparent liberalization of merchandise trade, services trade, and investment plays a pivotal role in creating more opportunities.

Table 9.1 Average GDP growth (%), 1996–2016

	1996–2000	2001–2005	2006–2011	2011–2016
Brunei	1.35	2.08	0.94	−0.48
Cambodia	**7.18**	**9.36**	**6.80**	**7.22**[*]
Indonesia	1.06	4.71	5.86	5.44
Lao PDR	**6.17**	**6.33**	**7.99**	**7.87**[*]
Malaysia	4.99	4.76	4.57	5.11
Myanmar	**8.35**	**12.87**	**10.30**	–
Philippines	3.59	4.60	4.75	6.08
Singapore	5.84	4.83	6.33	3.76
Thailand	0.87	5.45	3.09	2.96
Vietnam	**6.96**	**7.51**	**6.83**	**5.96**

Source: Data for 2006–2011 are cited in ERIA (2014). Data for 2011–2016 are calculated from IMF International Financial Statistics.

Note: [*]: For 2011–2014 only.

Such liberalization at the border is complemented by joint and harmonized efforts to facilitate trade and investment at behind-the-border level. That is, ASEAN member countries should seek to reduce transaction costs associated with production networks and value chains. In another direction, coordinated connectivity enhancement constitutes an important work agenda for the Master Plan for ASEAN Connectivity (MPAC) to 2025. This agenda is wide-ranging, resting on a three-pronged approach to promote the development of institutional connectivity, physical connectivity, and people-to-people connectivity. Ultimately, this agenda will work towards the easier access to new opportunities and reduction of transaction costs. Besides, development cooperation is asserted as a framework for capacity building efforts. The substance of development cooperation is specifically tailored to support the ASEAN integration process (Vo and Nguyen 2010).

Notwithstanding the limited information on the detailed progress of RCEP negotiation and position of each member economy, there are several aspects of RCEP that can be envisaged. First, although the structure of the RCEP remains ambiguous – especially on whether the arrangement involves a hub-and-spoke structure – ASEAN remains the driving force for the process. The AEC Blueprint (2007: 33) states that "ASEAN shall work towards maintaining 'ASEAN Centrality' in its external economic relations, including but not limited to, its negotiations for FTAs and CEPs agreements". More importantly, as argued in the Expert Roundtable for RCEP in May 2013, the agreement needs to be consistent with the AEC's four pillars. These requirements have a couple of implications. On the one hand, ASEAN should play an active leading role in coordinating and harmonizing integration commitments with different partners. On the other hand, the development levels and needs of the CLMV countries should be maximally addressed so that ASEAN adheres closely to its objective of reducing the intra-regional development gap, among others.

In another aspect, the RCEP should be appropriately designed to attain "significant improvements over the existing ASEAN+1 FTAs". The Guiding Principles and Objectives of the RCEP are already aligned with this purpose, specifically to achieve a modern, comprehensive, high-quality, and mutually beneficial economic partnership agreement among ASEAN members and ASEAN's FTA partners. The Guiding Principles and Objectives still reflect some ambiguities, particularly about the meaning of "significant improvements" over the existing ASEAN+1 FTAs and whether the RCEP allows for a hub-and-spoke structure. Nonetheless, the RCEP also reflects the substance of flexibility, which by no means contradicts the gradualism approach of ASEAN. The process may take some time, but the cumulative progress so far can certainly compensate for the wait. In fact, liberalization levels under ASEAN Economic Community (AEC) in terms of trade in goods and services as well as investment are the highest in East Asia, particularly compared with most of the ASEAN +1 FTAs (ERIA 2014).

From ASEAN's experience, merely focusing on the traditional liberalization of goods and services trade may not help realize the full benefits of economic integration. Various surveys by ERIA on NTMs and the utilization of FTAs already show major impediments to such a realization process. In this regard emerges room for more meaningful liberalization by increasing efforts toward trade and investment facilitation. Therefore, the RCEP also needs to concretize trade facilitation programs that can strengthen regional production networks. Similarly, ASEAN and its partners need to commit to a development and cooperation agenda that is tied to connectivity under the RCEP. For consistency, this enhancement of connectivity should be built upon the past and renewed MPAC. More importantly, the framework for development cooperation under the RCEP should also incorporate substances of inclusivity and sustainability.

Potential impact of RCEP

Several studies have attempted to quantify the economic impacts of RCEP. Itakura (2012) presents the simulation results that show greater benefits for ASEAN member countries if East Asian economic integration attains more depth. Specifically, the benefits were quite small with ASEAN Free Trade Area alone. Meanwhile, the scenario with all members of RCEP liberalizing trade among themselves will lead to the largest projected benefits for all ASEAN members. This finding should make sense, as the largest scope of trade and investment liberalization will enhance transparency and consolidate the production network that is already in operation in the RCEP region.

Petri and Plummer (2013) provide an extract of the projected income gains for various countries/regions under RCEP, TPP, and a broader economic integration in the Asia-Pacific (Free Trade Area of Asia-Pacific (FTAAP)). Evidently, RCEP, TPP, and FTAAP have different impacts, including trade diversion, on all major economies. Asian economies reap the majority of benefits under all scenarios, though the benefits are understandably larger under FTAAP (relative to RCEP and TPP). The FTA for the whole Asia-Pacific region will provide the ideal case, with benefits being several times larger than those under RCEP. This result is also consistent with the expectation as distortions-related trade diversions are smaller under FTAAP (widest membership) than under RCEP.

Several considerations of the above-simulated benefits are noteworthy. First, the figures may overestimate the actual net benefits due to: (i) the overlapping of RCEP and FTAAP (among themselves and with existing ones) that induce a complex web of commitments and arrangements with huge distortions to all economies; and (ii) the use of maximal liberalization commitment under each scenario which may not happen in practice. Meanwhile, the benefits could arguably be larger since the domestic institutional reforms accompanying the implementation of FTAs – which leads to more opportunities and/or better capacity to realize those opportunities by economic agents – are excluded from the model-based quantitative analysis.

Second, RCEP leads to minimal extent of distortion and trade diversion, thanks to its wide membership, thus making way for ample benefits for member economies. Nevertheless, even if the agreement is agreed upon and comes into force, it still runs the risk of producing unequal benefits for different members. As an instance, Table 9.1 shows that under RCEP some countries could acquire small income gain of less than 2 percent (compared with baseline), while the top gain could be up to 11.5 percent (relative to baseline).

Finally, the possibility of RCEP achieving a more rigorous and comprehensive set of commitments remains a major question. Kawasaki (2017) estimates that the benefits induced by RCEP could be much smaller than that by TPP 12 if RCEP arrangement does not cover NTM reductions. This could be explained by the depth of commitments under TPP, should it come into force, which covers reduction of tariff and NTMs, and also the behind-the-border areas such as competition, e-commerce, government procurement, etc.

Major issues and challenges

Still, RCEP is not problem-free. Nor should RCEP be expected to help alleviate contemporary challenges to the region in the absence of more information about its design. First, the region as a whole and each member country are facing a more complex web of regional cooperation arrangements and stakeholders' engagements. Regarding regional and bilateral FTAs involving ASEAN member countries, the so-called "spaghetti-bowl" syndrome already embodies huge inconsistencies in the rules of origin (RoO) and the depth of investment and services trade liberalization. There is a need to harmonize trade and investment regimes, particularly in the aspects of behind-the-border regulations, national single windows, standards, and conformance. Progress in each area may, however, be countered or even reversed with proliferation of protectionist measures since 2016. Coping with these inconsistencies is no easy task and the extent of such inconsistencies may even increase with new FTAs in the region.

Second, even with its hard-earned achievements by 2015, ASEAN still faces a major challenge in strengthening its connectivity and centrality. It is important that ASEAN's centrality be seen as the facilitator of process and driver of substance. Nevertheless, even the meaning of "centrality" remains ambiguous. Specifically, whether such centrality requires external agreements to be jointly concluded, centrally overseen, or negotiated in consultation with other members is far from clear. MPAC is well and broadly defined with three major pillars of connectivity (physical infrastructure, institutions, and people-to-people) and specified projects under each pillar,[2] yet the coordination of external development partners and the mobilization of technical and financial resources still encounter difficulties.

Third, RCEP still lacks a number of mechanisms to support and enforce its implementation. Its dispute settlement mechanism is a challenge, notwithstanding its necessity to induce proper compliance with future provisions. The process of reviewing progress and issues represents another area of deficiency. Setting up relevant committees in the ASEAN Secretariat also requires material efforts, even though resources may not be the key constraint. The relevance of the current ASEAN Secretariat for the RCEP presents another issue for consideration in the RCEP. Upgrading the ASEAN Secretariat to support the RCEP has its own advantages, though subject to capacity improvement and consensus within itself in settling issues with external partners.

Fourth, ASEAN and its partners under the RCEP also need to mount a joint effort to address the regionally common challenges related to non-traditional security. Food security constitutes a material issue as it has implications for income and employment in agriculture and access to food at reasonable prices. Meanwhile, energy security is another concern with various impacts for the RCEP region, being both a major consumer and exporter of energy. Other issues include the spread of infectious diseases and human trafficking. However, the scope of impacts varies between countries, which may undermine the consensus on the priorities and practical measures to address the above issues.

Finally, enhancing the feasibility of an East Asian Cooperation and Development Fund is no easy task, though it may help extend the Initiative for ASEAN Integration into the Initiative for East Asian Integration. This process should incorporate effective cooperation and coordination to support the CLMV countries, particularly in the areas of institutional reform, capacity building, and development of small and medium-sized enterprises.

The RCEP, TPP, and Vietnam

Vietnam is among the few countries that holds membership in both the TPP and the RCEP. There are several reasons for this. First, there have been significant developments in the regional geopolitical arena that requires careful consideration from Vietnam. Balancing relationships (including economic relations) with major powers is almost unavoidable. Second, pursuing a development paradigm that relies on exports and investment, Vietnam is striving for the expansion of and easier access to major markets. Opportunities for trade, FDI, transfers of technology, and management skills are among the top inducements for Vietnam. Finally, given their tough requirements, the TPP and the RCEP can serve as credible sources of pressure for spurring domestic reforms. The lessons from Vietnam's preparation for World Trade Organization accession show that institutional reforms may not be appropriately designed and/or enforced in the absence of such pressures.

The TPP and the RCEP are also expected to produce ample positive impacts on Vietnam's economy. Table 9.1 shows that its GDP in 2025 may increase by up to US\$48.7 billion (14.3 percent) and US\$17.3 billion (5.1 percent), respectively, under the TPP or the RCEP.[3] Wider membership of the TPP also increases Vietnam's income gains. Notably, under the various possible scenarios of the TPP (with 12 members or 16 members), Vietnam has the largest income gains in percentage terms (10.5 percent and 14.3 percent, respectively).

The above-projected benefits of the TPP and the RCEP can be explained by several reasons. First, the TPP and the RCEP include many of Vietnam's important economic partners such as China, Japan, Australia, and ASEAN. These also represent the markets for Vietnam's major export commodities; access to these markets may be enhanced due to further tariff reductions. Second, FDI inflows to Vietnam are likely to increase considerably so as to take advantage of the new opportunities and incentives created by the TPP and the RCEP. In particular, the FDI projects from many advanced partners may bring about substantial positive spillovers, including the transfer of technology and management know-how. Finally, the fulfilment of TPP and RCEP commitments will help build a transparent and competitive investment environment in Vietnam, thereby facilitating the efficient allocation of capital resources.

Still, the above figures and arguments are only presented on an *ex ante* basis. As Vietnam's ten years of World Trade Organization membership show, opportunities may instead become challenges in the absence of appropriate macroeconomic policy responses and necessary domestic reforms. Hence, the realization of TPP- and RCEP-induced opportunities depends crucially on whether Vietnam can overcome the challenges in implementing its commitments. Unlike the context of the early 1990s, economic reforms in the country – still at a low development stage – now interact very closely with the economic integration process. The gap between the requirement of new-generation FTAs[4] and the actual capacity of Vietnam, meanwhile, remains material. As such, the country needs to make further efforts to improve economic institutions, especially its legal framework and enforcement structure, so as to internalize the commitments made under those FTAs.

At the same time, Vietnam also has to harmonize its commitments under various integration tracks. As discussed previously, Vietnam's memberships in many FTAs show a commitment to establish a more favorable investment environment in the country. Yet, the benefits of such agreements may be reversed if the commitments under those FTAs are inconsistent or developed without sequential consideration. Should this happen, businesses will encounter difficulties in developing appropriate investment strategies if adjustment costs turn out to be high.

In the meantime, Vietnam needs to restore and further consolidate market confidence. This again depends importantly on political will as well as consistency in macroeconomic stabilization and the long-term economic restructuring process. The TPP and the RCEP may produce significant net benefits, yet the pattern of impact may vary across sectors and enterprises. The previously protected and/or weak ones may experience contraction or even bankruptcy, resulting in associated social consequences. In general, minimizing adjustment costs and social risks in the economic integration process such as the TPP and the RCEP should be the main priority in Vietnam's agenda.

The TPP and Cambodia, Laos, Myanmar (CLM)

The CLM countries and some other ASEAN member countries are currently not in TPP negotiations. Given its depth and scope of its liberalization commitments, the TPP may be expected to produce investment and trade diversion effects on the CLM countries. This impact may even be undesirable from the perspective of the ASEAN member countries that currently hold TPP negotiations.

Still, mitigating the adverse impacts and disadvantages for non-TPP negotiating members is not impossible. Several lines of effort may be proposed, which necessarily require active involvement of the CLM countries. First, efforts to realize the post-2015 commitments in the AEC and the RCEP need to be harmonized with comparable depth. Second, harmonization can be even promoted further by gradually incorporating some new areas covered in the TPP to the AEC and the RCEP processes. Here, the experience of the four ASEAN member countries involved in TPP negotiations will be valuable (ERIA 2014). Third, the CLM countries should be encouraged to implement unilateral liberalization and domestic reforms. Finally, capacity building efforts should be provided to support the CLM countries.

Conclusions and recommendations

This chapter elaborates on the prospects and implications of RCEP on the CLMV. The idea of RCEP is not new, but recent progress in East Asian economic integration and quantitative evidence has shown that realization of the idea would significantly benefit the CLMV. However, the CLMV to a different extent may experience diversion effects due to RCEP (and possibly TPP). In this regard, adhering to long-term structural reforms, preferably on a unilateral basis, alongside capacity building support should be essential.

The chapter then draws out some recommendations. First, the CLMV should perceive RCEP as a process, rather than a definite target by any specific timing. Expert Roundtable for RCEP (ERIA) (2014) asserts that RCEP is about liberalization with various development agenda with a philosophy of community-building. Building on AEC, RCEP should also be seen as a process to the approach which can entail certain advantages. For instance, Kimura and Chen (2016) contend that mega FTAs require beyond-the-border actions and, therefore, a gradual approach may lower the associated adjustment costs and smoothen the transition. Only with this view can the CLMV affirm longer time path and dynamic consistency for building capacity and competitiveness.

Second, the CLMV should work with other RCEP members in trying to maximize the substance of a bottom-up approach. Maria (2017) elaborates on the need to engage the public, apart from other issues such as RCEP impact and benefits, issue of the Investor-State Dispute Settlement, and small and medium-sized enterprises. RCEP could well be the model for integrating the least developed countries with developing and developed economies. Given the range of new and/or complicated issues, RCEP as a mega-FTA would certainly induce drastic behavioral changes in the business and people's communities. Engaging these actors right from the preparatory stage for RCEP would then allow for meaningful outcomes from the process.

Third, RCEP should reflect a reasonable balance between the depth of liberalization commitments (relative to existing ASEAN+ arrangement) and the flexibility equipped to members, especially developing ones such as the CLMV. RCEP should mean more than just opening markets to all members. It is about building a community and enhancing the welfare of all its members. The vision of ASEAN Community Vision 2025, should be constantly in the thoughts of those entrusted with creating RCEP (ERIA Research Institute Network Meeting (RINM) 2017). The priorities of RCEP need to be to ensure that international production networks can spread prosperity throughout the region and continue development.

Notes

1 Consisting of: (i) A highly integrated and cohesive economy; (ii) A competitive, innovative and dynamic ASEAN; (iii) Enhanced connectivity and sectoral cooperation; (iv) A resilient, inclusive and people-oriented, people-centred ASEAN; and (v) A global ASEAN.
2 See ASEAN (2011).
3 Measured at 2007 dollar.
4 Such as TPP and RCEP, not to mention EU-Vietnam FTA, Vietnam-Korea FTA, etc. The benefits from TPP may arguably be smaller after the US withdrew from the agreement.

References

ASEAN (2007), "ASEAN Economic Community Blueprint", ASEAN Secretariat, Jakarta.

ERIA (2014), *ASEAN Rising-ASEAN and AEC beyond 2015*. Jakarta: ERIA.

ERIA RINM (2017), RIN Statement No X: The Regional Comprehensive Economic Partnership, June (final draft).

Expert Roundtable for RCEP, ERIA (2014), "Recommendations on the Approaches to be Adopted in the Negotiations of RCEP and its Implementations", Jakarta, June (Draft).

Fukunaga, Y.D., Narjoko, I. I., and Intal, P. (2013), "ASEAN as Fulcrum of East Asia Integration", (mimeo).

Kawasaki, K. (2017), "Emergent Uncertainty in Regional Integration", *GRIPS Discussion Paper 16–28*.

Kimura, F., and Chen, L. (2016), "Implications of Mega Free Trade: Agreements for Asian Regional Integration", *ERIA Discussion Paper*, Dec 2016.

Petri, P.A., and Plummer M.G. (2013), "ASEAN centrality and the ASEAN-US economic relationship", *East-West Center, Policy Studies* 69, November.

Tan Sri Dr Rebecca Fatima Sta Maria (2017), "RCEP: More relevant now than ever", ERIA Note, January.

Vo, T.T., and Nguyen, A.D. (2010), "Development Cooperation in East Asia", Paper presented at the conference on 'East Asia Economic Integration in the Wake of Global Financial Crisis', Seoul, Korea. July 07.

10 South Asia's greater integration in Asia

Looking beyond the RCEP

Selim Raihan

Introduction

Regional integration and cooperation initiative in South Asia started with the formation of the South Asian Association for Regional Cooperation (SAARC) in 1985. SAARC includes Afghanistan, Bangladesh, Bhutan, India, Nepal, the Maldives, Pakistan and Sri Lanka. SAARC countries signed the SAARC Preferential Trading Arrangement (SAPTA) in April 1993 which came into force in December 1995, with the aim of promoting intra-regional trade and economic cooperation within the SAARC region through the exchange of concessions. SAPTA was replaced by the South Asian Free Trade Area (SAFTA) in January 2006, designed to more proactively promote and facilitate intra-regional trade among the SAARC members. Besides SAFTA there are three bilateral free trade agreements (FTAs) in South Asia, which are India-Sri Lanka bilateral FTA, India-Bhutan bilateral FTA and Pakistan-Sri Lanka bilateral FTA. Furthermore, the Bangladesh-Bhutan-India-Nepal (BBIN) is an initiative for a sub-regional cooperation. Despite these, South Asia is one of the least integrated regions in the world. The proportion of within-South Asia trade in the region's global trade hovers around the 5 percent mark. From a non-Indian and political economy perspective, there are concerns that a clear and visible leadership from India is yet to be seen to move the regional integration agenda forward in South Asia.

Despite the aforementioned 'pessimistic' scenarios, there are aspirations for greater regional integration in South Asia. Also, countries in South Asia aim for expanding integration with the rest of Asia, especially with the East and Southeast Asian countries. The most comprehensive regional integration initiative in Asia so far has been the Regional Comprehensive Economic Partnership (RCEP) which is a proposed FTA between the ten member states of the Association of Southeast Asian Nations (ASEAN) and the six states with which ASEAN has existing FTAs (Australia, China, India, Japan, South Korea and New Zealand). RCEP is one of the proposed mega trading blocs of recent time. RCEP negotiations were formally launched in November 2012 and until now 18 rounds of negotiations have taken place. RCEP represents 49 percent of the world's population, accounts for about

30 percent of the world's Gross domestic product (GDP), and makes up 29 percent of the world trade (Wignaraja, 2013). However, in the RCEP only India from South Asia is taking part and all other South Asian countries are excluded.

Against this backdrop, this chapter explores South Asia's greater integration in Asia with a special emphasis on looking beyond the RCEP. Section II of the chapter provides an overview of the regional integration initiatives in South Asia; Section III analyses the attempts for greater regional integration in Asia and the Pacific and the role of the RCEP; Section IV explores the implications of RCEP for the South Asian countries; and finally Section V concludes.

Regional integration process in South Asia

Despite several initiatives, the significance of intra-regional trade among the South Asian countries has remained low. Throughout the 1990s the share has been less than 4 percent (Raihan, 2015). There were some encouraging trends in the 2000s, with the proportion of within-South Asia trade in the region's global trade rising to more than 6 percent in 2003. More recently, however, the share has hovered around the 5 percent mark (Raihan, 2015). Compared to other regional arrangements, such as North American FTA, ASEAN and EU, within-region trade in South Asia remains very low.

Table 10.1 records regional exports as a percentage of a country's total exports in South Asia in 2014. The shares vary widely, from 74 percent in the case of Bhutan to only 2 percent for Bangladesh and 7 percent for India and Maldives. Intra-regional exports account for 61 and 62 percent, respectively, of Afghanistan's and Nepal's total exports. Similar to exports, there are wide variations in the relative importance of intra-regional imports for South Asian countries. Approximately 73 percent of Bhutan's imports and 52 percent of Nepal's imports are from South Asian countries. In sharp contrast, only 1 percent of India's imports are from other South Asian member countries. Low intra-regional dependency is also evident for Pakistan, where imports from other SAARC member countries account for only 4 percent of total imports. Furthermore, while Bangladesh imports around 16 percent of its total import from South Asia, the country exports only 2 percent of its total exports to this region.

There are a number of challenges and tasks ahead for greater integration in South Asia. The presence of the long 'sensitive lists', slow process of tariff liberalization under SAFTA, non-tariff measures/barriers (NTMs/NTBs), lack of trade facilitation and political relations between countries appear to be major barriers to intra-regional trade in South Asia (Raihan, 2015). Raihan et al (2015) suggested that there is a need to review and analyse the core NTMs, for example, Sanitary and Phytosanitary Measures, Technical Barriers to Trade, Port Entry Restrictions, and Para-Tariffs for their trade-restricting effects, and undertake appropriate steps to address

Table 10.1 Intra-regional trade in South Asia in 2014

From / To	Thousand US$										Regional export as % of country's Total export
	Afghanistan	Bangladesh	Bhutan	India	Maldives	Nepal	Pakistan	Sri Lanka	Total intra-regional export	Total export	
Afghanistan	0	1820	0	220129	0	0	177582	24	399555	659410	61
Bangladesh	4977	0	2949	461964	0	14212	53466	21146	558713	3019025	2
Bhutan*	0	22985	0	383000	0	4782	304	0	411072	555000	74
India	443055	6579875	749000	0	139835	4405078	2181823	6433181	20931847	317733218	7
Maldives	0	409	0	4061	0	0	10	8802	13282	191716	7
Nepal	0	20044	3379	547310	12	0	1247	32	572023	919640	62
Pakistan	2221769	494037	0	481204	5838	1157	0	253976	3457981	27052102	13
Sri Lanka	159	89849	12	610294	88632	4824	73173	0	866943	10923239	8
Total exports									27211415	388233348	7
Total intra-regional imports	2669960	7209019	755340	2707963	234317	4430052	2487604	6717160	27211415		
Total Imports	7990761	45610279	1040000	460512283	1700454	8486418	58945173	20537789	604823157		
Regional imports as % of country's total imports	33	16	73	1	14	52	4	33	4		

Source: IMF, Direction of Trade Statistics (DOTS). The data for Bhutan is mirror data from ITC and http://stat.wto.org/CountryProfile/WSDBCountryPFView.aspx?Language=E&Country=BT.

them at the SAARC level. Raihan and Ferdous (2015) further observed that tariff reduction/elimination provisions in the India-Sri Lanka FTA and Pakistan-Sri Lanka FTA are broader and deeper relatively to SAFTA. A more proactive policy initiative would be needed for SAFTA to match the deeper tariff cuts of bilateral FTAs.

Liberalization of the services trade has also become a critical economic agenda for the South Asian countries. At the 16th SAARC Summit in Thimpu in April 2010, the South Asian Agreement on Trade in Services (SATIS) was signed with the aim of liberalization of intra-regional trade in services. However, Member States are yet to schedule their specific liberalization commitments under SATIS and there has not been much progress in this front.

Also, South Asia remains one of the lowest recipients of Foreign Direct Investment (FDI) among the developing regions, with around 90 percent of the FDI inflow in South Asia destined to India (Moazzem et al., 2015). Like trade, intra-regional FDI in South Asia comprises of only less than 5 percent of the total FDI flow and India is the dominant investor within the region (Moazzem et al., 2015). The major reasons behind poor intra-regional investment are high regulatory restrictions on FDI, specific restrictions placed on doing business with other countries in the region, weak institutions to protect foreign investors, tariff and NTBs, bureaucratic delays, lack of cross-border facilities and absence of an effective banking network.

The initiative which created the opportunity for the majority of the South Asian countries (Bangladesh, Bhutan, India, Nepal, and Sri Lanka) to integrate with two Southeast Asian countries (Thailand and Myanmar) is the Bay of Bengal Initiative for Multi-Sectoral Technical and Economic Cooperation (BIMSTEC) which was initiated in 1997.[1] The regional group constitutes a bridge between South and Southeast Asia and represents a reinforcement of relations among these countries. BIMSTEC has also established a platform for intra-regional cooperation between SAARC and ASEAN members. The objective of building such an alliance was to harness shared and accelerated growth through mutual cooperation in different areas of common interests by utilizing regional resources and geographical advantages. Unlike many other regional groupings, BIMSTEC is a sector-driven cooperative organization. Starting with six sectors—including trade, technology, energy, transport, tourism and fisheries—for sectoral cooperation in late 1997, it expanded to embrace nine more sectors—including agriculture, public health, poverty alleviation, counter-terrorism, environment, culture, people-to-people contact and climate change—in 2008. However, even after 21 years of existence, the achievements under the BIMSTEC has been rather minimal.

In order to take forward the regional integration process in South Asia, a good and effective initiative is the BBIN initiative, a sub-regional coordinative architecture of countries in South Asia. In light of economic interdependence across Asia, and hitherto unaddressed concerns of eastern subcontinent nations, the Council of Ministers in May 1996 approved a sub-regional body of Bhutan, Nepal, northeast India and Bangladesh, forming the South Asian Growth Quadrangle.[2] BBIN operates through Joint Working Groups comprising official representation from each member state to formulate, implement and review quadrilateral agreements. Areas of cooperation include water resources management, connectivity of power grids, multi-modal transport, freight and trade infrastructure. Focusing on the subcontinent's northeast, it endeavours to cooperate on trade, investment, communication, tourism, energy and natural resource development. Its objectives were expanded over the years to incorporate substantial land and port connectivity. Although such initiatives further augment trade ties and commerce, the importance accorded this architecture over others, in a region deemed one of the least integrated with the world, is considered to have significant political and strategic undertones.

India also has bilateral FTA with the ten member states of the ASEAN, which came into effect in January 2010. Furthermore, under China's Belt and Road Initiative (BRI), the Bangladesh-China-India-Myanmar economic corridor (BCIMEC) paves the opportunity for greater economic and trade integration between two economic giants in Asia, namely China and India. BCIMEC also provides an opportunity for Bangladesh to exploit huge potential benefits from such an economic and trade integration. However, BCIMEC has not yet been launched due to the political tension between India and China, and subsequently India's opposition to this initiative. Among all the BRI initiates, the China-Pakistan economic corridor (CPEC) is in operational now. Yet, being a bilateral economic corridor, CPEC, has not been able to draw interest from other neighbouring countries. Also, India has a strong reservation against CPEC as it passes through the disputed territory of Pakistan-occupied-Kashmir.[3]

Greater regional integration in Asia and the Pacific and the RCEP

Mega trading blocs are increasingly important given the changing patterns of global trade. The RCEP, the Trans-Pacific Partnership (TPP), the Trans-Atlantic Trade and Investment Partnership (TTIP), and the Pacific Alliance are some examples of these emerging mega trading blocs. RCEP is a proposed FTA between ASEAN and Australia, China, India, Japan, South Korea and New Zealand. RCEP negotiations were formally launched in November 2012 at the ASEAN Summit in Cambodia. At the launch of negotiations on Tuesday, 20 November 2012, the leaders of each relevant country endorsed the "Guiding Principles and Objectives for Negotiating the Regional Comprehensive Economic Partnership." The agreement will encompass trade in goods and services, economic and technical issues, intellectual property and investments, and dispute settlement mechanisms. As expected, ASEAN will be in the 'driver's seat' of this multilateral trade arrangement (though the idea was initially given by Japan, it has been repeatedly endorsed by India). The joint statement issued at the end of the first round of negotiations also reiterated "ASEAN Centrality" in the emerging regional economic architecture. The RCEP will have broader and deeper engagement with significant improvements over the existing ASEAN+1 FTAs, while recognizing the individual and diverse circumstances of the participating countries.

Wignaraja (2013) suggested that RCEP will have important implications for the Asian countries. The RCEP can help regionalize the sophisticated global production networks that make Asia the world's factory. It will also reduce the overlap among Asian FTAs, lest Asia becomes a confusing 'noodle bowl' of multiple trade rules. If a comprehensive agreement can be reached, trade barriers in Asia will come down and the new rules will be consistent with WTO agreements. Rules of origin could be rationalized and made more flexible and be better administered through electronic means. In the area of investment rules, where no WTO agreement exists, the RCEP will promote easier FDI flows and technology transfers by multinational corporations. However, Palit (2014) cautioned that till now, mega trading blocs largely exclude least developed countries (LDCs) and small states. The latter also appears unprepared for tackling the various implications of the RTAs ranging from potential loss of market access from trade preference erosion and growth of new standards to trade governance.

Implications of RCEP for the South Asian countries

This chapter uses the Global Trade Analysis Project (GTAP) global general equilibrium model to explore the trade and economic impact of FTA and trade facilitation between Bangladesh and East and Southeast Asia. The global Computable General Equilibrium (CGE) modelling framework of the GTAP (Hertel, 1997) is a useful tool for the ex ante analysis of the economic and trade consequences of multilateral or bilateral trade agreements. The GTAP model is a comparative static model, based on neoclassical theories.[4] The GTAP model is a linearized model, and it uses a common global database for CGE analysis. The model assumes perfect competition in all markets, constant returns to scale in all production and trade activities, profit-maximizing behaviour by firms and utility-maximizing behaviour by households. The model is solved using the General Equilibrium Modelling Package software (Harrison and Pearson, 1996). The Annex provides the details of the GTAP model.

This chapter undertakes the following three scenarios in the GTAP model:

Scenario 1: The RCEP scenario – an FTA among RCEP countries
Scenario 2: The 'extended RCEP' scenario – the other South Asian countries also join the RCEP FTA
Scenario 3: The RCEP-BBIN scenario, where the BBIN countries join the RCEP FTA

Table 10.2 presents the results from three simulations with respect to the potential impacts on the real GDPs of the countries under consideration. Under the RCEP FTA scenario, all the RCEP member countries would accrue gains, in terms of the rise in real GDP. The largest gain, in terms of the percent change in real, would be for South Korea (2.89 percent) and smallest gain would be for New Zealand (0.19 percent). India's real GDP would rise by 0.73 percent. In contrast, all the non-member countries would experience loss in real GDP from the RCEP FTA scenario. Among the South Asian countries, the largest loss would be incurred by Nepal (−3.13 percent) followed by Bangladesh (−0.39 percent), Sri Lanka (−0.38 percent), Pakistan (−0.24 percent) and Rest of South Asia (−0.1 percent). The major reason for the negative impacts on the other South Asian countries is that these countries would experience some important losses in preferences of their exports in the markets of the RCEP countries once the RCEP FTA comes into the picture.

However, under the Scenario 2 – the extended RCEP FTA – where all other South Asian countries can also join the RCEP FTA, the gains in terms of the rise in real GDP for all the original RCEP member countries become larger than those under Scenario 1. In addition, all the other South Asian countries would also experience the rise in real GDP. Among the other South Asian countries, the largest gain would be for Nepal (2.87 percent), followed by Bangladesh (1.8 percent), Sri Lanka (1.08 percent), Pakistan (0.37 percent) and Rest of South Asia (0.33 percent).

Given the current deadlock in the South Asian regional integration process, if all other South Asian countries can't be taken in the extended RCEP FTA, a realistic alternative could be to consider the BBIN countries to be in the RCEP. The Scenario 3, shows that under the RCEP-BBIN FTA, the BBIN countries would also have a large rise in their real GDPs, though the gains would be smaller than those under the extended RCEP FTA scenario. Being the excluded countries, Pakistan, Sri Lanka and the rest of South Asia would incur losses in real GDP.

Tables 10.3, 10.4 and 10.5 presents the simulation results for the three aforementioned scenarios with respect to the change in sectoral and total exports from all countries to the RCEP region. Table 10.3 shows that under the RCEP FTA scenario, the intra-regional trade among the RCEP countries would increase considerably. All RCEP member countries would experience a rise in exports to the RCEP region by varying degrees. The largest percent rise would be observed for India (35.4 percent) followed by South Korea (24 percent). India would experience a very high increase in exports of agriculture and livestock and meat products. Also, India's exports of processed food, textile and clothing, light manufacturing and heavy manufacturing would increase by large margins. In contrast, the excluded countries, especially the other South Asian countries, would experience significant decline in exports to the RCEP region. The largest fall in exports would be for Nepal (27.7 percent) followed by Bangladesh

Table 10.2 Percentage change in real GDP

Regions	Scenarios 1: RCEP FTA	Scenario 2: Extended RCEP FTA	Scenario 3: RCEP-BBIN FTA
RCEP countries and region			
ASEAN	0.70	0.73	0.70
Australia	0.61	0.62	0.60
New Zealand	0.19	0.21	0.20
China	0.32	0.33	0.32
Japan	0.48	0.49	0.48
South Korea	2.89	2.91	2.89
India	0.73	0.75	0.74
Non-member countries and regions			
Bangladesh	−0.39	1.80	1.67
Nepal	−3.13	2.87	2.55
Pakistan	−0.24	0.37	−0.09
Sri Lanka	−0.38	1.08	−0.09
Rest of South Asia	−0.10	0.33	−0.07
North America	−0.01	−0.01	−0.01
European Union 25	−0.01	−0.01	−0.01
Rest of World	−0.02	−0.03	−0.03

Source: GTAP model simulation.

(13.4 percent). In the case of Nepal, the major negative impacts would be observed for exports of minerals, processed food and livestock and meat products. In the case of Bangladesh, the exports from sectors like processed food and textile and clothing would incur major losses. Similarly, for Pakistan and Sri Lanka, processed food, textile and clothing and light engineering would experience sizeable fall in exports to the RCEP region.

In contrast, under the extended RCEP FTA scenario, as presented in Table 10.4, the exports from other South Asian countries to the RCEP region would increase significantly. The largest increase in exports would be observed for Pakistan (45.7 percent) with sizeable increase in exports from agriculture and livestock, processed food and light engineering. Also, other South Asian countries would experience rise in exports in agriculture, textile and clothing, light and heavy manufacturing.

Under the RCEP-BBIN FTA scenario, as presented in Table 10.5, the exports from other BBIN countries to the RCEP region would increase significantly. Among the other BBIN countries, Nepal would have a larger increase in exports than Bangladesh with sizeable increase in exports of livestock and meat products, light and heavy manufacturing and different services. Bangladesh would experience substantial increase in exports minerals, of textile and clothing, and light manufacturing. Being excluded countries, Pakistan, Sri Lanka and rest of South Asia would experience fall in exports to the RCEP region.

Table 10.3 Percent change in export to RCEP region (Scenario 1: RCEP FTA)

	Grains and Crops	Livestock and Meat Products	Mining and Extraction	Processed Food	Textiles and Clothing	Light Manufacturing	Heavy Manufacturing	Utilities and Construction	Transport and Communication	Other Services	Total
RCEP countries and region											
ASEAN	53.3	11.8	-0.1	46.6	-3.5	9.4	8.2	6.1	0.8	-0.4	10.1
Australia	0.3	162.7	-1.0	95.0	6.0	1.3	4.3	-1.0	-3.1	-3.4	9.2
New Zealand	11.9	51.0	2.7	26.4	-20.5	-10.7	0.4	1.4	0.6	0.6	10.6
China	125.1	14.5	31.9	36.0	30.8	27.5	15.2	5.1	3.9	4.0	20.4
Japan	10.4	-4.6	57.6	38.5	43.0	72.5	13.8	-8.9	-8.0	-8.7	22.7
South Korea	251.3	193.3	24.9	251.9	39.5	61.5	16.5	3.1	1.1	-6.0	24.0
India	247.4	98.8	6.2	16.0	23.0	34.3	21.8	13.2	6.0	5.6	35.4
Non-member countries and regions											
Bangladesh	-13.1	-11.8	7.8	-49.4	-23.7	1.5	-3.5	11.6	6.8	7.6	-13.4
Nepal	-15.3	-27.7	-88.8	-63.9	-5.0	-17.9	-11.1	-19.4	-8.5	-1.4	-27.7
Pakistan	-3.3	-13.8	4.3	-21.5	-14.2	-7.1	-1.5	9.9	6.3	6.5	-7.4
Sri Lanka	-15.0	-6.6	6.9	-19.8	-22.4	-15.4	-3.6	11.8	7.6	7.6	-7.8
Rest of South Asia	-17.1	-21.0	1.0	-7.7	-23.8	-12.3	-11.1	6.8	5.4	5.9	-3.8
North America	-13.0	-31.3	1.3	-13.7	-18.8	-8.0	-0.2	11.0	5.8	6.7	-2.0
European Union 25	-11.7	-28.4	-0.9	-13.0	-20.3	-9.4	-2.2	7.9	4.1	4.7	-2.4
Rest of World	-5.8	-27.2	1.0	-18.0	-14.5	-9.8	-3.3	6.7	4.4	4.9	-1.1

Source: GTAP model simulation.

Table 10.4 Percent change in export to RCEP region (Scenarios 2: Extended RCEP FTA)

	Grains and Crops	Livestock and Meat Products	Mining and Extraction	Processed Food	Textiles and Clothing	Light Manu-facturing	Heavy Manu-facturing	Utilities and Construction	Transport and Communi-cation	Other Services	Total
RCEP countries and region											
ASEAN	52.2	11.4	-0.4	46.6	-4.5	9.3	8.0	5.9	0.6	-0.7	9.8
Australia	0.1	163.1	-1.0	94.0	5.3	1.7	4.6	-0.8	-2.9	-3.2	9.3
New Zealand	11.3	50.0	2.5	25.8	-21.8	-11.0	-0.1	1.0	0.3	0.2	10.1
China	124.5	14.4	31.7	35.4	29.9	27.6	15.2	5.2	3.9	4.0	20.3
Japan	9.5	-4.7	57.2	37.4	41.0	71.9	13.4	-9.1	-8.2	-8.9	22.3
South Korea	249.8	194.4	24.7	252.7	38.6	61.6	16.6	3.3	1.1	-6.0	24.0
India	245.9	98.1	5.2	15.7	21.1	34.1	21.7	13.1	5.7	5.3	34.9
Non-member countries and regions											
Bangladesh	1.2	7.9	14.4	0.7	13.1	28.4	9.6	1.9	2.9	-1.5	11.6
Nepal	3.5	40.2	45.3	-55.9	4.9	33.7	36.9	28.2	20.9	20.2	15.3
Pakistan	93.1	125.5	22.6	88.0	39.9	51.9	27.9	20.3	12.7	12.4	45.7
Sri Lanka	100.2	5.2	7.3	5.7	37.7	14.8	24.4	14.8	7.9	5.8	22.7
Rest of South Asia	-9.5	29.4	3.6	24.9	58.1	74.0	6.4	14.1	10.9	10.7	7.0
North America	-12.8	-30.9	1.4	-13.6	-19.2	-7.6	0.2	11.4	6.1	7.0	-1.7
European Union 25	-11.7	-28.0	-0.7	-12.9	-20.6	-9.0	-1.9	8.3	4.4	5.0	-2.1
Rest of world	-5.7	-26.8	1.1	-17.8	-15.0	-9.4	-2.9	7.0	4.7	5.2	-0.9

Source: GTAP model simulation.

Table 10.5 Percent change in export to RCEP region (Scenario 3: RCEP-BBIN FTA)

	Grains and Crops	Livestock and Meat Products	Mining and Extraction	Processed Food	Textiles and Clothing	Light Manu- facturing	Heavy Manu- facturing	Utilities and Construction	Transport and Communi- cation	Other Services	Total
RCEP countries and region											
ASEAN	53.2	11.6	-0.2	46.7	-3.8	9.3	8.2	6.0	0.7	-0.5	10.0
Australia	0.4	162.9	-1.0	95.1	5.9	1.4	4.4	-1.0	-3.0	-3.3	9.2
New Zealand	11.9	50.7	2.6	26.2	-20.9	-10.9	0.2	1.2	0.5	0.4	10.4
China	125.3	14.3	31.8	35.9	30.5	27.4	15.1	5.1	3.8	4.0	20.3
Japan	10.7	-4.3	57.6	38.5	42.8	72.6	13.8	-8.9	-8.0	-8.7	22.8
South Korea	251.5	193.7	24.8	251.9	39.4	61.4	16.5	3.1	1.0	-6.0	23.9
India	246.9	98.3	5.6	15.8	22.3	33.9	21.6	13.0	5.8	5.4	35.0
Non-member countries and regions											
Bangladesh	2.6	8.1	16.1	1.5	12.3	28.9	10.0	2.4	3.1	-1.0	11.7
Nepal	3.6	42.1	49.1	-64.9	5.4	34.7	38.9	29.4	21.6	20.5	16.7
Pakistan	-2.2	-12.2	5.1	-20.8	-13.2	-5.7	-0.3	10.7	7.1	7.4	-6.4
Sri Lanka	-14.5	-5.5	7.9	-19.4	-22.0	-15.0	-3.1	12.4	8.1	8.2	-7.3
Rest of South Asia	-16.5	-20.7	1.5	-7.5	-23.8	-12.2	-11.0	6.9	5.5	6.0	-3.5
North America	-12.8	-31.1	1.3	-13.6	-18.8	-7.9	-0.1	11.1	5.9	6.8	-1.9
European Union 25	-11.5	-28.2	-0.8	-12.9	-20.2	-9.2	-2.1	8.0	4.2	4.8	-2.3
Rest of world	-5.5	-27.0	1.0	-17.9	-14.5	-9.7	-3.2	6.8	4.5	5.0	-1.0

Source: GTAP model simulation.

Conclusion

The analysis in this chapter suggests that as the sole party from South Asia, RCEP has created significant opportunities for India to integrate with the advanced economies in Asia and the Pacific and to participate further with the global value chains. RCEP can help reduce the overlaps among Asian FTAs, rationalize rules of origin, and promote FDI flows and technology transfers by multinational corporations. However, being the non-members, RCEP has led to some important implications for the other South Asian countries. There are concerns that the RCEP will lead to the escalation of bars in standards and trade governance which might work as significant NTBs for the South Asian countries, especially for the Least Developed Countries, while exporting to the RCEP countries. Therefore, there is a need for strong efforts to improve the quality of trade infrastructures, capacities and institutions in these countries.

There are also risks of other South Asian countries with respect to the potential loss of market access from the erosion of trade preferences. Simulations using the global general equilibrium model (the GTAP model) suggest that the RCEP FTA would lead to gains, in terms of the rise in real GDP, for all RCEP member countries including India. In contrast, all other South Asian countries would experience a fall in real GDP, and the major affected countries would be Nepal and Bangladesh as these two countries enjoy the largest trade preferences both in India and China. A hypothetical 'extended RCEP' scenario, where all other South Asian countries could join the RCEP FTA, would lead to gains for all South Asian countries, and India's gain would become larger than what would be observed under the RCEP. Therefore, other South Asian countries should negotiate for their participation in the RCEP. The 'extended RCEP' scenario would certainly lead to the meaningful integration of South Asia, East Asia, Southeast Asia and the Pacific.

Notes

1 https://bimstec.org/.
2 https://aric.adb.org/initiative/south-asia-growth-quadrangle.
3 https://economictimes.indiatimes.com/news/defence/india-expresses-strong-opposition-to-china-pakistan-economic-corridor-says-challenges-indian-sovereignty/articleshow/57664537.cms.
4 Full documentation of the GTAP model and the database can be found in Hertel (1997).
5 Savings enter into the static utility function as a proxy for future consumption.

References

Harrison, W. J., and K. R. Pearson. 1996. "Computing Solutions for Large General Equilibrium Models Using GEMPACK". *Computational Economics* 9 (2): 83–127.
Hertel, T. W. 1997. *Global Trade Analysis: Modeling and Applications*. Cambridge: Cambridge University Press.

Moazzem, K. G., M. I. Chowdhury, and F. Sehrin. 2015. "Regional Investment Cooperation for a South Asia Economic Union." Background Paper prepared for the Asian Development Bank and SAARC Secretariat.

Palit, A. 2014. *Mega Trading Blocs and New Regional Trade Architectures: Implications for Small States and LDCs*. The Commonwealth Trade Hot Topics Issue 107, London: Commonwealth Secretariat.

Raihan, S. 2015. "South Asian Economic Union – Challenges and Tasks Ahead". *South Asia Economic Journal* 16 (2): 3S–18S.

Raihan, S., and F. B. Ferdous. 2015. "How Can SAFTA Embrace Bilateral Trade Agreements in South Asia?" Background Paper prepared for the Asian Development Bank and SAARC Secretariat.

Wignaraja, G. 2013. "Why the RCEP Matters for Asia and the World." *East Asia Forum*. www.eastasiaforum.org/2013/05/15/why-the-rcep-matters-for-asia-and-the-world/.

Annex: the description of the GTAP Model

In the GTAP model each region has a single representative household, known as the regional household. The income of the regional household is generated through factor payments and tax revenues (including export and import taxes) net of subsidies. The regional household allocates expenditure to private household expenditure, government expenditure and savings according to a Cobb–Douglas per capita utility function.[5] Thus, each component of final demand maintains a constant share of total regional income.

The private household buys commodity bundles to maximize utility, subject to its expenditure constraint. In the GTAP model the constrained optimizing behaviour of the private household is represented by a constant difference of elasticity (CDE) expenditure function. The private household spends its income on consumption of both domestic and imported commodities and pays taxes. The consumption bundles are constant elasticity of substitution (CES) aggregates of domestic and imported goods, where the imported goods are also CES aggregates of imports from different regions. Taxes paid by the private household include commodity taxes for domestically produced and imported goods and income tax net of subsidies.

The government also spends its income on domestic and imported commodities, and it collects taxes. Taxes consist of commodity taxes on domestically produced and imported commodities. Like the private household's, government consumption is a CES composite of domestically produced and imported goods.

The GTAP model considers the demand for investment in a particular region as savings. In a multi-country setting, the model is closed by assuming that regional savings are homogenous and contribute to a global pool of savings. This global saving is then allocated among regions for investment in response to changes in the expected rates of return in different regions. If all other markets in the multi-regional model are in equilibrium, if all firms earn zero profits, and if all households are on their budget constraint, such a treatment of savings and investment will lead to a situation in which global investment must equal global savings, and Walras' Law will be satisfied.

In the GTAP model producers receive payments for selling consumption goods and intermediate inputs both in the domestic market and to the rest of the world. Under the zero-profit assumption employed in the model, these revenues must be precisely exhausted by spending on domestic intermediate inputs, imported intermediate inputs, factor income and taxes paid to the regional household (taxes on both domestic and imported intermediate inputs and production taxes net of subsidies).

The GTAP model postulates a nested production technology, with the assumption that every industry produces a single output, and constant returns to scale prevail in all markets. Industries have a Leontief production technology to produce their outputs. Industries maximize profits by choosing two broad categories of inputs – namely, a composite of factors (value added) and a composite of intermediate inputs. The factor composite is a CES function of labour, capital, land and natural resources. The intermediate composite is a Leontief function of material inputs, which are in turn a CES composite of domestically produced goods and imports. Imports come from all regions.

The GTAP model employs the Armington assumption, which makes it possible to distinguish imports by their origin and explains intra-industry trade of similar products. Following the Armington approach, the import shares of different regions depend on relative prices and the substitution elasticity between domestic and imported commodities.

Version 9 of the GTAP database uses 2011 as the base year. Several pre-simulations are conducted to update the base year to reflect the situation in 2015, using updated national economic and trade data and updated protection data. GTAP data on regions and commodities are aggregated to meet the objectives of this study. Version 9 of the GTAP database covers 57 commodities, 140 regions/countries and 5 factors of production. The current study has aggregated 57 commodities into 10 and 140 regions into 15, as shown in Annex Tables 10A.1 and 10A.2.

Table 10A.1 GTAP commodity aggregation in the present study

No.	Sector	Comprising
1	Grains and crops	Paddy rice; wheat; cereal grains n.e.c; vegetables, fruit, nuts; oil seeds; sugar cane, sugar beet; Plant-based fibers; crops n.e.c; processed rice
2	Livestock and meat products	Cattle, sheep, goats, horses; Animal products n.e.c; Raw milk; Wool, silk-worm cocoons; Meat: cattle, sheep, goats, horse; Meat products n.e.c
3	Mining and extraction	Forestry; fishing; coal; oil; gas; minerals n.e.c.

No.	Sector	Comprising
4	Processed food	Vegetable oils and fats; dairy products; sugar; food products n.e.c; beverages and tobacco products
5	Textiles and clothing	Textiles; wearing apparel
6	Light manufacturing	Leather products; wood products; paper products, publishing; metal products; motor vehicles and parts; transport equipment n.e.c; manufactures n.e.c.
7	Heavy manufacturing	Petroleum, coal products; chemical, rubber, plastic prods; mineral products n.e.c; ferrous metals; metals n.e.c; electronic equipment; machinery and equipment n.e.c.
8	Utilities and Construction	Electricity; Gas manufacture, distribution; Water; Construction.
9	Transport and communication	Trade; transport n.e.c; sea transport; air transport; communication
10	Other services	Financial services n.e.c; insurance; business services n.e.c; recreation and other services; Pub Admin/Defence/Health/Educat; Dwellings

Source: GTAP Database 9.

Table 10A.2 GTAP region aggregation in the present study

No.	Aggregated Regions	Comprising Regions
1	Australia	Australia
2	New Zealand	New Zealand
3	China	China
4	Japan	Japan
5	South Korea	Korea
6	ASEAN	Brunei Darussalam; Cambodia; Indonesia; Lao People's Democratic Republic; Malaysia; Philippines; Singapore; Thailand; Vietnam; Rest of Southeast Asia
7	Bangladesh	Bangladesh
8	India	India
9	Nepal	Nepal
10	Pakistan	Pakistan
11	Sri Lanka	Sri Lanka
12	Rest of South Asia	Rest of South Asia
13	North America	Canada; United States of America; Mexico; Rest of North America
14	European Union 25	Austria; Belgium; Cyprus; Czech Republic; Denmark; Estonia; Finland; France; Germany; Greece; Hungary; Ireland; Italy; Latvia; Lithuania; Luxembourg; Malta; Netherlands; Poland; Portugal; Slovakia; Slovenia; Spain; Sweden; United Kingdom

(Continued)

No.	Aggregated Regions	Comprising Regions
15	Rest of World	Rest of Oceania; Hong Kong; Mongolia; Taiwan; Rest of East Asia; Argentina; Bolivia; Brazil; Chile; Colombia; Ecuador; Paraguay; Peru; Uruguay; Venezuela; Rest of South America; Costa Rica; Guatemala; Honduras; Nicaragua; Panama; El Salvador; Rest of Central America; Dominican Republic; Jamaica; Puerto Rico; Trinidad and Tobago; Caribbean; Switzerland; Norway; Rest of EFTA; Albania; Bulgaria; Belarus; Croatia; Romania; Russian Federation; Ukraine; Rest of Eastern Europe; Rest of Europe; Kazakhstan; Kyrgyzstan; Rest of Former Soviet Union; Armenia; Azerbaijan; Georgia; Bahrain; Iran Islamic Republic of; Israel; Jordan; Kuwait; Oman; Qatar; Saudi Arabia; Turkey; United Arab Emirates; Rest of Western Asia; Egypt; Morocco; Tunisia; Rest of North Africa; Benin; Burkina Faso; Cameroon; Cote d'Ivoire; Ghana; Guinea; Nigeria; Senegal; Togo; Rest of Western Africa; Central Africa; South Central Africa; Ethiopia; Kenya; Madagascar; Malawi; Mauritius; Mozambique; Rwanda; Tanzania; Uganda; Zambia; Zimbabwe; Rest of Eastern Africa; Botswana; Namibia; South Africa; Rest of South African Customs; Rest of the world

11 Economic integration in the emergent global landscape

An argument for Asian integration

Pranav Kumar and Jhanvi Tripathi

Introduction

The resurgence of protectionism in the developed world is a typical response to slow growth and therefore lesser job creation. It is an automatic response that nation-states have to serve what they deem the nation's self-interest but becomes unusually populist. The BREXIT referendum is one such case. The America First policy of the new US Administration is another.

The latest annual meeting of the World Economic Forum (WEF) in Davos, in January 2017, highlighted this concern with what is being termed 'de-globalisation'. Growing protectionism has been recognised as a response to the inequalities and inconsistencies created by globalisation. In fact, rising income and wealth disparities have been recognised as one of the Top 5 Trends that determine global developments, according to the WEF's Global Risks Report. The report notes that

> While we should be wary of attributing too much influence to a series of very recent electoral results, the consequences of which are still unknown, major unexpected events can serve as inflection points. Long-term trends – such as persistent inequality and deepening polarization … can build to a point at which they become triggers for change.
>
> (The Global Risks Report- 12th Edition, 2017)

An insight report by the G20 Task Force found that rising demands for economic nationalism may be owing to the rising inequalities within countries even as inequalities among countries have reduced. This is especially true for advanced economies, leading to a public backlash against economic globalisation in these nations. Noting the findings of the Global Trade Alert report, 2016 – that found that 81 percent of protectionist measures implemented worldwide in 2015 were by G20 nations – the task force warned that the situation could get worse due to the popularity of import tariffs as well as 'buy national' provisions (Akman et al., 2017).

Scholars have pointed out how bilateral and regional Free Trade Agreements (FTAs), while not a new phenomenon, have become central to trade policy. This has been attributed to the deadlock at the Doha Round of development negotiations at the World Trade Organization (WTO). The inconsistencies of the multilateral trading system and the overdependence on developed nations as export markets has led to an impasse in global trade. In a globalised world, protectionism is inefficient and not feasible as a policy choice. This is because production too is a globalised process taking place at multiple points along Global Value Chains (GVCs).

Protectionism in the west has reiterated the need for economic integration in Asia. The dependence on western markets has become a hindrance to further growth. Since the multilateral trading environment has become more cumbersome, regional trade agreements (RTAs) to further the goal of regional integration, could become a viable alternative for enabling trade.

Asia and the west: current trade scenario

The developed western nations are the biggest trading partners for most countries, especially in the developing world. This is why their threat of withdrawal from multilateral commitments is of serious concern to the global community and has created ripple effects. It has also created the space and impetus for greater regional integration. There is a recognition that dependence on the west and a select few rich countries must reduce.

All of these countries count the US and the EU as one of the top five destination countries for all their exports. These are also important destinations for them in terms of services trade. The same data sources show that Japan's services exports to the US account for 24.6 percent of the country's total services exports and 16.8 percent goes to the EU. In the case of Singapore's services exports, 11.4 percent go to the US and 13.7 percent to the EU. So, 25.1 percent, that is, a quarter of all services exports from Singapore goes to these two regions.

Table 11.1 Top 10 non-oil exporting economies in Asia (by GDP)

Country	GDP (US$ million) (2015)	Trade (% of GDP) (2013–2015)	Merchandise exports to US (in %) (2015)	Merchandise exports to EU (28) (in %) (2015)
China	11,064,665	22.3	18.0	15.6
Japan	4,383,076	18.9	20.2	10.6
India	2,088,841	24.8	15.2	16.9
Korea, Rep.	1,277,873	47.8	12.3	9.1
Indonesia	861,934	21.6	9.41	9.6
Thailand	395,168	65.3	11.2	10.3
Malaysia	296,283	69.3	9.45	13.0
Singapore	292,739	174.6	6.70	8.3
Philippines	292,451	27.6	15.0	12.2
Pakistan	271,050	15.3	16.6	30.1

Source: generated using data from World Bank and WTO and the World Integrated Trade Solutions (WITS) database.

The above data clearly shows how important these two markets are for major Asian economies. Any move towards protectionism seen in these markets will have far-reaching consequences for trade, not just for these select economies, but globally. In modern times, the global north has traditionally been the growth-pole-driving trade. Even if no concrete policy moves have been made yet, just the possibility of increased protectionism causes ripples in the global trading system. The goal then becomes to reduce any shocks that a move towards protectionism might create.

Ostensibly, the most serious challenge that the global system faces is the withdrawal of these trade poles from the system. The new US administration's decisions to leave the Trans-Pacific Partnership (TPP), is a concrete example of the same. The move caused a lot of disquiet at the international stage, with major world leaders having to come forward and reiterate their commitment to the multilateral system. Statements from the German chancellor, Angela Merkel and President Xi Jinping of China are cases in point. In fact, for the first time since its inception, the Chinese president attended the WEF's annual conference in Davos in January 2017, he noted the need to keep the commitments made towards global free trade and investment.

Evidently, the withdrawal of the West, or even the threat of withdrawal, will create a vacuum. One way to pre-empt the consequences of this gap is continuing down the path of greater regional integration. It is also necessary to ensure that integration is not unbalanced and does not make smaller or weaker nations beholden to the rules set by the few. The proliferation of GVCs and Regional Value Chains, also need to be accounted for. Different countries, depending on their levels of development and capacity, are consolidated to different levels within these value chains.

GVCs and international trade

As Hank Lim and Fukunari Kimura observe,

> Production networks and regional economic integration are accelerating in Southeast Asia and Northeast Asia within the framework of GVCs and expanding production networks in East Asia. These trends are being driven by competition, the rise of the PRC and India, the political stability of the region relative to other regions, and the availability of productive labour forces and resources, all buttressed by individual countries' macroeconomic regimes and liberal trade and investment regimes that promote economic development.
>
> (Lim & Kimura, 2010)

The above implies that the countries in Asia, which are so-called latecomers to the international stage, are finally coming into their own in terms of bargaining power and their move towards greater liberalisation. Asia, is on a sure path to replacing the west as the centre for growth in terms of trade. The region has continued to register high growth rates despite the economic slowdown in the west. It also survived the 2008 economic crisis largely unscathed.

However, as these countries become more integrated into GVCs and regional value chains, their ability to remain insulated will automatically reduce. There is also the matter of attaining greater diversification in terms of production and exports and increasing trade in value added, all necessary elements to ensure that growth continues at a consistent pace.

As the April 2015 regional economic outlook for Asia and the Pacific notes, the proliferation of GVCs has led to "faster growth of trade in intermediate inputs than of trade in final goods. Asia has especially exemplified this new pattern of production" (International Monetary Fund (IMF), April 2015). The same report notes that an emerging challenge for policymakers is to ensure greater upstream[1] GVC participation while reducing the 'spillover risks' of more trade interconnectedness.

The question may arise about the need for GVCs. The fact is, GVC participation is no longer a choice. Globalisation, as has been noted, not only led to greater interlinkages in terms of final trade transactions, it has also led to the inevitable interlinking of production systems with each country adding value in the area where it has an ostensible comparative advantage. Also, as the IMF report notes, "Integration into GVCs brings benefits beyond those traditionally associated with international trade in final goods, reflecting the more granular division of production and task specialization ... and raises the benefits from economies of scale and scope" (IMF, April 2015). Referring to empirical evidence, the report found that GVCs also lead to productivity gains. The question then should be how to ensure greater and more effective participation for emerging Asian markets, having the positive effect of saving them from the middle-income trap and having stronger growth for low-income economies.

Protectionism in any form has also a negative impact on GVCs and therefore on productivity. In a global system where the production process is fragmented within GVCs, protectionism will not protect jobs. Rather, it could make 'job-replacing technologies' more competitive in comparison. This would mean a greater rate at which labour could be replaced by capital in the production process (Akman et al., 2017). Hence, protectionism in the current trade scenario, will be counterproductive. It will not have any revitalising effects on trade growth but lead to a reduction in overall productivity and competitiveness. Turning protectionist will only be disruptive as it might increase the costs of production besides making trade more cumbersome. This is because protectionism will not only negatively impact market access, but also will restrict production destinations.

Competitiveness in GVCs is crucial to improving the performance of economies. "Exporting in the global market today requires continuously enhancing firm- and industry-level competitiveness by increasing cost-effectiveness, product or service quality, and openness to global innovation and emerging market demands" (Singh & Gupta, March 2016). These requirements cannot be met by turning protectionist. On the contrary, ways must be found to ensure that nations can utilise the benefits of being part of GVCs and, in the long run, move more downstream.

The space for regional integration: ASEAN +

Over the last two decades, there have been various significant changes in the global economic order. These changes have led to specific trends in the consumption and production patterns around the globe. Asia is no exception.

> In addition to being the global economic driver … the region became a growing market of almost half of the world's population and a rapidly rising middle class … the international trade in Asia was governed by the development of cross-border production networks with each country specializing in a particular stage of the production sequence.
>
> (Das, 2014)

The centre for production firmly shifted from the west to Asia in this time. Sanchita Das argues that Asian economies and especially the Association of Southeast Asian Nations (ASEAN), consciously started down a path of economic regionalism (Das, 2014). This was around the time when the slowdown in the US and EU economies began and Asian economies like China, India, and Indonesia started growing stronger. This was in addition to the value chains that were developing in the region.

"The Asia-Pacific region is renowned for its active intra-industry trade and considerable lengths of several GVCs run through the region. The ASEAN economies play prominent roles in these GVCs" (Palit, 2015). As Das points out, 'cross-border production networks', started playing a stronger role in determining how Asian countries conducted international trade. The AEC was expected to assist in the liberalisation of trade in both, goods and services. It was also intended to help increase the intra-firm trade and investment in the region (Das, 2014). Thus, Regional Value Chains would start to take precedence.

Value chains do not work in vacuums. They are affected by traditional trade tools like tariffs and exchange rate changes.

> Tariffs on intermediate goods significantly increase costs associated with trade in intermediate goods, thereby reducing participation… GVC's tend to amplify the distortionary impacts of tariffs, as these are compounded along GVCs when intermediate inputs are traded across borders many times throughout the entire production chain.
>
> (IMF, April 2015)

Evidently, barriers to trade need to be reduced not just for traditional liberalisation goals but also to ensure that GVCs become more productive and realise their optimum potential.

Scholars have observed that trade through GVCs are essential to promoting trade growth in both developed and developing countries. They find that 'trade-enabling policies' besides high levels of interconnectedness and integration are necessary for attaining high growth (RIS, 2015). This helps reiterate the fact that GVCs can be vitalised through regional integration and trade policies which help reduce both tariff and non-tariff barriers to trade. As has been established, tariffs on imports, particularly on imports of intermediate goods decreases a country's GVC participation. The country also becomes unable to move to more downstream positions in value chains.

Having trade-enabling policies is also necessary for effective regional integration. Reducing hindrances to cross-border trade is a necessary element of this. Especially since production too has become dependent on free movement of the various factors of production. One method through which this has been done is the creation of supranational regional organisations like the EU, ASEAN et al. The other ostensible method to vitalise GVCs is through trade agreements.

FTAs in Asia

FTAs are a legitimate means to increase bilateral or pluri-lateral trade, sanctioned by the WTO. These can have 'WTO-plus' provisions, which build on current WTO commitments to make them more far-reaching in terms of their liberalisation goals. The second kind of provisions are 'WTO-extra' provisions which create rules for those issues not yet covered within the WTO framework.

The project for greater regional integration in Asia is best exemplified by the ASEAN example. A series of bilateral FTAs in the region were galvanised in the hopes of capitalising on the new growth momentum Asia has achieved 1990s onwards. This is evident from the workings of the ASEAN over this time period. "The objective of ASEAN Free Trade Area (FTA) and later of the ASEAN Economic Community (AEC) ... was to increase the region's competitive advantages as against China" (Das, 2014). There was also the recognition that there was continuity in the policies they followed which implied that greater regional cooperation could lead to more stability. It would also mitigate the effects of any future financial crisis. There was a tacit recognition that greater cohesiveness among the members of the ASEAN would give them more bargaining power internationally (Das, 2014).

The ASEAN FTA (AFTA) had WTO-plus provisions as it aimed to reduce tariffs on all products in the region to 0–5 percent under the Common Effective Preferential Tariff (CEPT) scheme. It aimed to intensify regional integration by reducing barriers to trade. The goals of the AFTA were eventually broadened to enhance liberalisation in the services sector and in investment. This was done through the ASEAN Framework Agreement on Services (AFAS) and the ASEAN Investment Area (AIA). There is evidence to show that production networking in the ASEAN economies has increased as a result of AFTA (Das, 2014; Lim & Kimura, 2010).

ASEAN as a regional grouping signed a series of ASEAN + 1 FTAs between 2005 and 2010 with countries in Asia and the Pacific. These included China, Japan, Republic of Korea, Australia, New Zealand and India – the ASEAN +6. Discussing various political-economic reasons for the individual ASEAN nations to join FTAs, Das argues that a key consideration is undertaking domestic reform besides market access. Domestic reforms would have the effect of increasing investor confidence and therefore attract more Foreign Direct Investment (FDI). It also helps mitigate the diversion of trade from the region when trade blocs are formed elsewhere.

Countries also recognise the political imperative of strengthening strategic partnerships in the region through trade diplomacy. Besides this, Das identifies some economic motives for why countries prefer regional cooperation. Chief among these is the belief that as compared to multilateral negotiations, regional agreements allow for a degree of protectionism in sectors which may be 'politically sensitive' or 'non-competitive' (Das, 2014).

While remaining committed to multilateralism, India like many other countries, has negotiated a series of FTAs, notably with trading partners in Asia. Within Asia, India has signed bilateral FTAs with Sri Lanka (1998), Afghanistan (2003), Thailand (2004), Singapore (2005), Bhutan (2006), Nepal (2009), Korea (2009), Malaysia (2011) and Japan (2011). There have also been two RTAs, the South Asian Free Trade Agreement (SAFTA, 2004) and the India-ASEAN, 2010. Outside Asia, India has entered into preferential trade agreements with Chile (2006, in force 2007) and MERCOSUR (2004, in force 2009) (Ministry of Finance, Government of India, 2015).

Indian industry, however, has been sceptical about the gains accruing to India after the entry into force of these FTAs and is of the opinion that such agreements have helped the exporters of other countries while Indian exporters have not gained much or have been hurt by increased import competition. It has been pointed out that India's trade deficit with the FTA partners has increased after signing such agreements. For instance, with Korea, India's merchandise export increased from US$3.4 billion in 2009–2010 to US$4.2 billion only in 2016–2017, an increase of less than US$1 billion in eight years. As a result, India's merchandise deficit with Korea shot up steeply to US$8.3 billion in 2016–2017 from US$5.5 billion in 2009–2010.

Based on the findings of the Indian Ministry of Finance funded study of 2014, the FTAs are not the main reason for the observed trends in exports, imports and trade balance, though they may have contributed to them. The main factors have been:

- declining competitiveness of Indian manufacturing and various constraints faced by the sector;
- India's difficult business environment which makes it onerous to attract FDI and leverage it for trade flows;

- competition from other countries like China, which are more competitive than India in these FTA partner countries, or which may also be receiving preferential access in those markets and thus undermining India's concessional access under the FTAs;
- the design of the FTAs in terms of stringent rules of origin (RoOs), carve-outs and the structure of tariff concessions which make these agreements less relevant to India's exports in certain sectors;
- continued presence of non-tariff barriers which make it difficult to penetrate partner markets; and lack of changes in the structure of India's trade basket towards new products and in trade orientation towards other countries and regions (Chanda, 2014).

Impetus for RCEP

A problem that has been identified with having multiple FTAs is the competing standards regarding RoOs. This is one of the many competing expectations that competing FTAs create. Collectively, they have been termed 'noodle bowl' inefficiencies. These inefficiencies materialise due to the existence of an increased number of bilateral and pluri-lateral FTAs. The result is the "emergence of a complicated trading system ... which may reduce trade by raising trade costs. Recognition of such concern by East Asian countries has resulted in the discussion over establishing a region-wide FTA" (Urata, 2013).

Scholars identify multiple political-economic reasons for the impetus that mega-regionals have been given in recent times. A central factor identified is the interest that multinationals have in global supply chains. Things like legal protection for investments, reductions in shipping costs across multiple national borders, certification of products for multiple markets and harmonisation of product regulations, would all assist in reducing transaction costs. Mega-regional agreements would help harmonise trade rules, reducing inefficiencies (Bown, 2016).

The focus on the Regional Comprehensive Economic Partnership (RCEP) has increased ever since the US pulled out of the TPP and the negotiations on the Transatlantic Trade and Investment Partnership (TTIP) have come to a standstill. The RCEP has 16 negotiating members – the ASEAN countries and six others that ASEAN has bilateral FTA's with. Collectively, the members of the RCEP account for

> a third of the world's trade with a total population of 3 billion and a gross domestic product (GDP) of about US$ 20tn ... it will be the largest trading bloc in the world in terms of population ... the partnership also intends to facilitate engagement in global and regional supply chains.
>
> (Cote & Jena, 2015)

The negotiating members of the RCEP are divided in terms of levels of development, giving rise to different interests and expectations from the agreement. From the outset, the negotiators have made it a point to clarify that developing countries will be given space to manoeuvre. The principle of 'Special and Differential Treatment', enshrined in the WTO norms has been reiterated time and again in these negotiations. A problem that is seen in conflating the six ASEAN+ 1 FTAs is that they do not have a common template. This includes provisions regarding standards and RoOs. What is clear is that the agreement will not seek out the same high standards as the TPP or TTIP. Since trade between the negotiating nations already enjoys advantages of low tariffs, scholars observe that the focus now needs to be on reducing "beyond-the-border barriers that constrain production networks and supply chains" (Chia, 2015).

For India, given the tariff levels in the important RCEP markets are already low, the negotiated tariff reductions from the Indian side will be far greater. Therefore, there is a need for a balanced agreement through access to services market and investments. While domestic reforms are underway, and India is pushing the 'Make in India' initiative, investments and connecting to the Asian production networks would be of vital importance. The inclusion of China is proving to be a major threat to domestic manufacturing, particularly to sectors such as iron and steel, chemicals, textiles and clothing and auto and auto components. Given Indian manufacturers are already facing significant competition in these sectors from China even at most favoured nation (MFN) tariff rate, any gains from the RCEP negotiations can only be made by neutralising the China-effect.

RCEP and Asian integration

One of the considerations driving the RCEP is the recognised need for greater clarity in rules of trade in the region. Harmonising the rules in the region and cutting down ambiguities will have the effect of increasing productivity. This is because less complicated rules of trade will drive down transaction costs boosting investor and producer confidence. Making the trade architecture in the region more facilitative will vitalise supply chains and also create space for greater diversification in production and value chain participation. A so-called defining interest of the negotiations has been the integration of the economies and markets involved, especially the Asian markets, in order to create a more robust and cooperative economic neighbourhood (Cote & Jena, 2015).

The extent to which FTAs in general and the RCEP in particular will lead to greater trade liberalisation is moot. There is a question over whether RTAs, like the RCEP, lead to additional liberalisation or are they just 'stumbling blocks' to trade. Another area of dissonance is whether or not integration issues should be made part of these trade agreements to begin with (Bown, 2016).

Critics of FTAs elaborate on this and point to how these agreements actually lead to a shrinking of policy space. This is an argument which is inherently contradictory as they do not account for the fact that entering into FTAs is in itself a strategic policy decision. Governments do not enter into FTAs under duress but on the basis of various national interest considerations. They are able to define a framework within which government regulations can be formed in order to make trade freer. Therefore, it is not false to argue that they allow for wider integration.

Another argument made against FTAs and RTAs is the concern over unintended constraints on domestic policies and regulations. There is a need here to recognise that there is convergence in terms of policies. As discussed earlier in the paper, one of the various motives to enter FTAs is in fact to snowball domestic reform. Any government entering an FTA is already set on the path to greater liberalisation. FTAs are a tool to meet this domestic policy decision. Hence, not only is there no policy space lost, on the contrary, FTAs could be the means to achieve the goal of greater liberalisation and regional integration. Both of these goals will help increase trade and therefore help the economy to grow. This will also lead to job creation and facilitate diversification in production, helping nations move downstream in GVCs.

As Palit (2015) observes, India and New Zealand have the lowest levels of integration in GVCs. He also notes how this has slowly been changing in the Indian context. He credits this slight positive change to deeper economic integration in the region. He notes the necessity of ensuring that the RCEP puts forward rules that facilitate both upstream and downstream participation in value chains. Participation would be galvanised through making the exchange of raw materials as well as intermediates more efficient. Palit argues that the reason for the low levels of utilisation of FTAs may be due to inefficient information dissemination. He warns against repeating this mistake with the RCEP and reiterates the importance of involving the stakeholders, especially domestic industry, in a more active manner (Palit, 2015).

As is seen, there are various advantages that can be gleaned from greater regional integration. Chief among them is the strengthening of GVCs. The signing of FTAs is evidently not enough. Concrete steps to build infrastructure and connectivity would have to be taken in tandem to accommodate the anticipated increase in cross-border mobility of intermediate goods and services. The Mekong-India Economic Corridor, connecting Myanmar and India, is a case in point.

The Asia-Pacific Economic Cooperation (APEC) forum

Of the 16 countries negotiating the RCEP, 12 are part of the APEC. Since its inception, the APEC has been seen as the leading forum for enhancing integration in the region. Some have seen the emergence of the RCEP as a threat to APEC-led integration in the region. This need not necessarily be the case. The goals of the APEC coincide with what the RCEP hopes to achieve, namely, trade facilitation, reduction of non-tariff barriers to trade and the expansion of GVCs (Singh & Gupta, March 2016).

The RCEP has not been conceptualised as an alternative to the APEC, especially since it involves countries not yet part of the APEC. The moratorium on APEC membership, initiated in 1997, was only lifted in 2010. However, no new members have been added to the group so far. India has already shown interest in joining the group.

The case of India is a prime example of how far FTAs can be used for greater economic integration and regional integration. The country already has bilateral FTAs with a number of APEC members and is in the midst of negotiations with various others. The latest among these being Peru, with negotiations set to start in August 2017. Being part of the APEC would reinforce the commitments India makes under these FTAs besides the RCEP.

Further to this, the APEC forum has been debating the benefits of a future Free Trade Area of the Asia-Pacific (FTAAP). While the proposal is not new, it has gained momentum due to the stagnation of the Doha round at the WTO. With the emergence of mega-regionals like the TPP and the RCEP, the vision for an FTAAP took a new form. The new version would be a conflation of the TPP and RCEP membership. This would mean that the FTAAP would not be limited to the APEC but have a broader constituency. A conglomeration of all these trade agreements into a single agreement would help reduce trade diversions and make the global trading system more efficient. This would also help increase productivity and help in the harmonisation of standards and trade rules, especially RoOs.

However, in the drive towards greater integration, one thing that must not be forgotten is the differential capacities of the members involved. Involvement in the regional grouping would also have the positive effect of voluntary technology transfers in order to improve productivity. Transfers would be voluntary as all member countries would have a stake in the efficiency of others thanks to the proliferation of GVCs.

Regional integration has the added advantage of addressing common non-trade concerns as well. Challenges like food security, urban growth and the environment, are some examples of the same (Singh & Gupta, March 2016). While they have no direct effect on trade, there has been research to suggest that these issues might be addressed through greater trade and regional cooperation. In the long run, greater cooperation in this field would reduce dependence on specific markets as discussed in the earlier sections of this paper.

Agreements on WTO extra issues would also streamline future multilateral discussions. This could be the answer to the perennial problem that the WTO faces of effective consensus building. Smaller scale consensus building could set a precedent for larger negotiations, making them more effective.

Conclusion

In this chapter, we have discussed the over-dependence of the global south on markets in the global north. We have also acknowledged the issues that the tide of protectionism in these countries and the potential effects on the dependent economies. Given the rise of GVC's, we have discussed the merits of FTA's and regional integration. These discussions can lead us to a few specific conclusions.

First, ways must be found to reduce the dependence of the economies in the global south on the US and European economies. This is a need made more urgent by the increasing protectionist rhetoric that is being bandied about. Second, energising regional value chains and GVCs through the use of FTAs is a viable alternative for countries to explore. For countries in Asia, the RCEP has huge potential to achieve these goals.

A third conclusion that can be drawn and further studied is the potential effects that regional integration can have on building capacities. Overall, regional integration will have the effect of reducing any shocks that policy shifts in the west may create as it would move the focal point of production and distribution. A cohesive trading environment would create safety nets and balance out the negative effects of the externalities that these policy shifts in the west create.

Note

1 "Upstreamness (or downstreamness) refers to where an economy is located in a GVC ... (It) looks at how many stages of production remain before the final product reaches consumers ... A long distance to final demand suggests that a country is upstream in the production process, such as a producer of raw materials or product design and research" (IMF, April 2015).

References

Akman, M. S., Berger, A., Dadush, U., Evenett, S., Johnson, L., Mendez-Parra, M., . . . Schmuker, C. (2017, March 31). Key policy options for the G20 in 2017 to support an open and inclusive trade and investment system. *T20 Trade and Investment Task Force*.

Akman, M. S., Berger, A., Dadush, U., Evenett, S., Johnson, L., Mendez-Parra, M., . . . Schmuker, C. (2017, March 31). Key policy options for the G20 in 2017 to support an open and inclusive trade and investment system. *T20 Trade and Investment Task Force*.

Bown, C. P. (2016, September). Mega-Regional Trade Agreements and the Future of the WTO. *Council on Foreign Relations*, 1–14.

Chanda, R. (2014). *Impact Analysis of India's Free Trade Agreements*. IIM Bangalore.

Chia, S. Y. (2015). Emerging Mega-FTAs: Rationale, Challenges, and Implications. *Asian Economic Papers, 14*(1), 1–27.

Ciuriak, D., Singh, H. V. (2015, March). The E15 Initiative. *Mega-regionals and the Regulation of Trade: Implications for Industrial Policy*. World Economic Forum and International Centre for Trade and Sustainable Development.

Cote, K. R., & Jena, P. C. (2015, September). India's FTAs and RCEP Negotiations. *CUTS International Discussion Paper.*

Das, S. B. (2014). The Political Economy of the Regional Comprehensive Economic Partnership (RCEP) and the Trans-Pacific Partnership (TPP) Agreements: An ASEAN perspective. *Trends in Southeast Asia.*

Elms, D., & Tran, K. P. (2014). *RCEP Brings New Opportunities for Gradual Agricultural Reforms in India.* Asian Trade Centre, Singapore.

IMF. (2015, April). Reaping the Benefits from Global Value Chains. In IMF, *Regional Economic Outlook- Asia and Pacific: Stabilizing and Outperforming Other Regions* (pp. 73–92). IMF.

International Monetary Fund. (2017, April). *World Economic Outlook - Gaining Momentum.* IMF.

Lim, H., & Kimura, F. (2010). The Internationalization of Small and Medium Enterprises in Regional and Global Value Chains. *ADBI Working Paper 231.*

Marsh & McLennan Companies, Zurich Insurance Group, National University of Singapore, Oxford Martin School - University of Oxford, University of Pennsylvania. (2017). *The Global Risks Report- 12th Edition.* World Economic Forum.

Ministry of Finance, Government of India. (2015). *Union Budget: 2015–16: Ch 8: Preferential Trade Agreements.* New Delhi: Government of India.

Palit, A. (2015). Regional Value Chains, RCEP and India's Priorities. In R. A.-I. RIS, *ASEAN - India; Economic Relations: Opportunities and Challenges* (pp. 57–64). ASEAN - India Centre at RIS and RIS.

Research and Information System for Developing Countries (RIS). (2014). ASEAN-India Trade, RCEP and Trade Potential. In A.-I. C. RIS, *ASEAN - INDIA Maritime Connectivity Report* (pp. 7–16). ASEAN-India Centre at RIS.

RIS. (2015). Mega Regionals - Which Way? In *World Trade and Development Report - Mega Regionals, WTO and New Issues* (pp. 1–15). New Delhi: RIS.

Singh, H. V., & Gupta, A. (2016, March). *India's Future in Asia: The APEC Opportunity.* Asia Society Policy Institute.

Urata, S. (2013). Construction of RCEP by consolidating ASEAN+ 1 FTAs. In R. Baldwin, M. Kawai, & G. Wignaraja (Eds.), *The Future of the World Trading System: Asian Perspectives* (pp. 101–107). ADBI Institute and CEPR.

Index

Note: Boldface page numbers refer to tables; italic page numbers refer to figures and page numbers followed by "n" denote endnotes.